The Good Beach Guide 1993

The guide to over 500 of Britain's most popular beaches

Marine Conservation Society Limited

Edited, revised and updated by

Catherine Loretto, *Marine Science Officer*

and

Guy Linley-Adams, *Pollution Officer*

European research by

Sue Gregory, *Bournemouth University*

VERMILION
LONDON

Published by Vermilion, an imprint of Ebury Press
Random House UK Ltd, 20 Vauxhall Bridge Road, London SW1V 2SA

First impression 1988
Reprinted twice 1988
Revised and updated 1989, 1990, 1991, 1992 and 1993

Text copyright © 1993 by The Marine Conservation Society
Illustrations copyright © 1993 by Random House UK Ltd

All rights reserved. No part of this publication may be reproduced, stored in
a retrieval system, or transmitted in any form or by any means, electronic,
mechanical, photocopying, recording, or otherwise, without the prior permission
of the copyright owner.

The right of The Marine Conservation Society to be identified as the author of the
book has been asserted by them in accordance with the Copyright, Designs and
Patents Act, 1988.

Illustrations by Kate Simunek
Edited by Diana Vowles
Front cover photograph by Susan Gubbay

A catalogue record for this book is available from the British Library.
ISBN 0 09 177715 1

Typeset in Souvenir by Textype Typesetters, Cambridge
Printed and bound in Great Britain by Mackays of Chatham PLC, Chatham, Kent

This book is printed on recycled paper.

Contents

The Marine Conservation Society

The Marine Conservation Society (MCS) is the only environmental organisation that works exclusively to safeguard the marine environment across the whole range of conservation issues. The Society, a registered charity with an expanding membership (over 5,700 in 1992), encourages its members to take part in projects to help provide a sound scientific and factual base for its campaigns. The 'Seas Fit For Life' appeal has raised well over £150,000.

Membership is £12 per year (students £8) and members receive the colour magazine *Marine Conservation*, newsletters and details of the wide range of sales goods. The more readers of *The Heinz Good Beach Guide*, the more pressure the MCS can bring to bear on your behalf to change attitudes within government and industry alike. There is a loose-leaf membership form inserted in the Guide – use it today!

The Heinz Good Beach Guide forms only one part of the Society's work, but has had a massive impact on the debate over the state of Britain's beaches and the continuing pollution of the seas by raw sewage. By producing the Guide each year with the help of Heinz and Ebury Press, the MCS has forced the Government to take note of the problem.

Evidence given by the MCS to the House of Commons Environment Committee in 1990 was welcomed and adopted in the Committee's final recommendations to the Government. The National Rivers Authority described *The Heinz Good Beach Guide 1991* as 'excellent' – this one is even better!

At last, the MCS is having an impact! Help us to do even more – join today!

Heinz

Heinz is a major sponsor of British conservation programmes and has been closely involved with the Marine Conservation Society since 1988 as sponsors of *The Heinz Good Beach Guide*.

The Company has a long and on-going commitment to the environment and actively recognises its responsibilities both operationally and at a wider educational level.

Heinz cares about the quality of life and the world we live in; the development of best practice on environmental issues is an integral part of the company's business philosophy.

In 1986, Heinz launched a major conservation programme, entitled 'Guardians of the Countryside'. Aimed at protecting wildlife species and habitats, the programme has supported many projects, both land and marine based.

Projects have included the funding of coastal wardening at several sites in the UK, sponsorship of a marine conservation officer and the Marine Conservation Society's 'Coastal Directory'. Through the programme a large number of important sites have been protected including Helford River and sites in Devon, Dorset and Northumberland.

The purchase of Cape Cornwall (including Priest's Cove) and Dunwich Heath in Suffolk for the National Trust have been important steps for Heinz, underlining its commitment to Britain's environment. In 1991 Heinz became a Business Supporter of The Royal Society for Nature Conservation (RSNC).

The company is proud to be sponsors, for a sixth year, of *The Heinz Good Beach Guide* and will continue to support environmentally beneficial initiatives.

All information received from local authorities, the National Rivers Authority and water companies up to 1 January 1993 has been included in this revised edition. The Marine Conservation Society and Ebury Press take no responsibility for data that has been altered and amended after *The Heinz Good Beach Guide 1993* has been compiled.

**MARINE CONSERVATION
SOCIETY**

Foreword
by David Bellamy

A trip to the beach means different things to different people, from the rush to the coast on a Bank Holiday, a much-needed escape from the madness of commuter life, to the traditional British family seaside holiday.

Yet we have all heard the horror stories about the presence of sewage in the water, people contracting strange illnesses and finding sewage-related debris on the beach. This is not a new problem, and it is certainly not an insurmountable one.

We all know who produces the stuff in the first place, and that the technological knowhow exists to recycle and reuse it and to halt beach pollution. The water service companies are investing money under pressure from organisations such as the Marine Conservation Society, but we must keep up that pressure.

Quite simply, everyone who visits the seaside can make a difference. Until all the beaches of the UK are clean and the seas are free of raw sewage, we must:

- vote with our feet and not go to dirty beaches

- write to all in power to protest until the Post Office begs us to stop

- make it quite clear that sewage must be used in one of the many constructive ways already available – we expect no less

- shame those responsible into action!

And remember, if none of us acts, then we will all be responsible for the ruin of the seas, guilty by indifference of neglecting our marine heritage.

Introduction

Around the United Kingdom we have over 7,000 miles (11,000km) of coastline, with thousands of beaches. We are blessed with some of the most spectacular coastline in the world, from the chalk cliffs of the Seven Sisters to the saltmarshes of the Lincolnshire coast and the sandy beaches of the West Country. Many are remote beaches, of great nature conservation value, off the beaten track and largely undeveloped.

Others bustle with activity. Sun, sea and surf attract watersports enthusiasts and sunbathers alike. The beaches and bathing waters support immensely popular resorts such as Brighton, Bournemouth and Blackpool, while Atlantic rollers have made beaches in Cornwall central to world surfing.

The 1993 Heinz Good Beach Guide has attempted to give the reader a definitive guide to all the 'resort-style' or 'managed' beaches of Great Britain, Northern Ireland, The Channel Islands and The Isle of Man. At a time when holidays at home are becoming popular again, it is an essential ally in the hunt for clean, safe beaches and bathing waters – and, for the first time, this year's Guide also has a section about the most popular beaches in the rest of Europe.

The information from which we have compiled this Guide was supplied by (in no particular order):

Norwich Union Coastwatch UK based at Farnborough College of Technology
The National Trust
Members of the Royal Yachting Association Windsurfing Section
The National Rescue Training Council
Members of the British Sub Aqua Club
Surfers Against Sewage
Friends of the Earth local groups
The 10 Water Service Companies of England and Wales
The National Rivers Authority regional offices
UK District and Borough Councils
Regional Councils (Scotland)
River Purification Boards (Scotland)
Department of the Environment for Northern Ireland
Central Council for British Naturism
Radar – Royal Association for Disability and Rehabilitation
Readers of *Canoeist* magazine
The governments of Jersey, Guernsey and the Isle of Man
The European Commission
The Department of the Environment
and, finally, the many members of the Marine Conservation Society.

So What Is Wrong With Our Beaches?

The state of the beaches and bathing waters of the UK has been the subject of vociferous debate for the last four decades, ever since the establishment of the Coastal Anti-Pollution League by Tony Wakefield and his late wife Daphne. They lost their daughter to polio, contracted while swimming off a British beach. The water was heavily contaminated with sewage.

Thirty-four years after that tragedy, there are still bathing waters in the UK that present a real risk to human health. While it is thankfully very rare for potentially fatal illnesses to be caught, the government's own studies show us that we have a good chance of catching stomach bugs and ear, nose and throat infections in the water. We continue to receive many reports each year from members of the public who have been knocked flat by quite serious illness after windsurfing or diving in sewage-contaminated waters.

We pump 300 million gallons of sewage every day into the sea around our coasts – about two-and-a-half bucketfuls per person per day. Much of it is still untreated – it enters the sea in just the same state as it disappears round the U-bend in your toilet. That includes the bleach that you throw down the pan and the various plastic, rubber and sanitary items that get flushed away. Bear in mind the maxim 'bag it and bin it – don't flush it'.

Sewage is an amazing mixture of domestic wastewater, cleaning agents, industrial effluent, solid litter and stormwater (run-off from road surfaces). Typical sewage will contain viruses and bacteria that cause human diseases, engine oils from trade and domestic uses, fat balls and detergents from domestic and trade kitchens, old pesticides disposed of down the toilet and a range of heavy metal contaminants (mercury, lead, cadmium, arsenic, copper) from trade effluent.

When you consider just what sewage is and just how much of it is produced in the UK, comprehensive treatment seems essential in order to protect ourselves and the marine environment. But what is sewage treatment? And how much of our sewage do we treat?

Sewage treatment and the law on sewage pollution of the seas

The first stage of a comprehensive sewage treatment system is to remove all the larger solids, such as plastics, nappies and all manner of debris that finds its way into the sewers. This is done by screening the sewage, a type of very coarse filtering. This is called **preliminary treatment**. The material screened out is largely unrecyclable and may be landfilled or incinerated. Preliminary treatment may include a process called **maceration** – which is analogous to putting the sewage through a blender.

The sewage will still have between 220–500mg/litre suspended solids and so the next step in a comprehensive treatment system is to allow the solids to settle out. This is known as **primary treatment**. A standard sewage treatment works will allow for several hours of sedimentation before the effluent is passed on to the next stage. Primary treatment will remove 50–60 per cent of suspended solids, 30–40 per cent of oxygen demand (the amount of oxygen that the effluent will need to be broken down completely in the sea) and between 0–50 per cent of bacteria and viruses. A large volume of sludge is produced by primary treatment.

The effluent from primary treatment is then subjected to **secondary treatment**. This is biological treatment designed to reduce the oxygen demand of the sewage. Secondary treatment may be achieved by drip-trickle through gravel beds, or the use of activated sludge processes. Both methods generate more sludge. Secondary treatment can remove 90–95 per cent of suspended solids, 80–90 per cent of oxygen demand, 75–99 per cent of bacteria and viruses and about 50 per cent of heavy metal contamination.

In some cases, though this is very rare in the UK, **tertiary treatment** may be used to reduce the nitrogen and phosphorus levels in the effluent in order to reduce its 'fertiliser effect'. This process, also known as '**nutrient stripping**', is important since nutrients in sewage can severely disrupt the marine ecosystem, causing algal blooms and the death of marine life. Some algal blooms which cause shellfish poisoning can be enhanced by nutrient pollution.

There are now new methods of treating sewage to a very high standard indeed without the conventional stages just described. Write to the Pollution Officer at the Marine Conservation Society for factsheets about **membrane technology**. Please enclose an s.a.e. and a small donation to cover costs.

Sewage is discharged down **outfall pipes** which can be of varying length. Many discharge just a few yards below low water mark and consequently bathing waters may be badly contaminated with sewage. Some even discharge above the line of low tide. In the past, the **long sea outfall** was seen as the solution to contaminated bathing waters, but it is now regarded on all sides of the debate as no substitute for treatment. There are significant ecological problems with raw sewage wherever it is discharged. Sewage slicks from long sea outfalls may also be washed back towards beaches by wind, waves and currents.

The **sludge** generated by sewage treatment can be used in a variety of ways. It should not be regarded as a waste to be disposed of as quickly and cheaply as possible, but es a resource to be exploited for the production of agricultural fertilisers, soil conditioners, peat substitutes, methane production for electricity generation, and even oil production. The House of Commons Environment Committee Enquiry into Pollution of Beaches in 1989/90 adopted this recommendation proposed by the Marine Conservation Society and we now see the Department of the Environment showing enthusiasm in this area – evidence that we can make a difference! Indeed, in 1992 Wessex Water proved that a commercial fertiliser can be made from sewage sludge at a plant near Avonmouth.

At whatever stage the effluent is discharged to sea, be it raw or subjected to secondary treatment, **chemical disinfection** may be applied. The chemicals used may be sodium hypochlorite, peracetic acid or ozone. None of these systems has been adequately tested to ensure their safety to marine life and human health. As there is also doubt about the efficacy of these methods in killing disease-causing agents in the effluent, the water service companies may be lulling us into a false sense of security. Chemical disinfection is no substitute for comprehensive sewage treatment. Physical disinfection, using ultrafiltration or possibly ultraviolet light to kill off bacteria and viruses, presents no threat to the marine environment, since it is non-additive. The Marine Conservation Society actively supports physical disinfection systems to protect public health *and* the marine environment.

The table below gives a good idea of the extent of UK sewage discharges to sea.

COASTAL SEWAGE DISCHARGES AROUND THE UK
(populations over 10,000)

Type of Outfall Treatment	Pop'n Served	No of Outfalls	% of Outfalls
Raw sewage	1,645,000	49	42
Preliminary treatment	3,359,000	54	46
Primary treatment	395,000	11	10
Secondary treatment	43,000	3	2

(Redrawn from: Study of Coastal Discharges Vol 3. CES Ltd/DoE Oct 1990)

This table shows that about 88 per cent of outfall pipes carry raw or screened-only sewage. Forty-two per cent do not even have screens to remove large objects like sanitary towels, nappies and panty liners. It should also be borne in mind that there are many outfall pipes serving populations of less than 10,000 people that are not included in the table. The estimated number of such outfalls, the vast majority of which carry untreated raw sewage, is over 1,000.

Added to all these routinely discharging outfalls are the overflow outfalls. During storms, raw sewage is released from works that normally treat sewage. Works are usually designed to cope with three times the average daily flow of sewage, but this is often exceeded in the UK; on average, storm water and overflow outfalls are used 10 times a year as treatment works become overloaded and sewers fill up.

There is no doubt that improvements are being made, but progress is slow. The water service companies have control over all discharges and are directly responsible for cleaning up this deliberate mass pollution of our seas. Action is needed now, preferably unilateral, but by legal pressure if necessary. There are three main laws and legal systems that refer directly to the discharge of sewage to the sea:

The Water Act 1989 and the National Rivers Authority (consolidated by the Water Resources Act 1991)

Under this Act, the National Rivers Authority must give consents to discharge to the water companies for each sewage discharge to sea. These should be designed to protect the waters into which the sewage is being discharged. The NRA should put a limit on the amount of sewage that can be discharged to sea. In practice, the system does not always work effectively to reduce the polluting impact of sewage and can be undermined by political considerations.

A major review of sewage discharge consents is long overdue. Some coastal discharges regularly breach the consents. Many simply do not have numerical consents, meaning no limit is put on what volume of raw sewage goes down the outfall pipe – a licence to pollute.

One major problem still remaining is the ease with which industrial discharges to sewers may be made without the need for a direct licence from the National Rivers Authority. This loophole must be plugged at once.

The EC Urban Waste Water Directive

A new European Community law called the Urban Waste Water Directive was adopted by the UK government in 1991. It seeks to make secondary treatment the norm for all coastal sewage discharges serving populations of more than 10,000 people (or the equivalent amount of imported sewage) and estuarine discharges serving more than 2,000.

However, the numerous smaller outfalls are not covered. There is also an exception whereby primary treatment will be considered adequate for the large outfalls if the coastal waters are declared less sensitive, a description that has yet to be clearly defined. If the initial half-hearted approach to the EC Bathing Waters Directive is anything to go by, then we should expect the worst. The Department of the Environment's Implementation group should be reporting very soon. Meanwhile, it appears that much of the UK coastline has already been earmarked as 'less sensitive'.

Marpol Annex IV

The UK government is now considering the ratification of Annex IV of the International Agreement on the Prevention of Pollution from Ships (MARPOL). Annex IV makes it an offence in many cases to discharge sewage from ships, large boats and yachts without treatment. Holding tanks on ships are to be encouraged so that sewage can be discharged to land-based sewage treatment works at ports and harbours. Reception facilities and sewage works at ports must be adequate to cope – there is no point in bringing raw sewage back to land if the land-based treatment is simply to discharge it back to sea via an outfall pipe!

While this is a step in the right direction, many countries that have large shipping fleets operating around the UK coastline do not recognise the MARPOL Agreement and will still be discharging raw sewage.

Until ratification is secured, all boat owners and users should follow the RYA Clean Code (copies available from the Royal Yachting Association, RYA House, Romsey House, Eastleigh, Hants SO5 4YA).

Despite all these treatment methods available and the legal framework designed to protect the seas, the simple fact is that the vast majority of sewage from coastal populations is discharged raw or merely screened – and while that is the case, those using beaches and bathing waters will still suffer from illnesses caught in the water and be disgusted by the debris on the beach.

Litter on the beaches

Many beaches are still liberally littered with sewage debris. How do you explain to your kids what a sanitary towel or a condom is and what it is doing washed up on the beach? This may sound a little alarmist, but bear in mind that in 1991, out of 202 beaches in the south-west of England, only eight could be declared to be *completely* free of sewage-related debris. Many were found by the NRA to be 'objectionable'. If that can happen on what are often our most popular beaches, then it is not hard to see that the problem is indeed real and serious.

The Environmental Protection Act 1990 made it illegal to drop litter in public places including beaches, though it is impossible to find a beach around the coastline that has not been tainted by litter dropped not by the careless, but by the couldn't-care-less.

Under the International Agreement on the Prevention of Pollution from Ships (MARPOL) Annex V, it is also illegal to throw garbage overboard from ships and boats. Much illegal fly-tipping goes on around our coast. In 1991 the Marine Conservation Society was given a jar of Soviet coffee stamped with the date 1990, found at the foot of Beachy Head in East Sussex among plastic drums of ship's detergent and tubes of industrial lubricating grease, all obviously thrown overboard and washed ashore.

Despite very poor observance of these two laws and the difficulties of enforcing them, some effort has been made by government to tackle the problem. It is therefore strange and inconsistent of the authorities to continue to allow water companies to pump plastic and other debris out to sea with the sewage. The benefits derived from installing screening at all sewage discharges far outweigh the costs – and so the only conclusion to be drawn is that the water companies do not care enough about the seas.

However, we can all help with the sewage debris problem. Binning sanitary items and condoms instead of flushing them will help clean up the beaches and bathing waters, as well as making the water companies' treatment of sewage before discharge to sea (such as it is) easier; the machinery would be subject to fewer breakdowns with less debris in the sewers. The variety of items that get carried out to sea in domestic sewage defies belief. Remember that what goes round the U-bend may end up squashed between your toes on the beach or floating past your head in the sea!

When you go to the seaside, put all rubbish in the bin or take it home with you just as you should in the countryside or in the city centre. It is now a criminal offence to drop litter anywhere in public. Drink cans and glass bottles are particularly dangerous – there is no excuse at all for leaving these lying around as they can be taken for recycling in most towns.

Oil pollution at sea and on the beach

After the horrific oil spills in the Shetlands this year, the Gulf in 1991 and from the Exxon Valdez in Alaska in 1989, you could be forgiven for thinking that major disasters were the main source of oil pollution of the seas. The truth is very different. The bulk of oil that finds it way into the sea comes from routine losses and controllable discharges. Deliberate and illegal flushing of tanks at sea by the bulk oil carriers and other ships is probably the major source. Pipeline fractures and spills at on-shore and off-shore oil installations during the on- and off-loading of tankers also contribute to the tonnes of oil that escape into the seas each year.

The most visible sign of oil pollution is the sticky tar found on many UK beaches. Murphy's Law says that it will always manage to get on your clothes and your shoes, however careful you think you have been to tip-toe round it.

Tar on your clothes is a minor problem compared to the clogging and smothering effects of oil on seabirds. About 60 per cent of dead seabirds found around the UK are oiled. In the English Channel this figure rises to 75 per cent. Marine life under the water is also at risk. Not all oil floats; the heavier fractions of an oil slick will sink to the sea bed where bottom-dwelling animals and plants, unable to escape, die.

If you want information relating to the Shetland Islands' spill earlier this year, please contact the Marine Conservation Society direct.

You Still Want To Go To The Seaside?

After reading the preceding chapter you may be thinking that it would be best to stay at home and avoid the seaside with all its polluted waters and mucky beaches – but that is the last thing you should do. The more people use our beaches and bathing waters, the more they will learn to cherish the sea and take action with the Marine Conservation Society to protect it from all sorts of abuse.

The picture is not one of complete doom and gloom. There are beaches that have excellent water quality and are not badly contaminated with sewage. The water companies and local authorities are slowly beginning to clean up their act. Beaches and bathing waters are getting better. It is no longer a question of *if* we will get a major clean up, but *when*.

Yet there is still a long way to go and, while that is so, you need to be able to find out which beaches are and are not safe. Ever since Tony Wakefield published his first *Golden List of Britain's Beaches* the public has had access to informed advice on which beaches to visit. Many years on, *The Heinz Good Beach Guide 1993* is an essential read for swimmers, surfers, sailboarders and, most importantly, families visiting the seaside.

How To Use The Guide

The Guide can be used in many ways, but by far the best method of employing it is to sit down and plan your trip around a good beach and safe waters – a good beach is the central feature of a seaside holiday or weekend break, while the waters are the most important feature for surfers, sailboarders, divers and swimmers. Select one of the best 100 or so beaches that the Guide describes in detail, making sure the description matches your requirements.

If, however, you are limited by the difficulties of travel or have already chosen which beach you are going to visit, or if you wish to find out more about your own favourite beach, the Guide has a list, descended and considerably expanded from Tony and Daphne Wakefield's own 'Golden List'. This gives details, for over 600 beaches, of:

- water quality in terms of compliance with European law

- the number of outfalls found on or near the beach
- the type of treatment that the sewage has received
- whether the discharge is above or below low watermark
- a basic track record over the last 7 years, if available

There are also remarks about the type of beach (sandy, rocky or shingle) and any particular dangers at the beach that have been brought to our attention.

Information on water quality is given using our own Marine Conservation Society star system. This is based on the European Community Bathing Water Directive (1976). Under this law, about 450 designated bathing waters have been identified in the UK. These are regularly monitored for sewage pollution by the National Rivers Authority (NRA), River Purification Boards and DoE – Northern Ireland, throughout the bathing season from May to September inclusive. These bodies measure for the number of coliform bacteria in the water and in 1992, many monitored for faecal streptococcus too. They will also be taking 'discretionary' samples in a range of other factors such as pH, colour, phenols etc.

Coliform bacteria are found in the gut of every person. They do not cause diseases in man, but are used as an indicator of the amount of sewage contamination in the water. Sewage itself may carry enteric viruses, salmonella, hepatitis A virus and many other disease-causing agents. The Directive does allow for the monitoring of enteric viruses and salmonella but since the UK government bases its results only on the faecal and total coliform counts, the Marine Conservation Society is limited to the use of this data. However the MCS does divide the result into five water quality classes rather than the crude pass-fail used by the Department of the Environment.

Adding to the potential confusion, there are not one but two sets of standards laid down by the Directive. These are the Imperative standards (also called the Mandatory or Minimum standards) and the much stricter Guideline standards:

Number/100ml	Imperative	Guideline
Faecal coliforms	2,000	100
Total coliforms	10,000	500
Faecal streptococcus	–	100

It is only the Imperative standards that are referred to when a beach is given a pass or a fail by the DoE. It must always be remembered that if a beach achieves a pass, it is not declaring itself sewage-free. It simply means that the sewage has reached a certain dilution.

Scientific research being commissioned by the DoE at the tax-payers' expense strongly suggests that the Guideline standards should be regarded as the minimum target quality for UK beaches. The report costs £110 but a summary is available from the Marine Conservation Society – just send an s.a.e. to the Pollution Officer and mark it 'Summary of Bathing Studies'. Only beaches that have achieved the Guideline standard will be found in this year's recommended section.

The track record was a new feature of last year's *Heinz Good Beach Guide*. It is based simply on a pass or fail of the minimum standards of the Directive, and will help to highlight all those beaches whose waters have been consistently failing (such as Blackpool or Great Yarmouth's South Beach) and equally those that have been consistently passing (such as Poole's Sandbanks Beach).

A key to the star system precedes the listing section of the Guide.

Other Information

The Seashore Code

This is one of many educational packages produced by the Marine Conservation Society. It covers the seashore and how everyone should act when at the seaside (available from MCS Sales – 0989-62834).

- Show respect for sea creatures
- Take photos not living animals
- Take your rubbish home with you
- Drive on roads not beaches
- Be careful near cliffs
- Avoid disturbing wildlife

'Take nothing but photos, leave nothing but footprints, waste nothing but time.'

Seaside Awards – Should You Trust Them?

In 1992, we saw possibly the most outrageous piece of environmental trickery relating to beaches. As we predicted in last year's Guide, the Blue Flag Award was tightened up: the European Blue Flag Award was indeed moved to the Guideline standard of the EC Bathing Water Directive. This was a major step in the right direction. It at last appeared that the winners of this Award would really be the cleanest and best beaches and bathing waters in the UK.

It did mean, however, that the number of Blue Flags awarded in the UK would drop. Presented with this, the Tidy Britain Group, the English Tourist Board and the British Resorts Association, with the support of the Department of the Environment, cynically reinstated the old Blue Flag, called it the Seaside Award and ran this scheme alongside the European Blue Flag Award. Within the Seaside Award scheme there were four different flags, all blue, to be given away.

The seaside Awards were and are simply a tool by which a flag of sorts will fly at those UK resorts with borderline water quality – the same resorts that the Department of the Environment's own research shows carry an unacceptable risk to public health. Awards should not be given to those resorts which just achieve minimum legal requirements. The opposition to the Seaside Awards includes the Institute of Environmental Health Officers, Surfers Against Sewage, Friends of the Earth and the Consumers' Association (publishers of *Holiday Which?*).

Our advice to any member of the public is to take notice only of the European Blue Flag and to ignore the Seaside Award if you are worried about water quality. Better still, consult *The Heinz Good Beach Guide*.

The National Trust – Enterprise Neptune

In 1895 a Mrs Talbot gave 4 acres (1.6 hectares) of cliffland behind the Welsh seaside resort of Barmouth to a newly formed organisation called the National Trust. She said she wanted 'to secure for the public forever the enjoyment of Dina Oleu, but I wish to put it into the custody of some Society that will never vulgarise it or prevent wild nature from having its way . . . I wish to avoid the abomination of asphalt paths and cast iron seats of serpentine design'.

This sentiment has echoed down the decades as the National Trust has acquired stretches of unspoilt coastline in England, Wales and Northern Ireland. Ownership and management of the coast, secured through the Trust's Enterprise Neptune, currently covers 530 miles (853 km). This provides the opportunity for the Trust to protect it for permanent preservation and for the benefit of the nation, responsibilities placed on the National Trust by the National Trust Acts.

Many of the beaches described in this Guide are either in the care and direct management of the Trust, or the land adjoining the beach is owned by the National Trust and access has been improved for visitors to the shore. Busy and popular beaches, such as Studland on the Purbeck Coast in Dorset, are regularly cleaned and patrolled by Trust staff. In the wilder and remoter corners of the country there is also a Trust presence to maintain the beaches and keep them clean as well as to manage other coastal conservation interests, for example dune management work or cliff grazing schemes to improve the coastal flora or to maintain the habitat for coastal birds such as the chough.

If it is not a day for sitting on the beach there are always plenty of coastal walks that the Trust has established where you can discover the varied and dramatic scenery of the British Coastline.

If you would like more information about the National Trust, please write to The National Trust, 36 Queen Anne's Gate, London SW1H 9AS.

Naturist Beaches

There are a growing number of specialist naturist beaches in the UK and any information about them will be gratefully received. However, it is important to note that some people may not wish to visit naturist beaches and so these must be clearly signposted. Ask the Central Council for British Naturism for details. The list below gives several beaches used by naturists in the UK.

South-West:
Wild Pear Beach, near Combe Martin, Devon
Polgaver Bay, Carlyon Bay, Cornwall
Pilchard Cove, Slapton Sands, Devon
Studland Beach (mid-section), Dorset

South-East:
Brighton East Beach, Brighton, East Sussex
Fairlight Cove, Hastings, East Sussex
Long Rock Beach, Swalecliffe, Whitstable, Kent
Shellness, near Leysdown, Isle of Sheppey, Kent
St Osyth, Essex
Corton Sands, near Lowestoft, Suffolk
Holkham, Norfolk

East Coast:
Fraisthorpe Sands, Bridlington, North Humberside

Scotland:
Ardeer Beach, Stevenston, Ayrshire
Cleat's Shore, Lagg, Isle of Arran

RYA Windsurfing

RYA Windsurfing is the National Governing Body of the sport and operates as a department of the Royal Yachting Association. It is responsible for producing training schemes for children and adults which are taught in over 250 recognised centres in the UK and

Mediterranean. Competition training activities cover all aspects of the sport, from the Under 12s right up to Olympic representatives. Its main function, however, is to promote the sport of windsurfing to newcomers and look after the interests of participating sailors. Over the past few years the rights of windsurfers to access to clean water around our coasts has become a major concern. Because of a windsurfer's intimate contact with the water, the RYA Windsurfing sees it as being essential to support the MCS and other similar groups with, among other things, information on water quality at popular sailing beaches. It is their aim to help the MCS to expand *The Heinz Good Beach Guide* to include windsurfing access and suitability information for those recommended beaches. If you can provide any more information, please contact MCS or RYA Windsurfing for a reporting form. Write to: RYA Windsurfing, RYA House, Romsey Road, Eastleigh, Hants SO5 4YA.

Key To The Heinz Good Beach Guide Star System

In response to the latest scientific research we have revised the star system to reflect the state of the UK's beaches and the need to protect the public from sewage pollution.

****
80 per cent pass of Guideline coliform standards
80 per cent pass of Guideline faecal streptococcus

This new **** bracket illustrates those beaches that will get near the new standards for bathing water that recent scientific research strongly suggests should be our target. Only beaches achieving this can be awarded a European Blue Flag in 1993.
These are the cleanest bathing waters in the UK.

***
80 per cent pass of Guideline coliform standards

This bracket is regarded by the Department of the Environment as a Guideline pass. This is the minimum standard that a beach must reach to achieve recommended status in *The Heinz Good Beach Guide* 1993. It is hoped that these beaches will also be monitored for faecal streptococcus in the future. Nevertheless, the coliform counts for these bathing beaches suggest very little sewage pollution.
Come on in, the water's lovely!

**
100 per cent pass of Imperative standards

The very latest research suggests that beaches with water of this quality may not be adequately safe. Therefore, the Marine Conservation Society cannot recommend such beaches.
The water is almost certainly affected by sewage.

*

95 per cent pass of Imperative standards

The Department of the Environment regards this as a pass of the Directive. It is the minimum legal requirement and the UK has promised that all beaches will reach at least this 95 per cent Imperative pass by 1995. These waters are almost certainly contaminated by sewage and carry a significant health risk, according to research by Water Research Centre. Nevertheless, a beach achieving this can, amazingly, still get a Tidy Britain Group Seaside Award.

Vote with your feet – this bathing beach is only achieving the bare minimum legal requirements.

f (fail)

Even the Department of the Environment regards this as a fail. These beaches are heavily contaminated by sewage. The Marine Conservation Society would advise that these waters should not be used for bathing or any other water-contact sports.

Vote with your feet – this bathing beach is heavily polluted!

Track record
p=passed the legal minimum coliform standards of the EC Bathing Waters Directive.
f=failed those standards – badly polluted.

The track record shows how consistent the water quality has been at beaches around the UK. This is particularly useful for pinpointing those that have either failed or passed consistently for the last seven years.

Abbreviations
The following abbreviations are used in the lists (see pages 8–12 for details of sewage treatment).
HWM-high water mark
(all figures are in metres unless otherwise stated)
LWM=low water mark
UV = ultra violet

South-West England

Numbered beaches are included in the following chapter.

Long distance coastal paths
South West Coast Path
562 miles (904km), but made up of four main sections:
(1) Minehead to Padstow 131 miles (211km).
(2) Padstow to Falmouth 158 miles (254km).
(3) Falmouth to Exmouth 174 miles (280km).
(4) Exmouth to Poole 99 miles (159km).

Isle of Wight Coastal Path
A circuit of the island 60 miles (97km).

Solent Way
Milford on Sea to Portsmouth 60 miles (97km).

1 Woolacombe
Barns
2 Shipload Bay
5 Hayle Bay/Polzeath   3 Sandy Mouth
6 Constantine Bay   Bude
4 Widemouth Sand
■ Newquay
7 Crantock
16 Whitsand Bay
Bodmin ■
Plymout
■ Newquay
18
8 Hayle/The Towans   Truro
9 St Ives Porthmeor   15 Pendower
St Ives   14 Towan
Penzance   17 Wembury
Falmouth
10 Sennen Cove
(Whitesand)
13 Kennack Sands
12 Kynance Cove
11 Poldhu

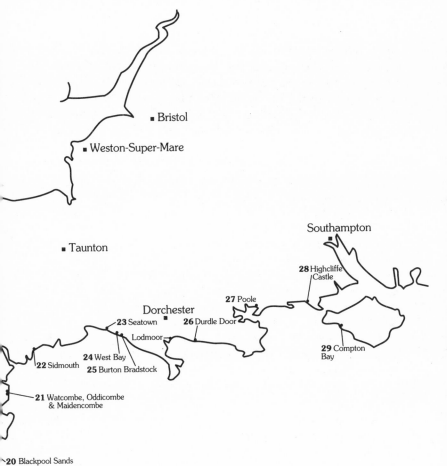

■ Bristol

■ Weston-Super-Mare

■ Taunton

Southampton

28 Highcliffe Castle

27 Poole

Dorchester

26 Durdle Door

23 Seatown

Lodmoor

24 West Bay

22 Sidmouth

25 Burton Bradstock

29 Compton Bay

21 Watcombe, Oddicombe & Maidencombe

20 Blackpool Sands
19 Slapton Sands

South-West England

There are hundreds of miles of glorious coastline along the south-west peninsula. Long, sweeping bays and small secluded coves are separated by rugged headlands; spectacular rocky cliffs contrast with smooth turfed slopes where wild flowers abound. Some of Britain's loveliest unspoilt scenery is to be found along this coast, as are many of the cleanest beaches and bathing waters in the country.

The area is not completely free of problems. Various forms of pollution affect several beaches and untreated sewage discharged close inshore is washed back on to the sands at popular resorts. Both South-West and Wessex Water have investment programmes to deal with the sewage problems of the region, but there is a long way to go. In the immediate future it appears that sewage is going to be an everyday obstacle faced by the surfers at Newquay.

In other areas, the china clay industry has covered once-pristine sand with a film of white dust and the Cornish tin mining industry has been responsible for chronic and acute pollution by mine waste. One of the most recent and dramatic demonstrations of this was the incident at the Wheal Jane tin mine (the term 'accident' cannot be applied as the flooding and subsequent pollution from the mine was foreseen in 1989). The NRA fears that there may be another major pollution incident at the Wheal Jane unless further action is taken.

Congestion problems on small country roads can build up in the summer as large numbers of tourists flock to the beaches. Long queues of traffic develop on the narrow lanes and the picturesque Cornish fishing villages heave with cars. The beaches become crowded and this can lead to damage, with paths over dunes becoming badly eroded and litter marring an otherwise beautiful area. To avoid some of these problems go to the beach by public transport or visit the area out of the holiday season. Remember, in winter you can have miles of golden sand to yourself.

The South-West   *See page 21 for further details*

Beach No on Map	Rating. The more stars the better. f=failed	Resort	Pass/Fail track record	Sewage outlets	Population discharging from outlet	Type of treatment	Discharge point relative to low water mark, unless otherwise stated. Distance given in metres	Remarks
AVON								
		Clevedon:		1	60,000	Fine	At HWM	Rocks and mud. Crude
	f	**Bay**	FFFFPFF			screening,		discharges now removed.
	f	Marine Lake	~~~~~~F			filtration,		All flow to sewage
	f	Layde Bay				settlement		treatment works at Kingston Seymour.
		Weston-Super-Mare:		1	75,000	Fine screening, disinfection	400m below LWM	Improvement scheme completed 1990. Reports of excessive littering, including syringes, 1992.
	★	Uphill Slipway	~~~~~PP					
	★	Sanatorium	~~~~~FP					
	f	Tropicana	~~~~~FF					
	f	Grand Pier	~~~~~FF					
	★★	Marine Lake	~~~~~PP					
	★	Weston Anchor Head (Birnbeck Pier)	~~~~~PP					
	★	Weston Sand Bay	PFPPPPP					
SOMERSET								
		Berrow:						
	★★★★	**North**	~~~~~PP					
	★★	**South**	PPFPPPP					Sandy.
	★★	**Brean**	PPPPPPP					Sandy.
		Burnham-on-Sea:		1	36,000	Fine screening, filtration, settlement	At HWM	All flow to West Huntspill sewage. treatment works.
	f	Yacht Club	~~~~~FF					
	★	Jetty	~~~~~PP					
	★★	Paddling Pool	~~~~~FP					
		East Quantoxhead		1	800	Maceration	At LWM	Rocks and sand. Water quality not monitored by NRA in 1992.
	f	Doniford	~~~~~FF	1	5,000	Fine screened	100 above LWM	Sand and mud.
	★	Watchet	~~~~~FP	1	4,500	Raw	100 above LWM	Sand and mud.
	★★	**Blue Anchor**	PFPPPFP					Sand and shingle. Flows to Minehead headworks.
		Dunster:						Sand and shingle. Flows to Minehead headworks.
	★	**North west**	~~~~~PP					
	★	**South east**	FFFFPPP					

Beach No on Map	Rating. The more stars the better. f=failed	Resort	Pass/Fail track record	Sewage outlets	Population discharging from outlet	Type of treatment	Discharge point relative to low water mark, unless otherwise stated. Distance given in metres	Remarks
		Minehead		1	35,000	Screening.	750 below LWM	Sandy. Headworks and outfall completed 1989. Long sea outfall and tidal discharge.
	★★	Terminus	~~~~~PP					
	★★	The Strand	~~~~~PP					
	★★	Warren Point	~~~~~PP					
		Porlock Bay:			850	Raw	At LWM	Pebbles.
	★★★★	**Porlock Weir**	PFPPPPP	3	1,200	Raw	At LWM	
					450	Raw	At LWM	
NORTH DEVON								
	★	**Lynmouth**	FFPFFFP	1	4,300	Raw	110 below LWM	Pebbles. New full treatment works and outfall planned for 1995.
	f	**Combe Martin**	FFFFPFF	1	3,600	Raw	65 below LWM	Pebbles and sand. New full treatment works and 500 m outfall planned by 1995.
		Ilfracombe:		2	22,000	Raw	235 below LWM	Sandy. Improvements planned to include full treatment works and medium sea outfall by 1995.
	f	**Hele Beach**	~~~~~FF					
	f	**Capstone Beach**	FFPPPPF		744	Raw	30 below LWM	
	★★	Tunnels	~~~~~PP					
		Rockham Bay						Rocky. Water quality not monitored by NRA in 1992
		Barricane Bay						Sandy cove surrounded by rocks. Water quality not monitored by NRA in 1992
1		**Woolacombe:**		1	13,200	Secondary	100 below LWM	Sandy. Surfing popular. Outfall extended 1990, remote from beach.
	★★★★	**Putsborough**	PPPPPPP					
	★★★★	**Village**	~~~~~PP					
	★★★★	**Croyde Bay**	PPPPPPP	1	6,400	Maceration	At LWM	Sandy. Surf bathing. Strong undertow at all times. Lifeguards. Problems with sewage-related debris. Improvements planned as for Instow.
	★★	**Saunton Sands**	PPPPPPP					Sandy. Lifeguards.

Beach No on Map	Rating. The more stars the better. f=failed	Resort	Pass/Fail track record	Sewage outlets	Population discharging from outlet	Type of treatment	Discharge point relative to low water mark, unless otherwise stated. Distance given in metres	Remarks
f		*Instow*	FFFPFFF	2	8,500	Screened	LWM	*Polluted by River Taw and Torridge. £62.4 m scheme to provide secondary treatment, long sea outfall and sludge digestion by 1997. Sewage related debris reported 1992.*
	**	*Westward Ho!*	PPPPPPP	1	4,600	Fine screens	10 below LWM	*Sand and pebbles. Surf bathing. Transfer to treatment works as above for 1997.*
		Clovelly		1	259	Raw	At LWM	*Sand at low tide only. Water quality not monitored by NRA in 1992*
2		Shipload Bay						*Pebbles, sand at low tide. Water not monitored by NRA in 1992.*
	****	*Hartland Quay*	PPPPPPP					*Rocks and pebbles.*
		Welcombe Mouth						*Pebbles and rocks; some sand at low tide. Water quality not monitored by NRA in 1992.*
CORNWALL								
3	****	*Bude Sandy Mouth*	~~~~~PP					*Sandy. Swimming dangerous at low tide. Surf bathing. Lifeguards from Whitsun to August Bank Holiday.*
	*	*Bude Crooklets*	FFFPPFP					*Sandy. Surf bathing.*
	*	*Bude Summerleaze*	~~~~~FP	1	12,700	Primary	1000 below LWM	*New inland treatment works and outfall opened summer 1992.*
4	****	*Widemouth Sand*	PPPPPPP					*Sandy. Bathing dangerous at low tide. Lifeguards Whitsun to August Bank Holiday. Regular cleaning all year and dog ban.*

Beach No on Map	Rating. The more stars the better. f=failed	Resort	Pass/Fail track record	Sewage outlets	Population discharging from outlet	Type of treatment	Discharge point relative to low water mark, unless otherwise stated. Distance given in metres	Remarks
	f	*Crackington Haven*	~~~~~PF					Sandy. Lifeguards, reduced cover from 1 July to August Bank Holiday. Dog ban. Good walking area. Further information is available from the National Trust.
		Boscastle		1	1,300	Raw	At LWM	Harbour outfall inaccessible. Water quality not monitored by NRA in 1992. The National Trust owns much of the land surrounding Boscastle and a leaflet with further information is available from them.
		Tintagel		1	1,500	Raw	At LWM	Shingle. Water quality not monitored by NRA in 1992. The National Trust owns land on either side of Tintagel and a leaflet with further information on the area is available from them.
	★	*Trebarwith Strand*	~~~~~PP					Sand and rocks. Swimming can be dangerous. Lifeguards Whitsun to August Bank Holiday.
		Port Isaac		1	1,800	Secondary	At LWM	Fishing port. Water quality not monitored by NRA in 1992.
5	★★★★	*Polzeath*	PPPPPPP	1	700	Screened	At LWM	Sandy. Beach cleaned all year round. Dog ban. Bathing can be dangerous at low water. Lifeguards from Whitsun to August Bank Holiday. Transfer to inland treatment works completed summer 1992.
	f	*Daymer Bay*	PPPPPPF					Sandy. Reports of excessive dog fouling 1992.
	★	*Rock Beach*	FFPPPPP					Sandy. Good sailing. Swimmers beware currents.

Beach No on Map	Rating. The more stars the better. **f**=failed	Resort	Pass/Fail track record	Sewage outlets	Population discharging from outlet	Type of treatment	Discharge point relative to low water mark, unless otherwise stated. Distance given in metres	Remarks
		Padstow		1	3,800	Fine screens		Small harbour. No swimming. Water quality not monitored by NRA in 1992. Transfer to inland treatment works planned for 1995.
	★	**Trevone Bay**	FFFPPFP	1	1,000	Raw	At LWM	Sandy. Bathing can be dangerous. Lifeguards. Transfer to inland treatment works planned for 1995.
	★	**Harlyn Bay**	PPPPPP	1	4,900	Secondary	At LWM	Sandy. Lifeguards cover from Whitsun to August Bank Holiday. Beach cleaned all year. Transfer to inland treatment works planned for 1995.
	★	**Mother Ivey's Bay**	~PPPPPP					Sandy. Pedestrian access.
6	★★★★	**Constantine Bay**	~PPPPPP					Sandy. Bathing dangerous. Lifeguard cover from Whitsun to August Bank Holiday.
	★	**Treyarnon Beach**	PPPPPP					Sandy. beach cleaned all year. Surfing dangerous at low tide. Lifeguard cover from Whitsun to August Bank Holiday.
	★★	**Mawgan Porth**	FFPFFFP					Sandy. Surfing dangerous at low tide. Improvements planned to construct reed bed at St Columb. Major sewage treatment works by 1994.
		Bedruthan Steps						Sand and rocks. Steps to beach closed, access dangerous and bathing dangerous. Much of the land is owned by the National Trust. The South West Peninsula path runs along the top of the cliffs here. There is a leaflet available from the National Trust with further information about the area.

Beach No on Map	Rating. The more stars the better. **f**=failed	Resort	Pass/Fail track record	Sewage outlets	Population discharging from outlet	Type of treatment	Discharge point relative to low water mark, unless otherwise stated. Distance given in metres	Remarks
	★★★★	**Watergate Bay**	PPPPPFP					Sandy.
	★★	**Porth Beach**	~~~~~FP	1		Maceration/ screens	75 below	Sandy. Surfing. Lifeguards.
	★★★★	**Newquay Bay: Towan Beach**	PPPPPPP	1	50,000	Maceration/ screens	75 below LWM	
	★★	**Fistral Bay**	PPPPPPP					Sandy. Strong currents when rough. Litter and sewage pollution reported in 1992.
7	★★★★	**Crantock**	PPPPPPP					Sandy. Surfing. Swimming dangerous at low water and near Gannel estuary. The National Trust owns several miles of the coastline in the area and a leaflet with further information is available.
	★	**Holywell Bay**	~~~~~PP					Sandy. Surfing dangerous at low tide. Lifeguards.
	★★★★ ★	**Perranporth:** Penhale Village Village End	~~~~~PP ~~~~~FP	1	12,000	Maceration	At LWM	Sandy. Good surfing. Dangerous at low tide. Lifeguards. New full treatment works planned for 1995.
	f	**Trevaunance Cove**	FFPPPFF	1	4,000	Fine screening	At LWM	Sandy. Powerful surf. New £2.3 m improvement scheme; full treatment planned for 1995.
	★	**Porthtowan**	PPPPPPP					Sandy. Surfing dangerous at low water. Lifeguards.
	★★★★	**Portreath**	PPPPPPP	1	26,300	Fine screening	At LWM	Sandy. Surfing. Swimming dangerous near pier. Lifeguards. There is National Trust property in the area and a leaflet with further information is available.
		Deadman's Cove (Cambourne)		1	19,500	Raw	At LWM	Sand and rocks. Water quality not monitored by NRA in 1992.

Beach No on Map	Rating. The more stars the better. f=failed	Resort	Pass/Fail track record	Sewage outlets	Population discharging from outlet	Type of treatment	Discharge point relative to low water mark, unless otherwise stated. Distance given in metres	Remarks
8	****	**The Towans – Hayle**	~~~~~PP					Sandy. Surfing. Swimming dangerous at low water. Lifeguards.
	****	**The Towans – Godrevy**	PPPPPP					
		Carbis Bay:						Sandy and sheltered.
	****	Porth Kidney Sands	~~~~~FP					
	**	Station Beach	~~~~~PP					
	*	**St Ives Porthminster**	PPPFPPP		21,400			Sandy. Sheltered. Well managed beach. Transfer to upgraded treatment at Hayle and outfall planned for 1995; construction started.
	**	**St Ives Porthgwidden**	FPFFFFP					Sandy beach. All discharges ceased.
9	****	**St Ives Porthmeor**	PPPPPPP	1	50	Fine screened	150 from harbour wall	Sandy. Surfing. The National Trust owns property in the area; a leaflet is available with further information.
		St Just Priest's Cove						Shingle. Water quality not monitored by NRA in 1992.
10	****	**Sennen Cove (Whitesand Bay)**	PPPPPPP	1	1,500	Maceration	130 from sea wall	Sandy. Surfing north of beach is dangerous. Lifeguards.
		Porthgwarra						Sandy at low tide. All discharges ceased.
	****	**Porthcurno**	PPPPPPP	1	200	Maceration	At LWM	Sandy.
		Lamorna Cove		1	Tidal tank		At LWM	Sand and rocks. Water quality not monitored by NRA in 1992.
		Mousehole		1	2,000	Raw	At LWM	Fishing port. Water quality not monitored by NRA in 1992. Transfer to upgraded treatment works at Hayle and outfall planned for 1995.

Beach No on Map	Rating. The more stars the better. f=failed	Resort	Pass/Fail track record	Sewage outlets	Population discharging from outlet	Type of treatment	Discharge point relative to low water mark, unless otherwise stated. Distance given in metres	Remarks
		Marazion and Mount's Bay:		12	37,585	Raw	11 at LWM, 1 at 50 below	Sand and shingle. New £48.7 m scheme proposed for Newlyn and Penzance for completion in 1995 to provide secondary treatment, sludge treatment, two storm water outfalls and a long sea outfall.
	f	*Wherrytown*	~~~~~FF					
	★	*Heliport*	~~~~~FP					
	★	**Penzance**	FFFFFFP					
	★★	*Little Hogus*	~~~~~PP					
	★★★★	**Perran Sands**	PPPPPFP	1	1,000	Raw	At LWM	Sandy.
		Praa Sands:						Sandy. Surfing, frequent surf and rip currents, heavy dump at high tide due to steepness of beach. Lifeguards. Sewage-related debris and bathing-related illness reported 1992.
	★★★★	*West*	PPPPPPP					
	★★★★	*East*	PPPPPPP					
	★	**Porthleven West**	FFFPFFP	1	3,700	Raw	At HWM	Flint and pebbles. Bathing dangerous. £3.2 m improvement scheme planned to provide full treatment at inland sewage treatment works and discharge via medium sea outfall by 1995.
	★★★★	**Gunwalloe Cove**	PPPPPPP					Swimming dangerous in rough weather. Lifeguards. Marine litter reported 1992. The National Trust owns much of the land in the area; a leaflet with further information is available.
11	★★★★	**Poldhu Cove**	PPPPPPP					Sandy. Bathing dangerous at low tide. Lifeguards.
	★★★★	*Polurrian Cove*	PPPPPPP	1	2,700	Macerated	At LWM	Sandy. Weekend lifeguards.

Beach No on Map	Rating. The more stars the better. f=failed	Resort	Pass/Fail track record	Sewage outlets	Population discharging from outlet	Type of treatment	Discharge point relative to low water mark. unless otherwise stated. Distance given in metres	Remarks
12	****	Kynance Cove						Sandy. Safe bathing. Coastal land in the area is owned by the National Trust; a leaflet with further information is available from the National Trust.
		Polpeor Cove						Rock and shingle. Safe bathing. Water quality not monitored by NRA in 1992.
	****	Church Cove		1	4,400	Maceration	500 below	Rocky fishing cove.
13	****	**Kennack Sands**	PPPPPP					Silver sands. Safe swimming in calm weather.
	****	**Coverack**	PPPPPP	1	800	Primary	100 below LWM	Sand and shingle.
	****	**Porthoustock**	PPPPPP					Shingle with sand at low tide.
	★	**Porthallow**	FFFFPFP		100			Grey stones. Improvements planned by 1995 to intercept numerous minor raw sewage discharges and provide treatment and short outfall.
	★	**Maen Porth**	PFPPPPP					Sand and shingle. Lifeguards.
	f	**Swanpool Beach**	PFPPPPF	1	36,500	Maceration	At LWM	Sand and shingle. £14.5 m improvement scheme planned for new full treatment works for 1995. Interim fine screening to be put in place 1993.
	****	**Gyllyngvase (Falmouth)**	PFPPPPP					Sandy. Safe swimming. Lifeguards.
	****	Loe Beach Feock	~~~~~PP					Sand and shingle. Boating beach. Affected by the Wheal Jane incident in 1992.

Beach No on Map	Rating. The more stars the better. **f**=failed	Resort	Pass/Fail track record	Sewage outlets	Population discharging from outlet	Type of treatment	Discharge point relative to low water mark, unless otherwise stated. Distance given in metres	Remarks
		St Mawes		1	1,500	Secondary	100 below LWM	Sandy. Safe swimming. Water quality not monitored by NRA in 1992.
		St Anthony's Head						Sheltered bay; fine shingle at low tide. Water quality not monitored by NRA in 1992.
14	**★★★★**	Towan Beach,						Sand and rock.
	f	Portscatho		2	1,988 52	Raw Raw	At LWM At LWM	Sand and rock.
		Porthcurnick Beach						Sand, some rocks. Water quality not monitored by NRA in 1992.
15	**★★★★**	**Pendower Beach**	~~~~~PP					Sand and rock. Safe bathing.
	★★★★	Carne Beach (Pendower)						
		Portloe		1	450	Maceration	At LWM	Sand and rock. Fishing village.
		Portholland Beach						Shingle; sand at low tide. Old lime kilns on the shore.
	★	Porthluney Cove	~~~~~PP					Sandy.
		Hemmick Beach						Small sandy bay. Water quality not monitored by NRA in 1992.
	★ **★★**	**Gorran Haven:** **Bow (or Vault)** **Little Perhaver**	PFPPPPP ~~~~~PP	2	2,600	Raw	At LWM	Sandy, safe swimming. Improvements by 1995 to provide full treatment and an extension to the existing sea outfall.
	★★	**Portmellon**	PPPPPPP					Sand and shingle.
		Mevagissey		1	5,900	Raw	At LWM	Fishing harbour. No beach. New full treatment works and outfall planned for 1995. Water quality not monitored by NRA in 1992.

Beach No on Map	Rating. The more stars the better. f=failed	Resort	Pass/Fail track record	Sewage outlets	Population discharging from outlet	Type of treatment	Discharge point relative to low water mark, unless otherwise stated. Distance given in metres	Remarks
	★★	**Polstreath**	PPPPPP					Contaminated by the Mevagissey sewage outfall – improvements planned.
	★	**Pentewan**	FFFFPPP					Sandy. Sewage treatment works and 500m outfall to discharge effluent to St Austell Bay by 1994.
	★★★★	**Porthpean**	PPPPPPP	1	50	Raw	At LWM	Sandy.
	★	**Charlestown**	~~~~PPP	1	3,500	Raw	At LWM	Sandy. Flows transferred to inland treatment works at Par summer 1992.
	★★	**Duporth**	~~~~FPP					
	★★ ★★★★	**Crinnis Beach:** Golf Links Leisure Centre	PPPPPPP ~~~~~PP					Sandy. Swimming dangerous near stream. Improvements as above. Well managed beach.
f f		**Par Sands** Spit Beach	FPPPPPF ~~~~~FF	1	20,700	Primary	140 below LWM	Sandy. Dominated by china clay factory. Improvements as above.
	★	**Polkerris**	PFPPPPP	1	60	Raw	5 below LWM	Sandy. Interception and fine screening of flows installed summer 1992.
		Polridmouth Beach						Sandy beach with shelter from south-westerly winds. Water quality not monitored by NRA in 1992.
	★	**Readymoney Cove (Fowey)**	FFPPPFP	1	3,300	Raw	At LWM	Sandy. Transfer to new full treatment works planned for 1995.
		Lantic Bay						Sand and shingle. Strong undertow. Water quality not monitored by NRA in 1992. Coastal land owned by the National Trust; leaflet with further information available from the National Trust.
		Lansallos Bay						Sandy. Safe bathing. Water quality not monitored by NRA in 1992.
		Polperro		1	3,500	Maceration	At LWM	Pebbles. Water quality not monitored by NRA in 1992.

Beach No on Map	Rating. The more stars the better. **f**=failed	Resort	Pass/Fail track record	Sewage outlets	Population discharging from outlet	Type of treatment	Discharge point relative to low water mark, unless otherwise stated. Distance given in metres	Remarks
	★	**East Looe**	PPPFPPP					Sandy.
	★★	**Millendreath**	~PPFPPP					Sandy.
	f	**Seaton Beach**	FFFPPPF	1	1,337	Raw	At LWM	Grey sand and pebbles. Improvement scheme for completion in 1995 to provide sewage treatment and discharge via medium sea outfall.
	★★	**Downderry**	~FPPPPP	1	1,000	Raw	At LWM	Silvery sand. Scheme as above.
16 ★★★★		**Portwrinkle** (Whitsand Bay)	~FPPPPP	1	800	Macerated	At LWM	Grey sand. Bathing-related illnesses reported 1992. Flow interception and transfer to Seaton planned for 1995.
	★★	Cawsand Bay		2	500	Raw	At LWM	Pebbles and rocks. Improvement scheme to intercept and transfer flows to new inland works by 1995.
		Kingsands Bay		2	157 665	Raw	5 and 12 below LWM	Sand and shingle. Water quality not monitored by NRA in 1992. Improvement scheme to intercept and transfer flows to new inland works by 1995.

SOUTH DEVON

Beach No on Map	Rating	Resort	Pass/Fail track record	Sewage outlets	Population discharging from outlet	Type of treatment	Discharge point	Remarks
f		**Plymouth Hoe**	FFFPFFF	Many	10,400	Primary and Raw	From LWM to 50 below	£37.6 m improvement scheme due in 1998 will provide primary treatment at Millbay.
	★★	**Bovisand Bay**	PPPPPPP					Sand and rocks. Polluted by untreated sewage from Plymouth outfalls.
17 ★★★★		**Wembury**	PFPPPPP	1	4,400	Secondary	100 below LWM	Silvery sand and rocks. Discharge point remote from beach.
	★★	**Mothecombe**	PPPPPPP					Sandy. Bathing safe only on incoming tide.
	★★★★	**Challaborough**	PFPPPPP					Sandy and rocky. Bathing dangerous at low tide.

Beach No on Map	Rating. The more stars the better. **f**=failed	Resort	Pass/Fail track record	Sewage outlets	Population discharging from outlet	Type of treatment	Discharge point relative to low water mark, unless otherwise stated. Distance given in metres	Remarks
18		**Bigbury-on-Sea:**		1	1,260	Secondary	50 below LWM	Sandy. Swimming dangerous near river mouth. Popular with windsurfers.
	★★★★	North						
	★★★★	South	PPPPPPP					
	★★★★	**Bantham**	PPPPPPP					Sand and mud. Some bathing-related illnesses reported. Bathing dangerous.
		Thurlestone:						Red sand. Sheltered swimming. Improvement scheme completed 1992; sea discharge intercepted and pumped to inland works including tertiary treatment by reed-beds. Good for windsurfing.
	★★★★	**North**	~~~FFFP					
	★	**South**	~~~PPPP					
	★	**Hope Cove**	PPPPPPP					Sandy. Flows transferred for treatment inland.
		Soar Mill Cove						Stream-crossed sands, rock pools and cliffs. Water quality not monitored by NRA in 1992.
	★	**Salcombe North**	FPPFPFP	4	3,400	Macerated and raw	At LWM and 50 below	Sandy. Full treatment by 1995.
	★★	**Salcombe South**	FPFPPPP	1	21	Raw	7 below	Sandy.
	★★	**Mill Bay**	PFPPPPP					Sandy.
		Hallsands						Shingle. Interesting ruined village nearby. Water quality not monitored by NRA in 1992.
		Beesands						Shingle, steeply shelving.
	★★★★	Torcross	~~~~PPP	1	500	Raw	At LWM	Fishing port. Flow interception and transfer to full treatment works planned for 1995.
19 ★★★★		**Slapton Sands**	PPPPPPP	1	900	Secondary	To stream	Tiny red pebbles.

Beach No on Map	Rating. The more stars the better. f=failed	Resort	Pass/Fail track record	Sewage outlets	Population discharging from outlet	Type of treatment	Discharge point relative to low water mark, unless otherwise stated. Distance given in metres	Remarks
		Pilchard Cove		1	600	Raw	To stream	New full treatment works planned for completion in 1993.
20	****	Blackpool Sands	PPPPPP					White sand. Shelves steeply.
		Leonard's Cove		2	1,051 1,044	Raw Raw	At LWM At LWM	Shingle. Water quality not monitored by NRA in 1992.
	**	Dartmouth Castle and Sugary Cove	PPPPPP	5	11,900	Raw	At LWM to 50 below.	Shingle. New full treatment works, flow transfers and outfall planned for 1995.
	**	St Mary's Bay	PPPPPP	1	93,200	Raw/ maceration	220 below LWM	Sand and pebbles. New full treatment works, flow transfers and outfall planned for 1995.
	****	Shoalstone Beach	PPPPPP					Pebbles.
		Churston Cove						Shingle. Water quality not monitored by NRA in 1992.
	**	Broadsands Beach	PPPPPP					Muddy sand and pebbles.
	*	Goodrington Sands	PFPPPP	1		Screened	At LWM	Sand and pebbles. Storm water overflow.
	**	Paignton Sands	PPFPPP	1		Screened	200 below LWM	Red sands. Reports of oil on beach 1992.
	**	Preston Sands	~~~PPPP	1		Screened	At LWM	Red sands. Stormwater overflows.
	**	Hollicombe	PPPPPP					
	f	Torre Abbey Sands	PPPPPF					
	****	Beacon Cove	~PPPPP					
	****	Meadfoot Beach	PPPPPP					Sandy at low tide.
	**	Anstey's Cove/ Redgate Beach	PPPPPPP	1	99,400	Fine screened	At LWM	Sand and shingle. Outfall off Hope's Nose. Flows to be transferred and outfall planned for 1998.

Beach No on Map	Rating. The more stars the better. f=failed	Resort	Pass/Fail track record	Sewage outlets	Population discharging from outlet	Type of treatment	Discharge point relative to low water mark, unless otherwise stated. Distance given in metres	Remarks
	★★	**Babbacombe**	PPPPPPP	1	1,000	Transfered as previous entry		Shingle.
21	★★★★	**Oddicombe**	PPPPPPP					Shingle.
21	★★★★	**Watcombe Beach**	PPPPPPP					Sandy.
21	★★★★	**Maidencombe**	PPPPPPP					Red sand.
	★★★★	**Ness Cove**	PPPPPFP					Sandy. Sewage-related debris reported 1992. Improvements as below.
	★	**Shaldon**	FFFPPFP	1	1,700	Raw	At LWM	Sandy. New treatment provision, flow transfer and outfall, including removal of discharges to estuary, due for completion in 1993.
	★	**Teignmouth**	PFPPPPP	2	18,300	Raw	50 below LWM	Sandy. Improvements as above.
	★	**Holcombe**	~~~FPPP	1	3,000	Raw	At LWM/ 330 below	Rocky. Improvements a above.
	f ★★	**Dawlish** Town Coryton Cove	PPPPPPF ~~~~~PP	2	21,500	Raw	At LWM/	Red sand/shingle. Town beach affected by sewage-related debris. Sewage slicks and gross littering reported 1992.
	★★★★	**Dawlish Warren**	PPPPPPP					Sand and dunes. Bathing dangerous near river. Sewage-related debris a problem. Reconstruction works.
	★★★★	**Exmouth**	FPPPPPP	1	42,700	Primary	170 below LWM	Sandy. sheltered from all but easterly winds. Buoyed area dedicated to windsurfing, strong tides. Beach patrolled Sundays and Bank Holidays. Resewerage works, flow transfer from Lympstone due for completion in 1993. Transfer of Budleigh Salterton flows with upgraded treatment works planned for 1995. Sewage-related debris a problem, reports of bathing-related illnesses.

Beach No on Map	Rating. The more stars the better. f=failed	Resort	Pass/Fail track record	Sewage outlets	Population discharging from outlet	Type of treatment	Discharge point relative to low water mark, unless otherwise stated. Distance given in metres	Remarks
	****	**Sandy Bay**	PPPPPPP					Red sand.
	**	**Budleigh Salterton**	PFPPPPP	1	5,066	Raw	50 below HWM	Pebbles sloping steeply. (see Exmouth for improvements)
	**	**Ladram Bay**	~PPPPPP	1	3,055	Primary	At LWM	Pebbles.
	**	**Sidmouth**	~~~~PPP	1	15,600	Maceration/ screens	400 below LWM	Pebbles with sand.
22	****	**Sidmouth: Jacob's Ladder**	PPPPPPP					
		Branscombe						Pebbles. Water quality not monitored by NRA in 1992.
	*	**Beer**	PPPPPPP	1	3,016	Raw	At LWM	Pebbles. Steep beach.
	**	**Seaton**	PFPPPPP					Pebbles. Steep beach. Improvement scheme.
DORSET								
		Lyme Regis:		2	32	Raw	10 below LWM	Sandy. £8.7 m improvement scheme planned for 1995 to provide primary treatment and a long sea outfall. Also sludge digesters planned.
		Monmouth Beach	FFFFFF~		9,519	Raw	15 below LWM	
f		**Church Beach**	~~~~~FF					
f		**Cobb Beach**	~~~~~PF					
	**	**Charmouth West**	FPPPPPP					Sand and shingle. 1.3km outfall, fine screening, storage of flow, discharge pulse at ebb.
	**	Charmouth East	~~~~~FP					
23	****	**Seatown**	PPPPPPP					Pebbles.
	**	**Eypemouth**	FPPPPPP					Pebbles.
24	****	**West Bay**	PPPPPPP	1	30,000	Maceration/ screens	1500 below LWM	Shingle; steep beach. Littering and marine debris a problem.
25	****	Burton Bradstock						Shingle.
	****	Chesil Beach		1	86,000	Maceration/ screens	1300 below LWM	Pebbles. Swimming very dangerous. Reports of littering 1992.

Beach No on Map	Rating. The more stars the better. f=failed	Resort	Pass/Fail track record	Sewage outlets	Population discharging from outlet	Type of treatment	Discharge point relative to low water mark, unless otherwise stated. Distance given in metres	Remarks
	★★★★	**Church Ope Cove**	PPPPPP					Shingle.
		Portland Harbour:						
	f	**Sandsfoot**	PPPPPPF					Sandy.
	★	**Castle Cove**	~~~~~PP					Sandy.
		Weymouth:						
	★	South	~~~~~PP					
	★★	Central	PPPPPP					Sandy.
	★★★★	Lodmoor West	~~~~~PP					
	★★★★	Lodmoor	~~~~~PP					
	★	**Bowleaze**	PPPPPP					Fine shingle and sand.
	★★	**Ringstead Bay**	PPPPPP					Shingle and pebbles.
26		**Durdle Door:**						Sand and pebbles.
	★★★★	**West**	PPPPPP					
	★★★★	East	~~~~~PP					
	★★	Stair Hole	~~~~~PP					
	★	**Lulworth Cove**	PPPPPP	1	2,000	Raw	Below LWM	Shingle. Discharge is outside the cove. Screens planned for 1994.
		Worbarrow Bay						Sand and pebbles. Closed at times due to military range. Water quality not monitored by NRA in 1992.
	★	**Kimmeridge Bay**	PPPPPP					Rocky.
		Swanage:		1	20,000	Maceration	100 below LWM	Sandy. Outfall off headland.
	f	South	~~~~~PF					
	★	Central	PPPPPP					
	f	North	~~~~~PF					
	★★	**Studland Bay**	PFPPPPP					White sand. Naturist beach. A leaflet about Studland and the surrounding area is available from the National Trust.
	★★★★	**Shell Bay**	~~~~~PP					Sandy. Strong currents.

Beach No on Map	Rating. The more stars the better. f=failed	Resort	Pass/Fail track record	Sewage outlets	Population discharging from outlet	Type of treatment	Discharge point relative to low water mark, unless otherwise stated. Distance given in metres	Remarks
		Poole:						
	★	**Rockley Sands**	FPPPPPP					
	★	**Lake**	PPPPPPP					
	★	**Harbour**	PPPFPPP					
27	★★★★	**Poole Sandbanks/ Shore Road**	PPPPPPP					
	★	Branksome Chine	~~~~~PP					Sand and shingle. Muddy at low tide (Lake and Harbour)
	★★★★	Alum Chine						Windsurfing popular.
		Bournemouth:						Sand.
	★	Bournemouth Pier	PPPPPPP					
	★★	Boscombe Pier	~~~~~PP					
	★★	Southbourne	~~~~~PP					
	★★★★	Hengistbury East	PPPPPPP					
		Christchurch:						
	★★★★	Mudeford Sandbank	PPPPPPP					
	f	Mudeford Quay	~~~~~PF					
	★★	Avon Beach	PFFPPPP					
	★★	Friars Cliff	~~~~~PP					
	★★	Highcliffe Castle	~~~~~PP					
28	★★★★	**Highcliffe**	PPPPPPP					Sailing harbour. Shingle and mud. Rivers Avon and Stour contain treated sewage giving a high coliform bacterial count in the harbour.
ISLE OF WIGHT								
	★	**Totland**	FPPPPPP	1	2,000	Maceration	300 below LWM	Shingle. To be transferred to Norton by 1993.
	★	**Colwell Bay**	FPFPPPP					Shingle.
		Yarmouth		1	1,000	Raw	170 below LWM	Sailing harbour. Shingle beach. Water quality not monitored by NRA in 1992. Flows to be transferred to Norton by end of 1993.
	★★	Norton	~~~~~PP	1	15,000	Maceration	230 below LWM	Sandy.

Beach No on Map	Rating. The more stars the better. f=failed	Resort	Pass/Fail track record	Sewage outlets	Population discharging from outlet	Type of treatment	Discharge point relative to low water mark, unless otherwise stated. Distance given in metres	Remarks
f		**Gurnard Bay**	FFFPFFF	1	5,800	Maceration	400 below LWM	Shingle.
f	★	**Cowes:** West East	FFFFFFF ~~~~~PP	1	15,000	Screens	700 below LWM	Sailing centre.
f	★★	**Ryde:** West East	FFFFPFF ~~~~~PP	1	21,000	Maceration	3km below LWM	Sandy.
		Seaview						Sandy and rocks. Bathing safe. Sewage transfer to Ryde. Water quality not monitored by NRA in 1992.
★★		**Bembridge**	FFFFPFP	1	7,000	Maceration/ tidal tank	800 below LWM	Sailing centre. New scheme planned for 1995 to give preliminary treatment and a long sea outfall. Reports of sewage-related debris in 1992.
★★★★		**Whitecliff Bay**	PPFFPPP					Sandy. Safe bathing.
★★		Yaverland	~~~~~PP	1	50,000	Primary	250 below LWM	Sandy.
★		**Sandown Esplanade**	PPPPPPP					Sandy.
★★ ★		**Shanklin** Shanklin Chine	PFPPPPP ~~~~~PP					Sandy.
f		**Ventnor**	FFFFPFF	2	5,300	Maceration	At LWM	Sandy. Improvement scheme to give preliminary treatment and a long sea outfall by 1995. Littering by plastics and polystyrene reported 1992.
29 ★★★★		**Compton Bay**	PPPPPPP					Pebbles.
f		**St Helens**	PFFFPPF	1	1,500	Raw		Sandy.
f		**Seagrove Bay**	PPFFFFF					Connected to Ryde.

1 Woolacombe Sand, Woolacombe, Devon   OS Ref: SS4500

Two rugged headlands, Morte Point and Baggy Point, bound this magnificent, straight, west-facing beach. Two miles (3km) of flat sands extend south from the rocky shore at Woolacombe to the sandstone cliffs of Baggy Point at Putsborough. This beach has again achieved a four-star *Good Beach Guide* grading for its water quality. The 380-yard (350m) wide sands are backed by extensive dunes, behind which rise the shrub-covered slopes of Woolacombe Down. Woolacombe Sand is popular with surfers, because of the crashing waves that wash the shore, and with families wanting to relax on the beach. After building sand castles and exploring the rock pools you can escape from the crowds by taking a stroll on the headlands at either end of the bay. On the northern side of Woolacombe there is a pocket-sized beach, in complete contrast to the long sweeping sands to the south. The small sandy Barricane beach nestles within the rocky shore stretching to Morte Point and is overlooked by the hotels and guest houses of Woolacombe.

Water quality Water quality monitored by the NRA and found to meet the EC Guideline coliform standards for bathing water in 1992. **** in this year's listing section. One outfall serving 11,000 people discharges fully treated sewage 110 yards (100m) below low water, north of the beach.

Bathing safety It is dangerous to swim near the rocks or at low tide because of undertow currents. Lifeguards patrol part of the beach from Whitsun to the second week in September.

Access A turning off the approach road to Woolacombe from the B3231 leads to car parks behind the beach. There are paths through the dunes to the sands.

Parking There are several car parks behind the dunes which provide over 1,000 spaces. National Trust car park close to Baggy Point.

Toilets There are toilets in the car park behind the dunes and at the Putsborough end of the beach.

Food There are cafés and shops at the Woolacombe end of the beach and a shop at Putsborough car park.

Seaside activities Swimming, surfing, windsurfing, diving, sailing and fishing. Surfboards are available for hire. Hang gliding from Woolacombe Down.

Wildlife and walks The North Devon Coast Path leads in both directions from Morte Bay. To the south, the gorse-clad Baggy Point affords excellent views across the bay, as does the jagged slate headland of Morte Point. On a clear day you can see Lundy Island lying 15 miles (24km) away in the Bristol Channel. This island is a Marine Nature Reserve, renowned for the rich marine wildlife around its rocky shores. The steep cliffs that soar 390 feet (120m) above the sea are the haunt of numerous seabirds. Trips to the island to explore its superb shore in greater detail are available from Ilfracombe harbour.

2 Shipload Bay, Hartland Quay, Devon   OS Ref: SS2428

Far removed from the seaside resort or the quaint tourist attraction, this is a small unspoilt cove on the northern side of Hartland Point. Cliffs 330 feet (100m) high rise sharply above the half moon of shingle and low tide sand. There are rocky reefs at either side of the beach The steps down to this sheltered beach are steep and quite difficult.

Water quality No sewage is discharged in the vicinity of this beach. Water quality monitored by the NRA and found to meet the EC Guideline coliform standards for bathing water in 1992. **** in this year's listing section.

Bathing safety Bathing from the centre of the beach is safe, but beware of currents that may cause problems.

Access From Hartland take the road signposted to Hartland Point lighthouse. The bay lies just off the road a mile before the Point; there are steps down the steep cliffs.

Parking There is a National Trust car park on the cliff top.

Toilets None.

Food None.

Seaside activities Swimming.

Wildlife and walks The North Devon Coast Path leads along the cliff path to Hartland Point; the strenuous walk is rewarded with excellent views along the rocky shore to the south and to Lundy Island on the far horizon. From the point, you look down on to a lighthouse standing on a lower promontory (the lighthouse is not open to the public).

3 Sandy Mouth, near Bude, Cornwall   OS Ref: SS200100

The National Trust watches over this superb Cornish beach, which is in pristine condition and absolutely unspoilt. The beach consists of rocks and sand with many rock pools, while the somewhat unstable cliffs surrounding the beach are covered in beautiful wildflowers.

Water quality Water quality is monitored by the NRA and found to meet EC Guideline coliform standards for bathing water in 1992. **** in this year's listing section.

Litter There is much seaborne litter.

Bathing safety Swimming is dangerous at low tide because of currents. Lifeguards patrol from Whitsun to August Bank Holiday.

Access From the A39 going north, turn left to Stibb and continue through the village to the beach car park.

Parking National Trust car park 110 yards (100m) behind beach.

Toilets There are toilets, including facilities for disabled visitors, near the car park.

Food A beach shop/café.

Seaside activities There is a National Trust interpretation leaflet for the beach. Walking is recommended, but keep one eye on the tide. Some areas may be cut off by the incoming tide and the cliffs offer little escape.

Wildlife and Walks The area boasts an Area of Outstanding Natural Beauty, Heritage Coast, Cornish Trust for Nature Conservation and National Trust land. A valuable site indeed – please treat with great care.

4 Widemouth Sand, Widemouth Bay, Cornwall   OS Ref: SS2002

In contrast to a lot of the beaches in North Cornwall, the mile (1.6km) of flat sands at Widemouth Bay is backed by low cliffs and undulating grassy fields which stretch down to the beach from the whitewashed houses of Widemouth village. Flat rocks, which can be too hot to lie on, stretch away in either direction from this popular surfing beach. The relatively easy access, which can be so important if you do not wish to negotiate steep cliff paths, unfortunately means that in summer the beach often becomes very congested. The cliffs that rise on either side of the beach provide walks away from the busy sands.

Water quality Water quality monitored by the NRA and found to meet the EC Guideline coliform standards for bathing water in 1992. **** in this year's listing section. No sewage is discharged in the vicinity of the beach.

Litter There are reports of bottles and containers being washed up on the beach. The beach is cleaned all year round by the local authority and there is a dog ban.

Bathing safety Surf bathing is dangerous at low tide, and beware of currents near the rocks at each side of the beach. Lifeguards patrol the beach during the summer.

Access Widemouth Bay is signposted from the A39 south of Bude. Sandy slopes and steps lead from the car parks on to the beach.

Parking There are two car parks behind the beach at either end of the bay, with spaces for approximately 200 cars in each.

Toilets There are toilets at the car parks.

Food There is a a café at the southern car park and a beach shop at the northern.

Seaside activities Swimming, surfing, windsurfing and fishing. Surfboards are available for hire.

Wildlife and walks The coast path leads off the road south of the beach, climbing Penhalt cliff towards Dizzards Point. There are superb views looking back along the straight coast stretching north of Bude.

5 Polzeath, Cornwall   OS Ref SW930790

Situated in Hayle Bay in the Camel Estuary, Polzeath is a very popular small resort. The beach is flat and sandy and is cleaned regularly all year round by volunteers from the local Residents Association. There is an information board on the beach which gives details about the beach area and water quality.

Water quality Water quality monitored by the NRA and found to meet the EC Guideline coliform standards for bathing water in 1992. **** in this year's listing section. One outfall serving 656 people discharges primary treated sewage at low water mark. There is a dog ban at this beach.

Bathing safety Bathing can be dangerous at low water. Lifeguards patrol from Whitsun to August Bank Holiday.

Access A turning off the B3314 leads down a steep hill to Polzeath. The village is on a local bus route.

Parking There are two private car parks adjacent to the beach, one local authority car park on the beach and another at New Polzeath, close by. The Marine Conservation Society is not in favour of car parking on the beach.

Toilets Near the beach, with facilities for disabled visitors.

Food There are hotels, pubs, cafés and takeaways in the village.

Seaside activities Swimming, surfing.

Wildlife and walks There are good walks on the National Trust property north of Polzeath with superb views from Pentire Point and the Rumps headland where there is an Iron Age fort. Tamarisk grows well in this area and is spectacular in July and August.

6 Constantine Bay, Treyarnon, Cornwall   OS Ref: SW8575

This wide, sweeping arc of gently shelving soft pale sands, backed by large marram-covered dunes and bounded on either side by low headlands with rocky outcrops stretching seaward, is a picture to behold. There is very limited parking and there are few facilities available at the beach.The beach is cleaned all year round.

Water quality Water quality monitored by the NRA and found to meet the EC Guideline coliform standards for bathing water in 1992. ★★★★ in this year's listing section. No sewage is discharged in the vicinity of this beach.

Bathing safety Bathing is dangerous near the rocks. Lifeguards patrol from Whitsun to August Bank Holiday.

Access A road off the B3276 at St Merryn is signposted Constantine Bay.

Parking A private car park with space for 200 cars is located 2 minutes from the beach.

Toilets There are toilets at the entrance to the beach.

Food None.

Seaside activities Swimming, surfing.

Wildlife and walks The dunes behind the beach are under restoration, with marram grass being planted to stabilise the sands. There are interesting rock pools to explore. The coast path skirts the bay but the low cliffs do not provide the spectacular views that can be found elsewhere on this coastline.

7 Crantock, Cornwall   OS Ref: SW7761

An excellent sandy beach nestles between the twin headlands of Pentire Point East and Pentire Point West. The beach is backed by high dunes and Rushy Green, an area of undulating grassland behind the dunes. The tidal channel of the River Gannel bounds the northern side of the beach, below Pentire Point East. There is a deep inlet in the low cliffs on the south side of the bay, Vugga Cove, which can only be reached at low tide. There are also a number of caves; the one closest inshore – Piper's Hole – can be explored at low tide. There are many signs of man's activities around the bay; two slipways are cut into the rocks of Vugga Cove, a poem is carved on a rock in Piper's Hole and there is evidence along the Gannel of its past use as a natural harbour. The entire beach is owned by the National Trust.

Water quality Water quality monitored by the NRA and found to meet the EC Guideline coliform standards for bathing water in 1992. ★★★★ in this year's listing section. There is no sewage discharged in the vicinity of this beach.

Bathing safety Bathing is dangerous at low tide and near the Gannel. Red flags indicate where and when it is safe to swim. The beach is patrolled by lifeguards between mid-May and mid-September.

Access Crantock is signposted from the A3075 south of Newquay. A lane from the village leads to a car park behind the dunes. There is a path through the dunes to the beach. The beach can also be reached from West Pentire; a path leads from the village to steps down the cliffs. The Gannel can be crossed from Newquay by either ferry or tidal bridge at Fern Pit and Trethellan.

Parking National Trust car park behind the dunes and another in West Pentire.

Toilets There are toilets at both car parks.

Food Cafés, shops and pubs in Crantock and West Pentire.

Seaside activities Swimming, surfing and fishing.

Wildlife and walks There is a network of paths south of the beach providing pleasant circular walks. The footpath which follows the cliffs on the southern side of the beach passes Piper's Hole, a deep crevice in the cliffs where fulmars may be seen nesting. The path continues to the end of the headland where there is a collapsed cave and beautiful views to be enjoyed. Tucked below the headland is a tiny unspoilt cove, Porth Joke. The walker can either continue around the next headland, Kelsey Head, toward Holywell beach or make the return journey across Cubert Common.

8 The Towans, Hayle, St Ives, Cornwall   OS Ref: SW5639

St Ives Bay has a magnificent necklace of golden beaches, backed on its southern edge by high dunes and some rocky outcrops. The approach to the beach at Hayle is uninspiring; there has been a lot of development on the landward side of the dunes which is rather unattractive and an army of telegraph poles marches across the scene. However, once down on the beach all is forgotten; the 3 miles (5km) of rippled pale golden sands remain untouched by the development behind. From the mouth of the River Hayle the sands, fringed by magnificent dunes and rocky outcrops, stretch north towards Godrevy Point where Godrevy lighthouse stands on an island just offshore. Dogs are banned from Easter to 1 October. The beach is cleaned regularly.

Water quality Water quality monitored by the NRA and found to meet the EC Guideline coliform standards for bathing water in 1992. **** in this year's listing section. No sewage is discharged in the vicinity of this beach; an outfall is to be constructed at Gwithian to discharge St Ives and Penzance sewage.

Bathing safety There are strong currents around the river mouth which make bathing dangerous. Lifeguards patrol the beach during the summer.

Access The beach is signposted from the A30 through Hayle. The road leads up to the car parks behind the dunes and the sands are less than 5 minutes' walk away.

Parking Car parks behind the dunes provide plenty of spaces.

Toilets There are toilets at the car parks.

Food There is a beach shop and café at the car parks. A hotel provides snacks and meals.

Seaside activities Swimming and surfing. Surfboards are available for hire.

Wet weather alternatives Hayle Paradise Park and West Cornwall Leisure and Bowling Club.

Wildlife and walks Following the beach north brings you to the rocky shore towards Godrevy Point where the coast path leads along the cliffs to Navax Point. There are lovely views back across St Ives Bay and numerous seabirds can be seen nesting on the cliffs.

9 Porthmeor, St Ives, Cornwall   OS Ref: SW5241

The delightful old buildings which are crowded together on the narrow streets around the harbour spill directly on to the beach at Porthmeor. A row of stone houses faces on to the sands but they in no way spoil this most attractive of beaches. Below St Ives Head, also known as the Island, ⅔ mile (1km) of soft sand backed by low cliffs stretches west. Unlike the more sheltered beaches on the other side of the headland, Porthmeor is a surfer's beach with the waves from the Atlantic rolling on to the shore. A promenade at the foot of the cliffs provides all the facilities needed for a day on this lovely beach. St Ives is famous for the quality of light that has made it popular with artists, a fact reflected in the numerous art galleries and craft workshops to be found in the town. Dogs are banned from the beach from Easter until 1 October. The beach is cleaned daily in the summer.

Water quality Water quality monitored by the NRA and found to meet the EC Guideline coliform standards for bathing water in 1992. **** in this years listing section. One outfall serving 50 people discharges fine screened sewage into the sea 155 yards (150m) from the harbour wall.

Bathing safety Care must be taken when bathing during outgoing tides, as there is an undertow. The beach is patrolled by lifeguards in the summer. An area for use of surfboards is marked with buoys.

Access The beach is signposted within the town but it is best to use the large car park above the town and walk down to the beach. There are steps and a lane down on to the sands.

Parking The main car park for the town is signposted on the approach roads. There are car parks at either end of the beach; each has space for about 40 cars.

Toilets There are toilets at the car parks.

Food There is a beach shop and café on the promenade.

Seaside activities Swimming and surfing. Deck chairs, surfboards and beach huts are available for hire. Boat trips around St Ives Bay are available from the harbour.

Wet weather alternatives Art galleries, craft workshops, Barbara Hepworth Museum, St Ives museum, St Ives Leisure and Squash Club.

Wildlife and walks From the beach a coastal path leads west along the low rocky cliffs to a series of sandy and rocky coves.

10 Whitesand Bay, Sennen Cove, Cornwall   OS Ref: SW3626

On the rugged Land's End Peninsula the splendid sweep of Whitesand Bay is in sharp contrast to the many rocky coves that indent the cliffs. From the picturesque little harbour of Sennen Cove the beach stretches north 1 mile (1.6km) to Aire Point, with steep cliffs ringing the northern section. The southern end of this moderately shelving beach is good for swimming and surfing, being sheltered by offshore reefs. The northern end is open to the full force of the Atlantic and conditions can be wild and dangerous. Dogs are banned from the beach between Easter and 1 October. It is cleaned by the local authority.

Water quality Water quality monitored by the NRA and found to meet the EC Guideline coliform standards for bathing water in 1992. ★★★★ in this year's listing section. One outfall serving 1,489 people discharges macerated sewage at low water mark by the harbour. There have been some complaints of sewage slicks in the bay in the past.

Bathing safety Bathing and surfing are safe at the southern end of the bay. Lifeguards patrol the beach during the summer months.

Access A road from the A30 to Land's End leads steeply down to Sennen Cove. There is easy access to the beach.

Parking There is a car park in Sennen Cove and another on the approach road.

Toilets There are toilets in the village.

Food Shops, cafés and a pub in the village.

Seaside activities Swimming, surfing and angling. Fishing trips are available from the harbour. Surfboards can be hired.

Wildlife and walks The granite cliffs south from Sennen Cove to Land's End are owned by the National Trust. The coast path follows the cliff top which can be wild and windswept. It is probably the best way to approach Land's End, avoiding the severe summer congestion of the most westerly tip of Britain which has been rather spoilt by uncontrolled development.

11 Poldhu Cove, Mullion, Cornwall   OS Ref: GR6620

A stream crosses this sheltered, sandy cove backed by dunes and bordered by steep, turf-covered slopes. At high tide there is a fair-sized beach, and the falling tide reveals wide, gently sloping sands washed by clear green seas. This cove is easily accessible, making it popular and often busy. It can be a good starting point for reaching coves north and south which are quieter. The Cornwall South Coast Path leads south to the Marconi Memorial ¾ mile (1.2km) away, and north to Church and Dollar coves. Both are fine, sandy coves framed by low, rocky cliffs, but they are unsafe for swimming at low tide. On the rocks of Church Cove stands the 15th-century church of St Winwaloe.

Water quality Water quality monitored by the NRA and found to meet the EC Guideline coliform standards for bathing water in 1992. ★★★★ in this year's listing section. No sewage is discharged into Poldhu Cove.

Bathing safety Signs warn that it is unsafe to swim for one hour either side of low tide. The beach is patrolled by lifeguards during the summer season.

Access A lane north-west of Mullion, signposted to Poldhu, leads down to the car park behind the beach. There is a path to the sands.

Parking There is a car park with 100 spaces close to the beach and another car park behind Church Cove.

Toilets On the beach.

Food There is a beach shop/café.

Seaside activities Swimming, surfing, windsurfing and fishing from the beach, but no hiring facilities for boards etc.

Wildlife and walks There are pools among the rocks that fringe the beach, with plenty of marine life to be examined.

12 Kynance Cove, The Lizard, Cornwall   OS Ref: GR6912

A classic Cornish cove which is extremely well known for its magnificent cliff scenery and is therefore popular with visitors. The 200 foot (60m) cliffs shadow the golden sands which are revealed at low tide. Softer layers of rock between the richly-coloured serpentine have been eroded to form some spectacular cliff formations, impressive isolated stacks, arches and caves. The Devil's Bellows stacks tower as high as the cliffs; they are surrounded by the sands of the cove at low tide. The beach completely disappears at high tide, so take great care not to get cut off by the rising tide.

Water quality No sewage is discharged in the vicinity of this beach. Water monitored by the NRA and found to meet EC Guideline coliform standards for bathing waters in 1992. ★★★★ in this year's listing section.

Bathing safety Bathing is safe away from the rocks.

Access A toll road from the A3083 north of the Lizard leads to a car park on the cliff top. It is a 5-minute walk to the cove down a valley path to the north of the car park.

Parking National Trust car park on the cliff top.

Toilets There are toilets in the car park.

Food Beach café. There are seasonal refreshments in the car park.

Seaside activities Swimming.

Wildlife and walks There is good walking on the coast path along the cliffs, from which the seabirds nesting on the cliffs and stacks can be best appreciated. There are caves that can be explored at low tide.

13 Kennack Sands, Kuggar, Cornwall   OS Ref: SW7316

Probably the best swimming beach on the Lizard. Two separate 550 yard (500m) beaches merge at low tide to form one wide, gently sloping sandy beach. The pale sands, on the sheltered eastern side of the Lizard Peninsula, are fringed by dunes. At either end of the bay the sand gives way to shingle, which is bounded landwards by cliffs. This is a popular family beach.

Water quality Water quality monitored by the NRA and found to meet the EC Guideline coliform standards for bathing water in 1992. **** in this year's listing section. No sewage is discharged in the vicinity of this beach.

Bathing safety Bathing is safe.

Access A road from Kuggar village signposted for Kennack ends behind the beach; there is a short walk through dunes to the sands.

Parking There is a car park with 250 spaces at the beach entrance .

Toilets In the car park.

Food Cafés at the entrance to the beach.

Seaside activities Swimming, surfing, diving, windsurfing and fishing. Surfboards are available for hire adjacent to the beach.

Wildlife and walks The Cornwall South Coast Path proceeds east from the beach along the cliff tops towards Black Head with good sea views.

14 Towan Beach, Portscatho, Cornwall   OS Ref: SW8733

A safe and sandy beach south of the fishing village of Portscatho; 550 yards (500m) of sand and pebbles are encircled by low shale cliffs on which wild flowers abound. St Anthony Head, south-east of the beach, guards the entrance to Carrick Roads.

Water quality Water quality monitored by the NRA and found to meet the EC Guideline coliform standard for bathing waters in 1992. ★★★★ in this year's listing section. No sewage is discharged in the vicinity of this beach.

Litter Fishing materials and a lot of plastics are frequently washed up on the beach; however, it is periodically cleaned by the owners, the National Trust.

Bathing safety Bathing is safe.

Access From Portscatho take the road to St Anthony Head. The car park is off this road. There is a 330 yard (300m) level walk from the car park behind the beach to the sands.

Parking National Trust car park with 200 spaces behind the beach at Porth Farm.

Toilets There are National Trust toilets, including facilities for disabled visitors, 275 yards (250m) from the beach.

Food None.

Seaside activities Swimming, windsurfing, diving and fishing.

Wildlife and walks The beach lies on the Cornwall South Coast Path, which can be followed in either direction. There is a 6 mile (9.6km) circular route starting at the beach skirting land owned by the National Trust; follow the path inland along Froe Creek, turning east along the Percuil to Carricknath Point and beach. From there continue to the lighthouse on St Anthony Head, where there is a superb panorama of Falmouth Bay and the Black Rock. The path returns to Towan Beach along the cliff top.

15 Pendower Beach, Veryan, Cornwall   OS Ref: SW9038

A lovely, unspoilt beach with an attractive setting facing Gerrans Bay; there are good views from the beach towards the gorse-covered cliffs of Nare Head. There is a ⅔ mile (1km) strip of coarse sand fringed by dunes which have suffered from erosion. In order to repair the damage access is restricted, with areas fenced off. Further east the sand gives way to the rocky outcrops and sand of Carne Beach. There are rocky platforms below the steeply sloping cliffs towards Nare Head. A good family beach with easy access.

Water quality Water quality monitored by the NRA and found to meet the EC Guideline coliform standards for bathing water in 1992. ★★★★ in this year's listing section. No sewage is discharged in the vicinity of the beach.

Bathing safety Bathing is safe.

Access A turning off the A3078 leads to the car park behind the beach.

Do not take cars right to the end of the road as there is only parking for hotel patrons. There are two small slipways for launching water craft but there are difficulties when the beach is crowded. Carrick District Council has recently passed a bylaw restricting speeds close by the beach. At high tide the easiest access from Carne to Pendower beach is via the coast path which runs parallel to the beach.

Parking There are two car parks, one off the A3078 and the other through the village of Veryan. There are 200 spaces at the National Trust car park; access is from the Veryan side only. There are board walks across the dunes suitable for wheelchair users. A National Trust car park behind the dunes has about 200 spaces.

Toilets In the car park behind the dunes.

Food The Pendower House Hotel and café overlooks the beach.

Seaside activities Swimming and fishing.

Wet weather alternatives Veryan Sports Club.

Wildlife and walks There is abundant marine life to be found in the rock pools along the shore. The coast path follows the cliffs that rise to the southeast of the beach. Excellent views can be had from Nare Head and Carne Beacon. The panorama along the coast stretches from Zone Point in the west to Dodman Point in the east.

16 Whitsand Bay, Freathy, Cornwall   OS Ref: SX4052

A 3 mile (5km) sweep of sand backed by 250 foot (75m) cliffs stretches from Portwrinkle south-east to Rame Head. The rugged slate cliffs slope gently down to the beach where rocky outcrops dot the pale grey sands. Portwrinkle, with its tiny harbour, overlooks the rocky shore at the western end of the bay. Once a pilchard fishing village, it is now given over to the holiday industry with holiday development ranging over the cliff top. Further east the beach remains unspoilt by development. Access points to this long stretch of beach are few; there are paths down the cliffs at Tregantle and Freathy. The former provides the easiest route down but this part of the beach lies below the Tregantle Fort, which is used as a firing range. There have also been reports that this section of beach suffers considerably from marine litter washed on to the shore. At Freathy the path is steeper but the reward is a superb clean and quiet beach. There are excellent views along the bay to Rame Head, its seaward-pointing finger ending in a knoll topped by a small chapel. On a calm day the water may look very inviting but beware of strong rip currents.

Water quality Water quality at Portwrinkle monitored by the NRA and found to meet the EC Guideline coliform standards for bathing water in 1992. ★★★★ in this year's listing section. Three small outfalls discharge raw sewage at low water mark and one discharges treated sewage. A £900,000 scheme for a long sea outfall should be completed in 1995.

Litter There is a problem in some parts of the bay, with marine litter being washed on to the beach; a considerable amount of plastic includes bottles, old buckets and packaging.

Bathing safety Bathing is unsafe; the beach is valleyed which causes a tidal race and undertow. Life-saving teams are based at Tregonhawke and Tregantle in the summer.

Access Whitsand is signposted from the B3247. There are paths down the cliffs at Portwrinkle, Tregonhawke, Tregantle and Freathy. The area around Tregantle Barracks is used by the army as a firing range and a red flag indicates when access is prohibited.

Parking Cliff-top car parks at the access points; there are 150 spaces at Freathy.

Toilets On the beach at Freathy.

Food There is a café on the cliff top at Freathy and another at Tregonhawke.

Seaside activities Swimming, surfing and fishing.

Wildlife and walks Tregantle Cliffs and Rame Head are owned by the National Trust and provide good walks over the scrub headland with fine sea views.

17 Wembury, Devon   OS Ref: SX5248

Wembury is a Marine Protected Area set up to maintain its diverse marine wildlife. It is a particularly attractive and unspoilt bay. A valley opens to the back of the beach, where the only development is a car park and a small shop and café. Flanked on either side by low cliffs, a narrow strip of sand curves round the bay. Low tide reveals a series of sandy pockets between rocky reefs which contain numerous pools. This area is of significant marine biological interest and, while beach users should take the opportunity to investigate the shore life, a great deal of consideration is required so that the area remains unspoilt. The disturbance or collection of marine life should be avoided, as should littering, or any other type of damage to the beach and its surroundings. The view from the beach is dominated by the Great Mew Stone just off-shore. There is excellent snorkelling in the area.

Water quality Water quality monitored by the NRA and found to meet the EC Guideline coliform standards for bathing water in 1992. **** in this year's listing section. One outfall serving 4,383 people discharges secondary treated sewage. A £100,000 scheme for a sewage treatment works was completed in 1992.

Litter There is a small amount of marine litter.

Bathing safety   Bathing is safe, but beware of rocks off-shore.

Access   Wembury is signposted from the A379. A lane from the village leads down to the car park behind the beach, and a path approaches the beach about 33 yards (30m) away.

Parking   National Trust car park behind the beach.

Toilets   At the car park.

Food   There is a National Trust café and shop adjacent to the beach.

Seaside activities   Swimming, windsurfing, diving, sailing and fishing.

Wildlife and walks   The South-West Peninsula Coast Path skirts the bay, but the path to Wembury Point is frequently closed when the firing range around the point is in use.

18 Bigbury-on-Sea, Devon   OS Ref: SX6544

Bigbury-on-Sea is a pretty village with a sandy beach at the mouth of the South Devon Avon. Burgh Island, just off the beach, is connected by a causeway which is passable at low tide; at high tide there is a unique sea tractor which transports passengers to and from the island. The hotel on Burgh Island is reputed to have been the inspiration for Agatha Christie's *Ten Little Indians*. Dogs are not banned from the beach but must be kept under control.

Water quality   Water quality monitored by the NRA and found to meet the EC Guideline coliform standards for bathing water in 1992. ★★★★ (north and south) in this year's listing section. One outfall serving 1,286 people discharges primary treated sewage at low water mark.

Bathing safety   Bathing is safe, except near river mouth. Lifeguards patrol between May and September.

Access   From the village and car park.

Parking   There is a car park with space for 900 cars.

Toilets   In the village and on the island.

Food   There is a kiosk and café in the village and a pub and hotel on the island.

Seaside activities   Swimming, surfing, windsurfing, fishing, jetskiing.

Wildlife and walks   Bigbury is on the South Devon Coast Path and leaflets are available describing the area. Between the rivers Avon and Erme, the path follows the undulating cliff-line passing Burgh Island and the beaches of Bigbury and Challaborough. It leads on through one of the most strenuous sections of the coast path: after rounding Beacon Point walking becomes easier as the path drops down to Wonwell Beach and the Erme estuary. The many wild flowers attract numerous butterflies in summer.

19 Slapton Sands, Devon   OS Ref: SX8445

A 2 mile (4.5km) stretch of shingle beach extends from Pilchard Cove in the north to Torcross in the south. The main road from Dartmouth to Kingsbridge runs along the edge of the beach, with a large, reed-rimmed freshwater lake (Slapton Ley) on the other side. The village of Slapton itself is about a mile (1.6km) inland. The beach was used in 1943-4 as a practice area for the D-Day landings and all the local villages were evacuated while the US army took over the area. A Sherman tank has been salvaged from the sea and is on display in Torcross as a memorial, and opposite the lane to Slapton there is a stone obelisk put up by the US army as a 'thank you' to the local people. As can be expected on such a long, open beach, it is often very windy but the views all round Start Bay are spectacular. At low tide it is possible to walk round the headland from Torcross to Beesands, the next cove along, but if you get cut off there is an arduous walk back on the cliff path.

Water quality Water quality monitored by the NRA and found to meet the EC Guideline coliform standards for bathing water in 1992. ★★★★ in this year's listing section. One outfall serving 889 people discharges primary treated sewage 33 yards (30m) below low water mark.

Bathing safety Bathing is safe, but the beach shelves steeply – beware of the undertow.

Access The A379 runs along the edge of the beach; access is easy.

Parking There are car parks at Strete Gate, Torcross and approximately half way down the length of the beach.

Toilets In Torcross and at the car parks.

Food There are shops, cafés and pubs in Torcross.

Seaside activities Swimming, fishing and a children's play area at Strete Gate.

Wet weather alternatives Field Study Centre at Slapton Ley.

Wildlife and walks The area is rich in differing habitats and the Slapton Ley Field Centre organises guided walks throughout the summer. On the edges of the beach itself the unusual Yellow Horned Poppy can be found, which should be admired, not picked. Slapton Ley itself is the largest body of fresh water in the south-west of England and as a result is a mecca for many species of wildfowl and other animals. At Torcross there is a hide (with access for disabled visitors) to allow panoramic observation across the Ley and also a corner where children can feed the ducks and swans.

20 Blackpool Sands, Stoke Fleming, Devon OS Ref: SY8747

Blackpool Sands is a complete contrast to its Lancashire cousin. The only development of this beach, an unspoilt cove at the northern end of Start Bay, comprises a car park, a building serving takeaway food and drink and a toilet block. A crescent of coarse golden sand ⅔ mile (1km) long is flanked by steep, wooded cliffs. On the southern side of the cove below Matthews Point a valley opens to the shore, from which a stream, Blackpool Lake, flows across the moderately shelving sands into a pool, very popular among families with small children. Easy access and safe bathing make it a busy beach. Dogs are banned from the beach between May and September.

Water quality Water quality monitored by the NRA and found to meet the EC Guideline coliform standards for bathing water in 1992. **** in this year's listing section. No sewage is discharged in the vicinity of the beach.

Bathing safety Bathing is safe, but care is required because the beach shelves steeply.

Access Blackpool Sands are signposted from Dartmouth on the A379. South of Stoke Fleming a side road leads to the car parks where there is a promenade to the sands.

Parking There are three car parks adjacent to the beach.

Toilets At the car park.

Food There is a takeaway with off-licence and beach barbecue.

Seaside activities Swimming, windsurfing, sailing, fishing and diving. Toppers, windsurf boards and canoes are available for hire. Sailing and windsurfing school with RYA instructors. Beach shop offers deckchairs, parasols etc. for hire.

Wildlife and walks North of the beach the South Devon Coast Path can be followed, passing through Stoke Fleming to the entrance to the Dart Estuary. South, the footpath leads to Strete Gate and along the 5 mile (8km) sweep of Start Bay, fringed by shingle beaches, and on towards Start Point.

21 Oddicombe, Watcombe and Maidencombe, Devon OS Ref: SX9366

This is one of the most famous and popular seaside areas in Britain, known as the English Riviera on account of the mild climate and abundant palm trees. The large bay has numerous beaches, many of which passed the Guideline standards of the EC Bathing Directive (see the listing section). As should be expected in a large holiday area, there are a lot of things to do locally and on trips inland. Dogs are banned from most of the beaches between May and September. All the major beaches are cleaned daily over the summer season.

Water quality Water quality monitored by the NRA and found to meet the EC Guideline coliform standard for 1992 at Oddicombe, Watcombe and Maidencombe. **** in this year's listing section.

Bathing safety Bathing is generally safe. All beaches fly red flags when it is not.

Parking, food and toilets There are numerous facilities at most of the beaches.

Seaside activities There are many activities including swimming, fishing, sailing, and there are opportunities to hire boats and pedalos.

Wet weather alternatives The English Riviera Centre in Torquay, Kent's Cavern show caves, Paignton Zoo, Torbay Aircraft Museum, Compton Castle, Berry Pomeroy Castle, the Dart Valley Railway and the beautiful village of Cockington are all within reach. Leaflets available from the local tourist offices.

Wildlife and walks The South Devon Coast Path extends round the bay and offers some of the most glorious views on the south coast. More information is available from the local tourist offices.

22 Sidmouth, Jacob's Ladder, Devon   OS Ref: SY1287

An elegant Regency seaside resort overlooking Lyme Bay which has escaped over-commercialisation. Sidmouth has two beaches: the town beach and Jacob's Ladder beach to the west. There is great commitment on the part of the local authority towards the cleaning and maintenance of the beaches. The town sits in an open hollow between impressive sandstone cliffs facing a ⅔ mile (1km) long pebble and sand beach. To the west are the Chit Rocks and the Connaught Gardens, which give access to the 1 mile (1.6km) shingle and sand beach of Jacob's Ladder backed by the 500 foot (160m) west cliff. Sidmouth has all the amenities one may require of a quiet resort and is an ideal place for relaxing on the beach or walking in the surrounding countryside, but not a spot for those seeking bright lights and amusements. However, the town comes alive during the first week of August when it hosts an International Folk Festival. Dogs are banned on the town beach between 1 May and 30 September.

Water quality Water quality monitored by the NRA and found to meet the EC Guideline coliform standards for bathing water in 1992. Jacob's Ladder is four-star in this year's listing section. One outfall serving 15,880 people discharges screened and macerated sewage through a tidal tank 440 yards (400m) offshore.

Bathing safety Bathing is safe. The Sidmouth Inshore Rescue Club patrols at weekends.

Access Steps and a slope from the promenade lead on to the town beach. A sloping ramp gives access to Jacob's Ladder beach.

Parking Ham, Manor and Bedford car parks are close by in the town.

Toilets There are toilets in the Connaught Gardens and Port Royal.

Food Cafés and kiosks at the town beach and a kiosk at Jacob's Ladder beach.

Seaside activities Swimming, windsurfing, sailing and fishing. Deckchairs available for hire. Putting and golf courses.

Wet weather alternatives Sports centre, museum, theatre and indoor swimming pool.

Wildlife and walks There are some excellent walks on the surrounding hills and cliffs; the views of Sidmouth and the Heritage Coast from Peak Hill, Fire Beacon and Salcombe Hill are excellent.

23 Seatown, Bridport, Dorset   OS Ref: SY4292

This is an undeveloped and completely unspoilt beach in a most attractive setting. The green and lush Winniford valley opens to the coast at Seatown, where a lovely shingle beach shelves steeply to some sand at low tide. Steep sandstone cliffs rise on either side of the valley, the mellow-coloured sandstone making a pleasing contrast to the green grassland above. The cliffs show the distinctive signs of the sea's continual attack – sheer exposed rock at their summit with rock slumped at their base. To the west lies Golden Cap, the highest point on the southern coast, where the cliffs rise 626 feet (190m) above the shore. The beach is very popular with fishermen.

Water quality Water quality monitored by the NRA and found to meet the EC Guideline coliform standards for bathing water in 1992. ★★★★ in this year's listing section. No sewage is discharged in the vicinity of the beach.

Bathing safety The beach shelves steeply and great care is required when bathing.

Access A narrow lane from Chideock on the A35 leads to the shore.

Parking Car park behind the beach.

Toilets There are toilets in the car park.

Food The pub overlooking the beach serves food.

Seaside activities Swimming and fishing.

Wildlife and walks On either side of the beach the rugged sandstone and shale cliffs rise and fall steeply where river valleys cut through to the sea. To the west of the beach the Dorset coast path climbs on to the Golden Cap and from its flat table summit there are terrific views along the coastline and inland over the undulating patchwork of fields. To the east is Thorncombe Beacon, where a fire used to be lit to warn of potential invasion.

24 West Bay, Dorset   OS Ref: SY4690

West Bay is made up of two beaches, the East and West, separated by the twin piers of Bridport Harbour at the mouth of the River Brit. Both beaches are shingled, with West Beach having the larger pebbles. Towering cliffs run down steeply to either side of the beaches. West Bay has a small harbour providing facilities for fishing boats and pleasure craft. Once an important shipbuilding and sea-trading site, the village has buildings that date from the 17th century and a history that dates from Anglo-Saxon times.

Water quality Water quality monitored by the NRA and found to reach EC Guideline coliform standards for bathing waters in 1992. **** in this year's listing section.

Bathing safety No information was available at the time of publication.

Access West Bay is signposted off the A35 which bypasses Bridport and off the B3517 Weymouth to Bridport road.

Parking There are short-stay car parks on the esplanade and beside the harbour (240 spaces), close to both beaches.

Toilets Public toilets with facilities for disabled users are sited beside the harbour.

Food There are harbour-side kiosks, cafés and pubs.

Seaside activities Swimming, sailing, diving and fishing. Boats are available for fishing trips. Paddleboats may be hired at the mouth of the River Brit.

Wet weather alternatives The Harbour Museum illustrates the history of West Bay, as well as the rope and net trade for which Bridport is famous worldwide. There are also amusement arcades.

Wildlife and walks The coast path follows the cliffs, leading to Burton Bradstock in the east and Eype in the west. Spectacular views of Lyme Bay can be seen from both east and west cliffs. On clear days you can see as far as Portland in the east and Lyme Regis in the west.

25 Burton Bradstock, Dorset   OS Ref: SY4890

Chesil Beach officially begins here and runs the whole length of the coast as far as Portland. The shingle beach is backed by dramatic sandstone cliffs which are owned by the National Trust. At low tide a band of sand is revealed. The highly picturesque village of Burton Bradstock is worth exploring too, with its thatched, stone-built cottages set around a 15th-century church. Dogs (except guide dogs) are banned from the beach from June to September inclusive.

Water quality Water quality monitored by the NRA and found to meet the EC Guideline coliform standards for bathing water in 1992. **** in this year's listing section. No sewage discharged in the vicinity of this beach.

Bathing safety The beach shelves steeply and there is a strong under-tow which can make bathing dangerous.

Access The beach is signposted off the B3157 in Burton Bradstock, 3 miles (5km) east of Bridport.

Parking There is a 500-space car park close to the beach.

Toilets Public toilets with facilities for disabled visitors.

Food There is a beach café.

Seaside activities Swimming.

Wildlife and walks The coast path follows the cliff with fine views over Lyme Bay. As with most stretches of the Dorset coast, there are good geological exposures to be admired.

26 Durdle Door, Dorset   OS Ref: SY8280

This beach is famous for Durdle Door Arch, created by the great erosive power of the sea and probably the most photographed view along the Dorset coast. The eastern end of the beach (Durdle Door Cove) is protected by the arch while the rest of the beach is partially protected by a submerged offshore reef that dries in places along its length. The beach is a steep, narrow strand of mixed shingle, gravel and sand which makes a strenuous ⅔ mile (1km) walk to the western end where Bats Head, a chalk headland, forms an attractive boundary to the beach itself. All the cliffs backing the beach are steep and prone to occasional rockfalls – climbing them or sheltering underneath them is not advised.

Water quality Water quality each monitored by the NRA and found to meet the EC Guideline coliform standards for bathing water in 1992. **** in this year's listing section. No sewage is discharged in the vicinity of this beach.

Litter A small amount of marine litter, including plastic, rope and wood is washed up in Durdle Door Cove.

Bathing safety As with most shingle and gravel beaches, care is required since there can be sudden steep slopes underwater. The western end of the beach may be cut off under certain tide and wave conditions.

Access The beach is approached by steep 880 yard (800m) footpath from the cliff-top car park. Access on to the eastern end of the beach down a steep flight of steps cut into the cliff can be slippery in wet weather.

Parking There is a large cliff-top car park at Durdle Door Caravan Camping Park (with excellent views across Weymouth Bay to the Isle of Portland).

Toilets There are toilets at the caravan park.

Food Café and store in the caravan park.

Seaside activities Swimming, diving, snorkelling and fishing. The steep access to the beach means that heavy equipment, including picnic tables, should not be carried down.

Wildlife and walks The undulating cliffs form a challenging section of the Dorset Coast Path. To the east lies Lulworth Cove and the Isle of Purbeck, to the west White Nothe headland. However, the reward for tackling this stretch of Heritage Coast is a fine view across Weymouth Bay and to the glorious beaches below. The chalk habitat creates picturesque downland with its accompanying flora and fauna.

27 Sandbanks, Poole, Dorset   OS Ref: SZ0487

An extremely well managed and popular beach with consistently good or excellent water quality. From North Haven Point at the end of the Sandbank spit, the fringe of golden sand stretches 3 miles (5km) north-east to merge with the beaches of Bournemouth. The pedestrian promenade is backed by the steep pine- and shrub-covered Canford Cliffs. Flaghead Chine, Cranford Chine and Branksome Chine cut through the cliffs to the beach. South-west, the cliffs give way to the low-lying Sandbanks peninsula at the mouth of Poole Harbour. Here the beach is edged by dunes and overlooked by a holiday development and the Sandbanks Pavilion and recreation area. The whole of Poole Harbour is a centre for sailing and water sports, and there is an ever-changing boating scene at the harbour entrance. There are excellent views across the harbour and of Brownsea Island from Evenning Hill off the western shore road. A removal of canine faeces bye-law and dog ban between Sandbanks and Branksome Chine is in force from May to September, and dogs must be kept on a lead on the promenade. The beach is cleaned daily.

Water quality Water quality monitored by the NRA and found to meet the EC Guideline coliform standards for bathing water in 1992. ★★★★ in this year's listing section. No sewage is discharged in the vicinity of this beach.

Bathing safety Bathing is safe, except at the extreme western end of the beach near the harbour entrance. Warning signs indicate where not to swim. Segregation of bathers and powered vessels is actively encouraged, with a buoyed area in which boats must observe a strict speed limit. The beach is patrolled by lifeguards at weekends and on bank holidays from May to September and there is a first aid post manned by St John Ambulance at weekends.

Access There is easy access along the length of the beach; paths lead down the cliffs to the promenade. There is access for disabled visitors to the promenade at Sandbanks, Branksome Chine and Branksome Dene Chine.

Parking There are seven car parks with 1,400 spaces along the length of the beach. There is also parking available on adjacent streets.

Toilets There are toilets with facilities for disabled visitors and mother and baby rooms along the beach.

Food Cafés and kiosks close to the beach.

Seaside activities Swimming, windsurfing, sailing and fishing. There are windsurf boards and boats for hire. Poole harbour has several windsurfing and sailing schools. There is also a putting green, crazy golf and a variety of children's amusements.

Wet weather alternatives Tower Park leisure complex incorporating Splashdown, Ice-Trax, Mega-Bowl, multi-screen cinema and sports centre; swimming pool, aquarium, Guildhall Museum, Archaeological Museum, Royal National Lifeboat Museum, Maritime Museum, Waterfront Museum, Arts Centre and Poole Pottery, Poole Park.

Wildlife and walks There is a car and pedestrian ferry from North Haven Point to Shell Bay, where the extensive Studland Heath National Nature Reserve backs an excellent beach. There is also a pedestrian ferry to Brownsea Island. 200 acres (80 hectares) of this 500 acre (202 hectare) National Trust-owned island is a nature reserve run by the Dorset Trust for Nature Conservation. There are many different types of habitat to be found on the island including heathland, woodland, freshwater lakes, salt marsh and the sea shore. There is a nature trail and guided walks are available during the summer. Further information is available from the National Trust shop on the island's landing quay.

28 Highcliffe, Dorset   OS Ref: SZ2093

From Highcliffe Castle (which resembles the ruins of an impressive cathedral rather than a castle), steps lead down the gently sloping shrub- and tree-covered cliffs directly on to the sand. A lovely, long beach of sand and pebble extends from Highcliffe Castle to Highcliffe Crow's Nest. This is a clean, unspoilt stretch of beach which is ideal for a day relaxing in the sunshine. Between 1 May and 30 September dogs are permitted on Highcliffe Castle beach but not on Highcliffe Crow's Nest. On the promenade, cliff paths and adjacent car park, dogs must be kept on a lead. Owners are asked to clean up after their dogs and receptacles are provided. During the summer the local authority employs a team of litter-pickers to clean the beaches and surrounding area.

Water quality Water quality monitored by the NRA and found to meet the EC Guideline coliform standards for bathing water in 1992. ★★★★ in this year's listing section. No sewage is discharged in the vicinity of this beach.

Bathing safety   Bathing is safe, but care is required because the beach shelves quite quickly. A patrol boat operates daily from mid-July to early September. This stretch of coast has separate designated areas for swimming and windsurfing, which are signposted on the beach. There is a slight problem with weever fish.

Access   From the A337 through Highcliffe a side road leads to Highcliffe Castle. There are steps and a path down the cliff. The steps are quite gentle but access may be difficult for elderly and visitors with limited mobility, particularly the walk back up.

Parking   Car park at Highcliffe Castle with 100 spaces, 110 yards (100m) walk to the beach; at Steamer Point with 172 spaces, 330 yards (300m) walk to the beach; and at Highcliffe Top with 600 spaces, 440 yards (400m) walk to the beach.

Toilets   In Highcliffe Castle grounds and at Crow's Nest.

Food   During the summer there is often someone selling ices along the beach from a cool box. The newly refurbished Highcliff Castle Tea Rooms are now open throughout the year, depending on the weather.

Seaside activities   Swimming at Highcliffe Castle and windsurfing at Highcliffe Crows Nest. Fishing.

Wildlife and walks   There are woodland and nature walks on the cliffs at Steamer Point, where an information centre can provide details of the flora and fauna to be seen in the area.

29 Compton Bay, Isle of Wight   OS Ref: SZ3841

This is a lovely rural beach owned by the National Trust in an Area of Outstanding Natural Beauty. The beach itself is made up of shingles and extends for about ⅔ mile (1km). The cliffs are a part of the Hanover Point to St Catherine's Point Site of Special Scientific Interest (SSSI), renowned for its geological features as well as the fact that it supports a number of interesting plants and insects. There are superb views across the bay to Tennyson Down and in clear weather the Dorset coast at Purbeck can be seen.

Water quality   Water quality monitored by the NRA and found to meet EC Guideline coliform standards for bathing waters in 1992. ★★★★ in this year's listing section. No sewage is discharged in the vicinity of this beach.

Litter   The beach is cleaned regularly from Easter to the end of September and daily from the beginning of July to mid-September by the National Trust. It is sometimes susceptible to litter deposits after strong south-westerly winds, particularly in winter.

Bathing safety   The beach is considered to be safe. There are emergency telephones available, as well as lifebelts. There are no lifeguards but the beach is patrolled by National Trust staff from the beginning of July to mid-September. There is an inshore rescue boat station about 1 mile (1.6km) away at Freshwater Bay.

Access The beach can be reached from two places, although neither way is easy. Hanover Car Park provides the closest access to the beach but this is via a steep ramp which is sometimes destroyed by the tide in winter. The steps are rebuilt and maintained in the summer months. At the Compton Chine end of the beach the car park is situated beside the Compton Farm track. To get to the beach, cross the main road, follow a path round the edge of the field then descend several flights of steps.

Parking Two car parks provide space for about 400 cars.

Toilets There are toilets run by South Wight Borough Council in the Hanover Car Park. These are open from April to October and include facilities for disabled visitors.

Food A van supplies ice creams and a limited range of hot food at Hanover Car Park.

Seaside activities Swimming and surfing.

Wildlife and walks Compton Bay is on the Isle of Wight Coastal Path and adjoins many areas of National Trust land, including the downs behind the chalk cliffs at the western end of the Bay. It is the home of the glanville fritillary, a rare butterfly which lives on the eroding cliffs. Both the cliff and the adjoining downs are famous for many rare and interesting species of plant and insect.

South-East England

The south-east coast of England is rich in sharp coastal contrasts. The scenery ranges from long shingle banks to sand dunes and saltmarshes. Low clay cliffs predominate in Suffolk, creeks and mud flats are found on the Essex coast and also the Thames estuary, and the striking white cliffs of the south coast form an impressive setting to many busy holiday resorts and ferry terminals that are the gateway to Europe.

The south-east has some of the most heavily developed coastal regions and, as in most cases, with people and popularity come problems. The heavy shipping traffic in the Channel creates a continual problem with marine litter and oil being washed up on to the beaches, despite international legislation to stop such pollution. Extensive stretches of the coastline suffer from pollution by sewage, although action is being taken at many sites in the south and Southern Water are applying innovative ideas to their sewage treatment responsibilities. One major source of pollution, sewage sludge dumping off the Thames Estuary, must end by 1998 but other discharges, both nuclear and industrial, are still a cause for concern. The disturbance around Shakespeare Cliff from the construction of the Channel Tunnel will have a severe long-term effect on marine and coastal life. On a coastline under pressure from every type of human activity, tourism, industry, and residential development, continual effort is needed to ensure that those areas left unspoilt will remain so.

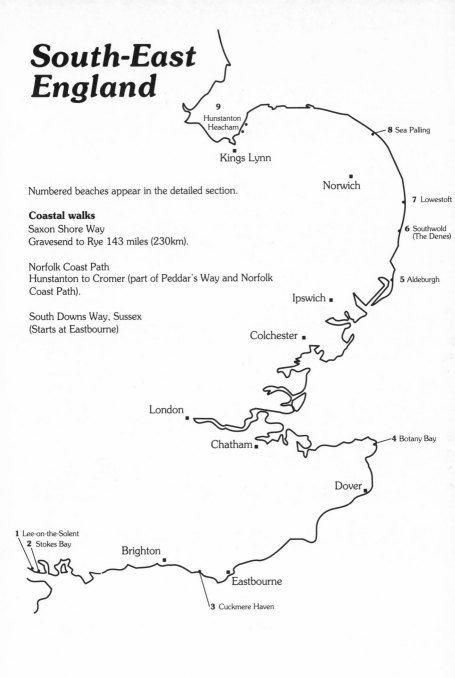

South-East England

9 Hunstanton Heacham

Kings Lynn

8 Sea Palling

Norwich

7 Lowestoft

6 Southwold (The Denes)

5 Aldeburgh

Numbered beaches appear in the detailed section.

Coastal walks
Saxon Shore Way
Gravesend to Rye 143 miles (230km).

Norfolk Coast Path
Hunstanton to Cromer (part of Peddar's Way and Norfolk
Coast Path).

South Downs Way, Sussex
(Starts at Eastbourne)

Ipswich

Colchester

London

Chatham

4 Botany Bay

Dover

1 Lee-on-the-Solent
2 Stokes Bay

Brighton

Eastbourne

3 Cuckmere Haven

The South-East   See page 21 for further details

Beach No on Map	Rating. The more stars the better. f=failed	Resort	Pass/Fail track record	Sewage outlets	Population discharging from outlet	Type of treatment	Discharge point relative to low water mark, unless otherwise stated. Distance given in metres	Remarks
HAMPSHIRE								
	★★	**Barton-on-Sea**	~~~PPPP	1	17,400	Flow transfer	At LWM	Pebbles and shingle. Scheme under construction to provide secondary treatment by 1995.
	f	**Milford-on-Sea**	FFFFPPF					Pebbles. Improvements as above.
	★★	**Lepe**	PPPPPPP					Sand and shingle.
	★★★★	**Calshot**	PFFPPPP	1	448	Maceration/ tidal tank		Mud. Existing flows are currently given primary treatment using a transportable waste water unit. Treated flows are stored in tidal tanks and released at high water. Scheme in progress to transfer waste to treatment works at Fawley.
	★★★★	Solent Breezes	~~~~~PP					
	★★★★	**Hill Head**	~~~~~PP					Dog fouling and sewage-related debris both a problem. Good winds for experienced windsurfers, big swell when winds high.
1	★★★★	**Lee-on-the-Solent**	PPPPPPP	1	200,000	Secondary	1100 below LWM	Sand and shingle. Good for all levels of windsurfing. Predominantly south-southwesterly winds giving good on- and cross-shore sailing.
2	★★★★	**Stokes Bay (Pier)**	PFPPPPP					Treatment as above.
	★	**Southsea (South Parade Pier)**	PFFPPPP					Shingle.
	★	**Eastney**	PPFPPPP	1	200,000	Screens	5 km below LWM	Shingle. New long sea outfall and improved fine screens.

Beach No on Map	Rating. The more stars the better. f=failed	Resort	Pass/Fail track record	Sewage outlets	Population discharging from outlet	Type of treatment	Discharge point relative to low water mark, unless otherwise stated. Distance given in metres	Remarks
	****	*Hayling Island (East)*	PPPPPPP					Shingle and some sand.
	****	*Hayling Island (West)*	PPPPPPP					Sandy. Some littering reported in 1992.
WEST SUSSEX								
	****	**West Wittering**	PPPPPPP					Sandy. Safe bathing.
	*	**East Wittering**	~~~~PPP					
		Bracklesham Bay						Sandy. Water quality not monitored by NRA in 1992.
	**	**Selsey Bill**	PFFPFPP					Shingle. Bathing unsafe.
	**	**Pagham**	PPFPPPP					Shingle.
	*	**Bognor Regis**	PPPPPFP	1	71,500	Screens	3km below LWM	Sandy.
	**	Felpham (Yacht Club)	~~~~~FP					Improvements planned to control storm water discharges for 1995.
	f	**Middleton-on-Sea**	FFFPPPF					Sand and shingle.
	**	**Littlehampton**	FFFPPPP	1	53,000	Maceration/ screens	2.5km below LWM	Sandy. Finer screens to be installed by mid 1993. Littering and sewage solids reported 1992.
		Goring-by-Sea		1	45,000	Primary	At LWM	Sand and shingle. Safe bathing. Scheme in progress to transfer waste water from Goring and West Worthing to current East Worthing site where flows will be given primary treatment prior to discharge via a new long sea outfall (4.5km). Improved storm water management will also be commissioned by 1995. Water quality not monitored by NRA in 1992.
		Worthing:		1	80,000	Primary	160 below LWM	Shingle and sand. Improvement scheme planned as above for 1995.
	f	**East**	~~~~~PF					
	f	**West**	FFFPPPF					

Beach No on Map	Rating. The more stars the better. **f**=failed	Resort	Pass/Fail track record	Sewage outlets	Population discharging from outlet	Type of treatment	Discharge point relative to low water mark, unless otherwise stated. Distance given in metres	Remarks
	f	*Lancing*	FFFFFFF					Shingle and sand. Improvement scheme planned as above for 1995.
	f	Shoreham (Kingston Beach)	~~~~~FF					Commercial port. Improvement scheme planned as at Goring-by-Sea by 1995.
	f	Shoreham-by-Sea Beach	F~~PPPF					
EAST SUSSEX								
	★	Southwick	FFFPFFP	1	54,000	Screens	50 below LWM	Shingle. Improvement scheme planned for 1995 as above.
	f	*Hove*	FFFFFFF					Pebbles and sand. Multi-million pound improvement scheme to be commissioned for 1995 to remove storm water outfalls from Hove and transfer all flows to Portobello.
		Brighton:		5		All storm water overflows		See above.
	★★	Kemp Town	~~~~~PP					
	★★	**Palace Pier**	PFFPFFPP					
	★★	**Saltdean**	PPPPPPP					Rocky with some sand.
		Portobello		1	300,000	Screens	1780 below LWM	New long sea outfall. Also see above. Water quality not monitored by NRA in 1992.
	★	**Newhaven**	PFFFFFP		7,500	Primary	Short sea outfall	Sandy beach within breakwater. Flows from East and West Newhaven have now been transferred to a new long sea outfall at Seaford.
	★★	Seaford (east of outfall)	~~~~~PP	1	21,500	Screens	Long sea outfall	Shingle beach is steep.
	★★	Seaford (Dane Road)	FFFFFPP					
3	★★★★	Cuckmere Haven						Pebbles. Bathing not safe at the mouth of the river.

Beach No on Map	Rating. The more stars the better. f=failed	Resort	Pass/Fail track record	Sewage outlets	Population discharging from outlet	Type of treatment	Discharge point relative to low water mark, unless otherwise stated. Distance given in metres	Remarks
	★★★★	Birling Gap	~~~~~PP					Steps down cliff to shingle beach. Many rock pools. Much marine litter in 1992.
	f ★	Eastbourne: East of Pier Wish Tower	~~~~~PF PPPPPP	1	90,000	Maceration/ screens	640 below LWM	Shingle and sand. Multi-million pound improvement scheme to be completed by 1995 to provide screening, primary treatment and improved storm water management.
	★★	Pevensey Bay	PFPPFPP	1	9,590	Maceration/ tidal tank	360 below LWM	Shingle with sand. Flows to be transferred to Eastbourne for 1995. Beach affected by sewage-related debris.
	★★	Norman's Bay	PPPPFPP					Shingle with sand at low water.
		Cooden Beach		2			150 above LWM	Shingle with sand at low tide. Flows from this area have been transferred to the long sea outfall at Bulverhythe. Improved storm water management planned for 1995. Water quality not monitored by NRA in 1992.
	★★	Bexhill (Egerton Park)	PPPPPPP	3	32,500	Maceration/ tidal tank	400 below LWM	Sand and shingle. Beware sand holes. Flows from this area have been transferred to the long sea outfall at Bulverhythe. Improved storm water management planned for 1995.
	f	Bulverhythe	~~~~~PF					Shingle. Long sea outfall.
	★★	St Leonards Beach	~~~~PPP	2	23,000	Maceration/ screens	2000 below LWM	Shingle, sand and rocks. Flows from this area have been transferred to the long sea outfall at Bulverhythe. Improved storm water management planned for 1995.

Beach No on Map	Rating. The more stars the better. f=failed	Resort	Pass/Fail track record	Sewage outlets	Population discharging from outlet	Type of treatment	Discharge point relative to low water mark, unless otherwise stated. Distance given in metres	Remarks
	f	**Hastings: Hastings (Queens Hotel)**	~~~~~FF	4	68,000	Screens/ maceration tank	140 below LWM	Shingle and sand. New long sea outfall. Improved storm water management for 1995.
	★★	**Hastings Beach (Fairlight Glynn)**	PFFPPFP					
	★★	**Winchelsea**	PPPPPPP					Shingle. Do not bathe when weather is rough.
	★★	**Camber Sands**	PFPPPFP					Sand dunes. Ridges in sand can be a danger.
		Broomhill Sands		1	9,500	Secondary	300 above LWM	Sandy and coarse shingle. Water quality not monitored by NRA in 1992.
KENT	f	Greatstone Beach	~~~~~PF					
		Littlestone-on-Sea	FFFFPFP					Sandy. UV disinfection.
	f	**St Mary's Bay**	FFFPFFF					Sandy. (As above).
	★	**Dymchurch: Dymchurch Hythe Road**	~~~~~PP	1	20,800	Secondary	Between HWM & LWM	Shingle and sand. New final tanks and UV disinfection.
	★★	**Dymchurch Beach**	FFFFPFP					
	★	Dymchurch Redoubt		1	3,000	Primary	At LWM	Pebbles and sand.
	★★	**Hythe**	FFFPFPP					Shingle and sand. New long sea outfall.
	f	**Sandgate: Sandgate Beach**	FFFPPPF					Shingle. Multi-million pound improvement scheme to give primary treatment, fine screening and long sea outfall in 1995. Improved storm water management will also be undertaken. The scheme will be commissioned by the end of 1995.
	f	Sandgate Town Centre	~~~~~PF					
	f	**Folkestone**	FFFFFFF	1		Screens	At HWM	Shingle. Improvement scheme as above.

Beach No on Map	Rating. The more stars the better. f=failed	Resort	Pass/Fail track record	Sewage outlets	Population discharging from outlet	Type of treatment	Discharge point relative to low water mark, unless otherwise stated. Distance given in metres	Remarks
		The Warren		1	20,000	Raw	584 below LWM	Danger from falling rocks. Improvement scheme as above. Water quality not monitored by NRA in 1992.
		Shakespeare Cliff		1	30,000	Maceration	635 below LWM	Sand and shingle. Multi-million pound improvement scheme being designed for the Dover area will include fine screening, primary treatment and discharge via long sea outfall. Improved storm water management in the lower Dour. To be commissioned by 1995. Start of the Tunnel. Water quality not monitored by NRA in 1992.
	★	Dover Harbour	~~~~PP					Windsurfing popular.
	★★	**St Margaret's Bay**	FPPPPPP					Shingle and rocks. Sewage-related debris a problem.
	★	**Deal Castle**	FFFFFFP	3	10,000	Screens/ maceration tank	731 below LWM	Steep shingle. Multi-million pound scheme to give secondary treatment, long sea outfall and improved storm water management by 1995. Path for wheelchair users installed in 1992; leaflet with further details of the route available from Dover District Council, Council Offices, Honeywood Road, Whitfield, Dover, Kent ME14 2LX.
f		**Sandwich Bay**	FFFFFFF					Sandy. Improvement scheme as above.
		Ramsgate:		3	20,000	Screens/ maceration	150 below LWM	Sandy. Improvement scheme to provide new inland treatment works at Ramsgate. Beach affected by sewage-related litter. Dog ban.
	★★	Ramsgate Sands	~~~~PP					
	f	**Ramsgate Beach**	PFFFFFF					

Beach No on Map	Rating. The more stars the better. f=failed	Resort	Pass/Fail track record	Sewage outlets	Population discharging from outlet	Type of treatment	Discharge point relative to low water mark, unless otherwise stated. Distance given in metres	Remarks
	★★ ★	Broadstairs **Broadstairs Beach**	~~~~~PP 1 FFFPFFP		24,000	Screens	3.6 km below LWM	Sandy. Improvement scheme commissioned 1991. Sewage-related debris a problem.
	★★★★	**Joss Bay**	FFPPPPP					Sandy. Poop scoop area. Reports of sewage-related debris and bathing-related illness 1992.
4	★★★★	Botany Bay	~~~~~PP 1		60,000	Screens	1.9 km below LWM	Sandy. Poop scoop area. New long sea outfall.
	★★	Palm Bay	~~~~~PP					Sandy. Poop scoop area. Watersports.
	★★★★	Walpole Bay	~~~~~FP					Sand, rocks. Dog ban.
	★★	**Margate (The Bay)**	PPPPPFP			Screens		Sandy. Sewage-related debris a problem.
	★	Westbrook Bay	~~~~~PP					Sandy. Poop scoop area.
	★	**St Mildred's Bay**	PFPPPPP					Sandy. Poop scoop area.
	★★	Westgate Bay	~~~~~PP					Sandy.
	★★★★	**Minnis Bay**	PPPPPPP			Fine Screens		Sand and rocks. Sewage-related debris reported 1992. Poop scoop area. Windsurfing popular, sailing area, café bar. Winds north to north-east – good variety of sailing at all times.
	f	**Herne Bay**	PFFFFFF 1		10,000	Screens	460 below LWM	Pebbles and sand. Improvement scheme planned for 1995.
	★★	**Whitstable**	PPPPPPP 1		10,000	Screens/ maceration	1.5 km below LWM	Shingle.
	★★	**Leysdown-on-Sea**	FFPFPPP					Sand, shingle and mud. Littered in 1992.
		Minster Leas						Water quality not monitored by NRA in 1992.
	★★★★	Sheerness	~~~~~PP					
ESSEX								
	★★	Canvey Island	~~~~~PP 1		45,500	Secondary	At LWM	Muddy sand.

Beach No on Map	Rating. The more stars the better. f=failed	Resort	Pass/Fail				
	★★	Leigh-on-Sea	~~~~~PP				
	★★	**Westcliff-on-Sea**	FFFPPFP				
	★★	**Southend-on-Sea**	~~~PPPP	1	210,000	Primar	
	★★	**Thorpe Bay**	FFFPPPP				
	★★	**Shoeburyness East**	~~~~~~PP				
	★★	Shoeburyness	~~~~~~PP				
	★	**West Mersea**	~~~~~FP	1	10,000	Secondary	To the colne
	★★★★	**Brightlingsea**	PFPPPPP				Muddy dangerou planned.
	★	*Jaywick*	PPPPPPP	1	38,000	Maceration	650 below LWM
	★	Clacton (off Coastguard Station)	~~~~~~PP	2			300 below LWM
	★	Clacton (Groyne 41)	~~~~~FP				50 below LWM
	★★	**Clacton (opposite Connaught Gardens)**	PFPPPPP				
	★★	**Holland-on-Sea**	PFPPPPP	1	70,000	Maceration	750 below LWM
	★★	**Frinton-on-Sea**	PPPPPPP	2			50 below LWM
	★	**Walton-on-the-Naze**	PFPPPPP	1	29,000	Secondary	50 below LWM
	★★	**Dovercourt**	PFFPPPP	1	39,000	Primary	At LWM
	★★	Harwich (Sailing Club)	~~~~~~PP				

Comments column:

- *Jaywick* — Sandy.
- Clacton (off Coastguard Station) — Sandy. Storm water outfalls only. Improvements planned for 1997.
- Clacton (Groyne 41) — 50 below LWM
- **Holland-on-Sea** — Sandy.
- **Frinton-on-Sea** — Sandy. Storm overflows only. Treatment planned for 1998.
- **Walton-on-the-Naze** — Sandy. See above.
- **Dovercourt** — Sandy. Treatment planned for 1997.

SUFFOLK

		Resort	Pass/Fail				
		Felixstowe:		1	4,262	Maceration	630 below LWM
	★★	**South Beach**	FPPPPPP				
	★★	**North Beach**	PPPPPPP				

Felixstowe comment: Red shingle and sand. Another outlet to docks serving 30,000. Improvement scheme for both beaches. Reports of sewage in water 1992.

Track record

Sewage outlets

Population discharging from outlet

Type of treatment

Discharge point relative to low water mark, unless otherwise stated. Distance given in metres

Remarks

500 below LWM

Sand, shingle and mud. Improvements as above.

Improvements as above.

Sand and shingle. Improvements as above.

n sand. Bathing . Improvements

Sandy. Improvements planned for 1998.

Small sandy beach.

...cliffs ...ed by

...A in ...ing

...ment ...ch for ...lors.

...stuary ...uth of

7 ****	**Lowestoft: South beach**	PPPPPPP				...ll ...s planned.
**	**Lowestoft: North beach**	FPPPPPP				
*	**Gorleston Beach**	~~~~~FP				

NORFOLK

	Great Yarmouth:		1	80,000 including screening discharge to river	Fine	1,050 below LWM	Sandy. Macerated sewage is discharged into the River Yare. Improvements to transfer all flows to outfall underway.
f	Power Station	~~~~~FF				
f	**Opposite Nelson Gardens**					
**	**Opposite Marine Leisure Centre**					
**	**Coastguard lookout**	~~~~~PP				
**	**Caister Point**	~~~~~PP				
*	**Hemsby**	~~~~~PP				
8 ****	Sea Palling						Sandy.
	Happisburgh						Sandy. Water quality not monitored by NRA in 1992.
**	**Mundesley**	PPPPPPP	1	14,000	Secondary/ other	1,420 below LWM	Sandy.

Beach No on Map	Rating. The more stars the better. f=failed	Resort	Pass/Fail track record	Sewage outlets	Population discharging from outlet	Type of treatment	Discharge point relative to low water mark, unless otherwise stated. Distance given in metres	Remarks
	★★	Overstrand	~~~~~PP					Sand and shingle.
	★	**Cromer**	PFFFPPP	1	13,500	Tidal tank	100 below LWM	Sandy. Improvement scheme underway.
		East Runton		1	1,400	Maceration	At LWM	Sandy. Improvement scheme underway. Water quality not monitored by NRA in 1992.
		West Runton		1	1,400	Maceration	At LWM	Sand and pebbles. Improvement scheme underway. Water quality not monitored by NRA in 1992.
	★★	**Sheringham**	FFFFPPP	1	10,000	Maceration	260 below LWM	Sand and shingle. Improvement scheme underway.
	★★	**Wells-next-the-Sea**	FFPPPPP	1	3,700	Secondary	To inland drain	Sandy. Improvement scheme underway.
9		**Hunstanton:**		1				Sand, stones and shingle. Storm overflow only. Sewage to Heacham treatment works.
	★★★★	Old Hunstanton Beach	~~~~~PP					
	★★★★	North Beach Sailing Club	~~~~~PP					
	★★	**Boat Ramp**	PPFPPPP					
	★★★★	South Beach Hunstanton Road	~~~~~PP					
		Heacham		1	24,000	Secondary/ tertiary	To river	Gravel. New treatment works completed 1990.
	★★★★	North Beach	~~~~~PP					
	★★	South Beach	~~~~~PP					
	★	South Beach (near River)	~~~~~FP					
	★★	Snettisham Beach	~~~~~PP					Near RSPB Reserve

1 Lee-on-the-Solent, Hampshire   OS Ref: SU5700

A long, gently curving ribbon of groyne-ribbed shingle with sand at low tide faces the Solent, with views of Southampton Water and across to the Isle of Wight. The residential development along Marine Parade overlooks this uncommercialised beach. Marine Parade West is separated from the beach by the Solent Gardens, which slope down to a promenade on two levels edging the shingle. Another promenade and flat lawns separate Marine Parade East from the beach. The steep shingle may not be the most comfortable for sunbathing on but it is popular with the more active beach user. There is a designated area for water skiing and jet skiing, and recommended launching areas for windsurfers. There is always something to watch offshore, whether it is the water sports or the continual shipping traffic plying the Solent. Dogs are banned from the central section of the beach from May to September inclusive. Dogs on the promenade must be kept on a lead and must not foul the footpaths or the adjoining grass verges.

Water quality Water quality monitored by the NRA and found to meet EC Guideline coliform standards for bathing water in 1992. ✶✶✶✶ in this year's listing section. One outfall serving 200,000 people discharges secondary treated sewage 1200 yards (1100m) below low water mark from Peel Common, to the north of Lee.

Litter The beach is cleaned regularly by the local authority. Heavy usage of the Solent leads to marine debris and oil being washed ashore.

Bathing safety Safe bathing. Water skiers and jet skiers must use the areas buoyed near the Daedalus slipway and windsurf boards should be launched from the Hill Head end of the beach.

Access Lee-on-the-Solent is signposted from the A32; the B3385 leads to Marine Parade, running parallel with the shore. There is level access and ramps to the promenade, from which steps and ramps lead to the shingle.

Parking Two car parks with approximately 250 spaces are signposted off Marine Parade; two other car parks with approximately 150 spaces are located at the Hill Head end of the beach.

Toilets At the Solent Gardens, Marine Parade East and Marine Parade West.

Food There are shops and cafés on Marine Parade opposite the Solent Gardens, a café and sheltered terrace garden off the promenade and a pub at Hill Head.

Seaside activities Swimming, waterskiing, jetskiing and windsurfing.

Wet weather alternatives In Gosport there is a local museum, Fort Brockhurst and the submarine museum.

Wildlife and walks The Solent Way coastal footpath can be followed in either direction from the beach. To the north it skirts the Titchfield Haven Nature Reserve and continues along the shore to the River Hamble, an extremely popular yachting centre. To the south it can be followed to Stokes Bay. A section of the grassland adjacent to the Daedalus slipway has been set aside as a conservation area.

2 Stokes Bay, Gosport, Hampshire   OS Ref: SZ5998

The arc of Stokes Bay curves from the No. 2 Battery Fort south to Fort Gilkicker – fortifications built in 1860 to protect the western approaches to Portsmouth docks. The narrow band of shingle, which shelves quite steeply to some sand at low tide, widens landward towards the south-east of the bay; the longshore drift currents continually move the shingle in this direction and this has led to the build-up of a wide area of flat shingle stretching towards Fort Gilkicker. The beach, overlooking Ryde on the Isle of Wight, has a wide-open feel about it. The promenade is level with the shingle and is backed by flat grassed recreational areas which are in turn bordered by the trees and shrubs of the adjacent park and school. It is a popular spot for water sports; windsurfers can be seen through-out the year. Dogs are banned from certain areas of the beach and, on the promenade, must be kept on a lead and should not be allowed to foul.

Water quality Water quality monitored by the NRA and found to meet the EC Guideline coliform standards for bathing water in 1992. ★★★★ in this year's listing section. One outfall serving 200,000 people discharges primary treated sewage ⅔ mile (1km) below low water mark from Peel Common, to the north of Lee-on-the-Solent.

Litter The beach is cleaned regularly by the local authority. Heavy use of the Solent by shipping leads to problems on the beaches; marine debris is frequently washed ashore.

Bathing safety Safe bathing. Swimming and windsurfing is restricted to specific areas of the beach which are signposted. There is a first aid post near the sailing club and an inshore rescue boat station at the southern end of the bay.

Access Stokes Bay is signposted from the B3333 between Lee-on-the-Solent and Gosport. There is easy parking off the road behind the beach and level access on to the shingle.

Parking Car parks are signposted at each end of the beach and at its centre, with over 300 spaces. There is also some parking along the promenade.

Toilets At the car park adjacent to the No.2 Battery Fort, on the promenade near the sailing club and at Gilkicker.

Food Café on the promenade.

Seaside activities Swimming, windsurfing, sailing, canoeing and diving. Two public slipways. Children's paddling pool, miniature golf and tennis courts behind the beach.

Wet weather alternatives In Gosport there is a local museum, the submarine museum and Fort Brockhurst.

Wildlife and walks The Solent Way footpath can be followed southeast past Fort Gilkicker towards Portsmouth Harbour or north-west to Lee-on-the-Solent and beyond.

3 Cuckmere Haven, Westdean, East Sussex   OS Ref: TV5298

A path from the Seven Sisters Country Park Centre leads through the lovely Cuckmere valley to this quiet pebble beach. The river, which meanders through the valley, disappears below the pebbles. The impressive white chalk cliffs of the Seven Sisters stretch away east to Beachy Head, while below them there are numerous rock pools which abound with marine life. This is an ideal spot for those who want to combine sunbathing with exploring the shore and surrounds. The nature trail starting from the superbly restored flint barn which houses the Country Park Interpretative Centre is well worth following.

Water quality No sewage is discharged in the vicinity of this beach. Water quality monitored by the NRA and found to meet the Guideline coliform standards for bathing water in 1992. **** in this year's listing section.

Litter A lot of plastic, metal cans and bottles, both washed up and left by visitors.

Bathing safety The swiftness of the incoming tide and associated currents can cause problems. Bathing is not safe at the mouth of the river.

Access Pedestrian access only; a 1 mile (1.6km) walk on a marked path through the Cuckmere Valley from the Country Park Centre at Exceat on the A259 leads to the beach.

Parking Car park at the Country Park Centre.

Toilets At the Country Park Centre.

Food The Golden Galleon pub at Exceat Bridge provides superb food.

Seaside activities Swimming and diving.

Wet weather alternatives The Country Park Centre and the Living World exhibition of animals from the countryside and seashore.

Wildlife and walks A 1 mile (1.6km) or 3 mile (5km) circular trail through the country park covers a selection of wildlife habitats, saltmarsh, river meadows and the chalk grassland above the cliffs. Leaflets describing the route are available at the Country Park Centre. The South Downs Way follows the cliffs and cuts through the valley. Survey work by the Marine Conservation Society showed that the shallow seas of this stretch of coast are particularly rich in marine life and the area has been designated as a Voluntary Marine Nature Reserve.

4 Botany Bay, Kent   OS Ref: TR4071

Botany Bay is a secluded, sandy and naturally sheltered bay with chalk cliffs. There was an archway of chalk here but it collapsed a few years ago as a result of erosion. A pleasant walk along the cliff top leads to Kingsgate Bay. Inland there is part of the North Foreland Golf Course and some picturesque 'ruins' built in the 18th century by Lord Holland.

Water quality Water quality monitored by the NRA and found to meet the EC Guideline standards for bathing water in 1992. ★★★★ in this year's listing section.

Bathing safety There are warning signs when it is unsafe to bathe and lifeguards patrol the beach.

Access Local buses run at least once every ten minutes and stop at Percy Avenue in Kingsgate; Botany Bay is at the foot of the Avenue. Access to the beach is via a steep slope. Assisted access by wheelchair is possible.

Parking There is a small cliff-top car park.

Toilets On the beach.

Food Pub on the cliff top and a café and ice-cream kiosk on the beach.

Seaside activities Swimming.

Wildlife and walks The Seven Bays of Broadstairs leaflet (price 20p from the local tourist office) features a 4½ mile (1km) walk around the seven bays from Botany Bay to Dumpton Gap.

5 Aldeburgh, Suffolk   OS Ref: TM4757

The long strip of unspoilt shingle beach falls within the Suffolk Coast and Heath Area of Outstanding Natural Beauty and the Suffolk Heritage Coast. A wide sea wall protects the charming town from the continual attack of the North Sea. Colour-washed houses and hotels face this 'working' beach from which a considerable number of boats fish, selling most of their catch of crabs, lobster and a variety of fish from sea-front huts. The local lifeboat can also be seen drawn up on the shingle. The beach has steep shingle ridges with some sand at low tide and stretches 2 miles (3km) north to Thorpeness. This Edwardian holiday village built around a man-made lake, the Meare, is a mixture of traditional weather-boarding combined with mock-Tudor elegance. The working windmill standing on the heathland behind the beach is also the Heritage Coast Visitors' Centre and it is well worth a visit to find out more about this curious village and adjacent stretch of unspoilt coast.

Water quality One outfall serving 4,000 people discharges macerated sewage ¾ mile (1.3km) below low water mark. Water quality monitored by the NRA and found to meet EC Guideline standards for bathing water in 1992. **** in this year's listing section.

Litter The beach is generally very clean, but subject to occasional spotting with tar and oil from passing ships. It is cleaned by the local authority.

Bathing safety The beach shelves quite steeply but evenly except at Thorpeness, where some ridges and pits in the sea bed can be a hazard. It is dangerous to swim near the groynes.

Access Level access from the road on to the promenade and across the shingle to the north.

Parking Car parks at each end of town adjacent to the beach. Car parks in Thorpeness can be busy on summer weekends.

Toilets At the Moot Hall and by the coastguard station at the southern end of the promenade.

Food Several cafés, pubs and hotels overlook the beach. Ice-cream vendor on the promenade; tea shop and inn at Thorpeness.

Seaside activities Swimming, diving, windsurfing, sailing and fishing.

Wet weather alternatives Moot Hall Museum, Thorpeness Windmill, Heritage Coast Visitors' Centre. Snape Maltings concert hall, on the banks of the River Alde a short distance inland, is the home of the Aldeburgh Festival. Gallery, craft centre, shops and restaurants at the Maltings.

Wildlife and walks A very good map available from tourist information details the network of paths that covers Aldeburgh and its surrounding area. The town lies on the Suffolk Coastal Path which runs from Felixstowe to Lowestoft. From the village of Snape the route follows the banks of the River Alde and joins the Sailors' Path. This crosses Snape Warren and the marshes north of the town to reach Aldeburgh beach, where shingle plants such as sea holly and sea pea abound. The path continues north along the beach to Thorpeness and beyond. The Meare at Thorpeness, a remnant heath with dry reedbeds, scrub and birch woodland, supports a wide variety of birdlife.

6 Southwold (The Denes), Suffolk   OS Ref: TM5076

Southwold once had a pier but all that remains is a short skeleton and the buildings on the promenade. Nevertheless, it is still the focal point for this

3 mile (5km) long beach of sand and shingle. To the north, rainbow-coloured beach huts line the sea wall which edges the groyne-ribbed beach of soft sand. The beach curves northwards below sand cliffs rising to replace the sea wall. South of the pier the groyne-ribbed beach of sand and shingle stretches to the harbour at the mouth of the River Blyth. Wheeled changing huts line the promenade below scrub-covered slopes. The attractive town of Southwold sits aloft, built around seven greens and overlooked by its lighthouse.

Water quality Water quality monitored by the NRA and found to meet the EC Guideline coliform standards for bathing water in 1992. ★★★★ in this year's listing section. One outfall discharges secondary treated sewage.

Bathing safety Safe bathing except near the groynes and at the river mouth. Life-saving equipment provided.

Access The sea front is signposted within the town; steps and a steep ramp lead down to the beach.

Parking Three car parks with a total of 300 spaces are adjacent to the pier and harbour.

Toilets On the promenade, including facilities for disabled visitors.

Food Café, bar, shop and takeaway at the pier.

Seaside activities Swimming, surfing, windsurfing, sailing and fishing. Boating lake.

Wet weather alternatives St Edmund's Hall and museum. Amusement arcade.

Wildlife and walks There are walks along the river and across the meadows. The climb to the summit of Gun Hill is well worth the effort for the reward of some good views. The Suffolk Coastal Path runs north towards Lowestoft and south to Dunwich Forest and Minsmere, approximately 3 miles (5km) from Southwold.

7 South Beach, Lowestoft, Suffolk   OS Ref: TM5491

Lowestoft is a popular resort and a busy port which is split in half by the narrow strip of Lake Lothing. The two sides are linked by a bridge which is occasionally raised to admit large merchant ships into the heart of town. South Beach is a 3 mile (5km) long pleasure beach, offering golden sand and all the normal paraphernalia of piers, stalls and amusements. It is cleaned every day by the local authority.

Water quality Water quality monitored by the NRA and found to meet the EC Guideline coliform standards for bathing water in 1992. ★★★★ in this year's listing section. Two outfalls serving 140,000 people discharge secondary treated effluent ⅔ mile (1km) below low water mark.

Bathing safety Safe bathing except near the harbour entrance. The beach is patrolled by lifeguards during the summer months.

Access Direct from the promenade.

Parking There are four car parks near the beach with approximately 800 spaces.

Toilets Four sets of toilets, including one with facilities for disabled visitors. Another set has showers and a baby-changing area.

Food A full range of catering outlets at a variety of prices.

Seaside activities Swimming, surfing, fishing, windsurfing, sailing. Punch and Judy shows, two piers.

Wet weather alternatives Multi-sports centre, large central library, Maritime Museum, two cinemas and theatres.

Wildlife and walks Guided walking tours of the fishing harbour start from the Tourist Information Centre on the Esplanade. Lowestoft marks the northern end of the Suffolk Coastal Path which runs for 50 miles (80km) south to Felixstowe. Lowestoft Ness is Britain's easternmost point.

8 Sea Palling, Norfolk   OS Ref: TG4327

This area has 10 miles (16km) of coastline that is undeveloped and not readily accessible. From Sea Palling the stretch of beach to Waxham can be reached – a beautiful, unspoilt beach, with gentle sloping sands fringed by substantial marram-covered dunes. It is ideal for a quiet day by the sea; no facilities, no razzmatazz, just sand, sea and sky. Three miles (5km) to the south the Broads come within a couple of miles of the dunes, the only protection that the flat, low-lying land has against the sea. The beach is cleaned daily during the season. Oil on the sand has been observed in winter.

Water quality No outfalls in the vicinity of this beach. Water quality monitored by the NRA and found to meet the EC Guideline coliform standards for bathing water in 1992. **** in this year's listing section.

Bathing safety Bathing can be dangerous on the ebb tide because of undertow currents.

Access From the village of Sea Palling, on the B1159, a road leads to a concrete ramp over the dunes.

Parking A car park behind the dunes provides spaces for 100 cars.

Toilets In Sea Palling village.

Food A tea shop and two pubs in the village serve food.

Seaside activities Swimming, windsurfing and fishing.

Wildlife and walks Fossils, jet and amber have sometimes been found in the area of the beach. The more remote parts of the beach are popular for birdwatching.

9 Hunstanton, Norfolk   OS Ref: TF6741

Hunstanton is famous for its striped red and white cliffs (chalk and carrstone) and for its sunsets – it's the only east coast resort that faces west! It is a small, friendly and well-kept resort where the attractive Edwardian Gardens overlook the sea. The sandy beach is 1 mile (1.6km) long and is protected by a dog ban. The beach is cleaned daily and there is adequate provision of litter bins. Though it is a popular resort it is large enough to accommodate many visitors. For those who want a slightly quieter time of it there is an alternative in the adjoining village of Old Hunstanton.

Water quality Water quality monitored by the NRA and found to meet the EC Guideline coliform standards for bathing waters in 1992. ✶✶✶✶ in this year's listing section.

Bathing safety Safe bathing except when there are offshore winds (warning flags are hoisted). Regular patrols by beach officers. Life-saving and first-aid equipment are available.

Access Direct from the promenade. There are access ramps for wheelchair users and a path running all along the promenade and round the town.

Parking Five car parks close to the beach provide around 3,800 spaces.

Toilets There are four sets of toilets, cleaned daily; showers and facilities for disabled users are available.

Food Many cafés, pubs etc. along the promenade and in the town.

Seaside activities Swimming, windsurfing, sailing, fishing, waterskiing, Punch and Judy, trampolines, funfair, crazy golf, bowls, tennis and croquet.

Wet weather alternative All-year entertainment at the Princess Theatre; tropical pools and giant aquaslide at the Oasis Leisure Centre; the Seal Hospital and North Sea fish at Kingdom of the Sea; new soft play facilities at the Jungle Wonderland. Nearby is the Queen's home at Sandringham.

Wildlife and walks Hunstanton is at the beginning of the Norfolk Coast Path and adjoins the Area of Outstanding Natural Beauty and the Heritage Coast. There are nature reserves at Snettisham, Holme and Titchwell. This is an area renowned for bird-watching.

The East Coast

Fabulous, spectacular, dramatic, remote, wild and mysterious have all been used to describe the east coast. Unfortunately, less complimentary terms have also been employed to describe parts of this coastline - polluted, spoilt, industrialised and scarred. Industry comes to the shore with steel works, power stations, oil and chemical works; they discharge toxic chemicals, polluting the coast and damaging wildlife.

Millions of tonnes of dredged spoil, sewage sludge and fly ash dumped offshore add to the problem, although the dumping of fly ash and sewage sludge is to end in 1998. Waste from coal mines blackens the beaches of Tyne and Wear, Durham and Cleveland.

Sewage pollution contaminates many of the bathing waters, particularly around the Tyne and the Tees. None of the beaches in the region escapes the problem of marine litter.

However, there are still beautiful beaches on the east coast and some wonderful cliff walks. Northumberland has bays of golden sands and unspoilt fishing villages, Yorkshire has rugged cliffs, and the magnificent chalk cliffs of Flamborough stretch for miles.

The East Coast

Berwick-
upon-Tweed

6 Bamburgh

5 Beadnell Bay

4 Newton Haven

3 Alnmouth
2 Warkworth
1 Druridge Bay

Newcastle ▪

Middlesborough ▪

Hull ▪

Numbered beaches are included in the detailed section.

Coastal walk
Cleveland Way. Coastal parts of the Cleveland Way mostly in
the North York Moors National Park.

Boston ▪

The East Coast   *See page 21 for further details*

Beach No on Map	Rating. The more stars the better. f=failed	Resort	Pass/Fail track record	Sewage outlets	Population discharging from outlet	Type of treatment	Discharge point relative to low water mark, unless otherwise stated. Distance given in metres	Remarks
LINCOLNSHIRE								
	★	**Skegness**	PPPPPPP					Sandy. Lindsey Coast improvement scheme.
	★★	**Ingoldmells**	PFPPPPP	1	122,000	Maceration/ screens	1420 below LWM	Sandy. Lindsey Coast improvement scheme.
	★★	**Chapel St Leonards**	PFPPPPP					Sandy. Improvements as above.
	★★★★	**Anderby Creek**	PPPPPPP					Sandy. Bathing safe. Improvements as above.
	★★★★	**Moggs Eye (Huttoft)**	PPPPPPP					Improvements as above.
	★	**Sutton-on-Sea**	FFFPPPP					Sandy. See improvements below.
	★	**Mablethorpe**	PFPFPPP	1	37,000	Secondary	To inland drain	Sandy. Improvements to existing full treatment plant planned in 1995.
HUMBERSIDE								
	f	**Cleethorpes**	FFFFFFF	1	66,000	Maceration/ screens	At LWM	Sand. Improvements planned in 1995 to give secondary treatment.
	★★	**Withernsea**	FFPPFPP	1	12,000	Primary	At LWM	Sand and shingle. £8m improvement scheme planned.
	★★	**Tunstall**	PPPPPPP					Sand and pebbles. Improvement scheme as above.
	★★	**Hornsea**	PPPPPPP	2	16,000	Screens/ maceration	1,000 below LWM	Sandy.
	★★	**Skipsea Sands**	PPPPFPP					Sandy.
	★★★★	**Barmston**	PPPPPPP					Sand and shingle.
	★★	**Earls Dyke**	PPPPPPP					Sandy.
	★★	**Fraisthorpe**	PPPPPPP					Sandy.
	★★	**Willsthorpe**	PPPPPPP					Sandy.
	★★	**Bridlington South**	PPPPPPP	1	56,000	Screens	1,600 below LWM	Sandy.

Beach No on Map	Rating. The more stars the better. f=failed	Resort	Pass/Fail track record	Sewage outlets	Population discharging from outlet	Type of treatment	Discharge point relative to low water mark, unless otherwise stated. Distance given in metres	Remarks
	★	**Bridlington North**	PPPPPP	2			At LWM	Sandy. Storm water overflows.
	f	**Flamborough South Landing**	FPFFFFF	1	200			Sandy. Bathing dangerous. Sewage works discharges to a stream which reaches the sea. £4m improvement scheme to be completed 1994 to give primary treatment and a long sea outfall.
	★	**Flamborough North Landing**	PPPPPFP					
		Thornwick Bay		1	300	Primary	At LWM	Rocky. Bathing very dangerous. Water quality not monitored by NRA in 1992.
YORKSHIRE								
	★	**Reighton Sands**	PPPPPPP					Sand and boulders.
	★	**Filey**	PPPPPPP	2	13,800	Maceration	200 below LWM	Red sand. One storm water overflow.
	★★	**Cayton Bay**	PPPPPPP					Sandy. Beware of incoming tide.
		Scarborough:		1	93,750	Screened	1.5 km long sea outfall	Sandy. £31m long sea outfall completed early 1991. Sludge contaminated with faecal micro-organisms found on North Beach in 1991. Much local debate.
	★★	**South Beach**	FFPPFPP					
	★★	**North Beach**	PFPFPPP					
	★★★★	**Marine Drive**						
	★★	**Robin Hood's Bay**	PPPPPPP	1	5,500			Rocky. Swimming dangerous. £5m improvement scheme to be completed 1994.
	★★★★	**Whitby**	PPPPPPP	1	20,000	Raw	At LWM	Sandy. Dog faeces, plastics, cans and fishing gear reported 1992.
	★★	**Sandsend**	PPPFPPP	1	450	Raw	At LWM	Sand and shingle.
	★★	**Runswick Bay**	PPPPPPP	1	480	Raw	At LWM	Sand and shingle.
	f	**Staithes**	~PPFFFF	1	4,000	Raw	At LWM	Sand and rocks.

Beach No on Map	Rating. The more stars the better. **f**=failed	Resort	Pass/Fail track record	Sewage outlets	Population discharging from outlet	Type of treatment	Discharge point relative to low water mark, unless otherwise stated. Distance given in metres	Remarks
CLEVELAND								
	⋆	Skinningrove	~~~~~FP	1	7,700	Raw	At LWM	Sandy.
	f	**Saltburn-by-Sea (Pier)**	FFFPPPF	2	13,850	Raw	At LWM	Sand and pebbles. Improvements planned to give long sea outfall by 1996, primary treatment in 1998 and secondary treatment by 2000. Sewage-related debris found 1992.
					6,800	Raw	At LWM	
	f	Saltburn Gill	~~~~~FF					
	f	Saltburn East (Sea at the Ship)	~~~~~FF					
	f	Skelton Beck (Beach)	~~~~~FF					Transfer of flow from Guisborough sewage treatment works, which discharges into the Beck, to Marske sewage treatment works. Long sea outfall planned.
	f	Skelton Beck (Footbridge)	~~~~~FF					
	⋆⋆	Marske-by-the-Sea	~~~~~FP	1	12,800	Raw	Long sea outfall	Sandy. Storm water outfall.
	⋆⋆	**Redcar (Stray)**	~~~~~PP	1	35,000	Screened.	1599 below LWM	Sand and rocks.
	f	**Redcar (Granville)**	~~~~~FPF					
	⋆	**Redcar (lifeboat station)**	~~~~~FP					
	⋆⋆	**Redcar (Coatham Sands)**	~~~~~PP	1	1,200	Raw	25 below LWM	Sandy. Storm water outfall only.
	f	**Seaton Carew North Gare**	~~~~~FF	2	31,300	Maceration	At LWM	Sandy. £11.4 m improvement scheme provided new long sea outfall in1991. Primary treatment is planned for 1994, secondary for 2000.
	f	**Seaton Carew Centre**	FFFFFFF		28,500	Maceration	25 below LWM	
	f	**Seaton Carew North**	~~~~~FF					
		Hartlepool		5	22,800	4 Raw 1 Screened/ maceration	2x25 below 3xLWM	Sandy. Water quality not monitored by NRA in 1992.
	f	The Stell	~~~~~FF					

Beach No on Map	Rating. The more stars the better. **f**=failed	Resort	Pass/Fail track record	Sewage outlets	Population discharging from outlet	Type of treatment	Discharge point relative to low water mark, unless otherwise stated. Distance given in metres	Remarks
DURHAM								
	f	**Crimdon Park**	FFF~FFF	1	4,000	Screened/ tidal tank	At LWM	Sandy. Improvements planned to provide screens in 1993, extended outfall in 1996, primary treatment in 1998 and secondary treatment in 2000.
	f	Crimdon South	~~~~FF					
		Blackhall		1	10,500	Raw	At LWM	Sand and pebbles. Water quality not monitored by NRA in 1992.
	f	Lime Kiln South	~~~~FF					
	f	Lime Kiln North	~~~~PF					
	f	Denemouth North	~~~~FF	1	31,500	Screened/ tidal tank	At LWM	Sand with stones and coal waste.
	f	Denemouth South	~~~~FF					
		Horden		2	6,900 / 8,100	Raw / Raw	Above LWM / Above LWM	Sand with coal waste. Water quality not monitored by NRA in 1992.
		Easington		1	8,500	Raw	At LMW	Sand with coal waste. Badly polluted coastline. Water quality not monitored by NRA in 1992.
	f	Dalton Burn	~~~~FF					
	f	**Seaham Remand Home**	~~~~FF	4	36,600	Raw	25 below LWM	Improvement scheme to reduce storm water outfall use and to provide primary treatment in 1995, secondary treatment by 2000. Badly polluted coastline.
	★	**Seaham Beach**	FFFFFFP					Sand.
	★	Featherbed Rocks	~~~~FP					
	f	Ice House Burn	~~~~FF					
TYNE AND WEAR								
	f	Ryhope South	~~~~FF	2		Raw	At LWM	Sandy. Storm sewage overflows only.
	f	Hendon South	~~~~FF					Sewage debris reported 1992

Beach No on Map	Rating. The more stars the better. f=failed	Resort	Pass/Fail track record	Sewage outlets	Population discharging from outlet	Type of treatment	Discharge point relative to low water mark, unless otherwise stated. Distance given in metres	Remarks
		Sunderland		2	500 175,000	Tidal tank Screened	At LWM 300 below LWM	Rocky outfalls situated south of Wear Estuary. Water quality not monitored by NRA in 1992.
	★ f	**Roker/ Whitburn South** Roker/ Blockhouse	PFFFPPP	1		Raw	25 below LWM	Sandy. Storm sewage overflows subject to extension and screening in 1994. Sewage solids reported 1992.
		Seaburn		1		Raw	At LWM	Sand. Storm sewage overflow. Water quality not monitored by NRA in 1992.
	f	**Whitburn**	~~~PFFF	1		Raw	At LWM	Sand. Storm sewage overflow.
	★★	**Marsden Bay**	PFFPPPP					Sand.
	★ f	**South Shields (Sandhaven)** South Shields (Inner Harbour)	FFPPFPP ~~~~~FF	2		Raw	At LWM	Sand. Storm sewage overflows only.
	f ★ ★★ ★	Tynemouth (Haven) **Tynemouth (King Edward's Bay)** **Tynemouth (Long Sands South)** **Tynemouth (Long Sands North)**	~~~~~FF ~~~~~PP ~~~~~PP ~~~~~PP	2		Raw	At LWM	Sand. Storm water overflow only. Sand.
	f	**Tynemouth** (Cullercoats)	~~~FPPF	1		Raw	At LWM	Sand. Storm water outfall only. Staff maintain beach facilities well.
	★	**Whitley Bay**	PPFPPPP	10		Raw	At LWM	Sand. Storm water outfall only. Improvement scheme to extend outfalls being considered for 1995.

Beach No on Map	Rating. The more stars the better. f=failed	Resort	Pass/Fail track record	Sewage outlets	Population discharging from outlet	Type of treatment	Discharge point relative to low water mark, unless otherwise stated. Distance given in metres	Remarks
	f	**Seaton Sluice**	FPFFPFF	1	43,000	Tidal tank	60 below LWM	Sandy. Improvement scheme to divert sewage to Howdon sewage treatment works scheduled for completion in 1992. Storm water will be screened and discharged down existing outfall.

NORTHUMBERLAND

Beach No on Map	Rating	Resort	Pass/Fail track record	Sewage outlets	Population discharging from outlet	Type of treatment	Discharge point	Remarks
	f	**Blyth: South Beach**	~~PPPPF	1	28,500	Maceration	30 below LWM	Sandy.
	f	Cambois South	~~~~~FF					
	f	Cambois North	~~~~~FF					
	f	**Newbiggin South**	FFFFFFF	2	29,000 5,000	Maceration Raw	At LWM At LWM	Sandy. Improvement scheme to provide primary treatment in 1995.
	f	**Newbiggin North**	~~~~~FF					
		Cresswell		1	1,800 summer (200 winter)	Other	At LWM	Sandy. Water quality not monitored by NRA in 1992.
1	****	**Druridge Bay**	PPPPPP	1	5,500	Screened/ maceration	At LWM	Sandy.
	****	**Amble (Links)**	~~~~~PP	1	8,000	Screens/ maceration	250 below LWM	Rocky.
2	****	**Warkworth**	PPPPPPP					Sandy.
3	****	**Alnmouth**	PFPPPPP					Sandy. Bathing very dangerous.
	f	River Aln Estuary	~~~~~FF					
		Longhoughton Steel		1	3,000	Screened/ Raw	At LWM	Sandy cove. Water quality not monitored by NRA in 1992.
		Craster		2	400	Maceration	30 below LWM	Water quality not monitored by NRA in 1992.
		Embleton Bay						Sandy. Water quality not monitored by NRA in 1992.

Beach No on Map	Rating. The more stars the better. f=failed	Resort	Pass/Fail track record	Sewage outlets	Population discharging from outlet	Type of treatment	Discharge point relative to low water mark, unless otherwise stated. Distance given in metres	Remarks
4	★★★★	**Low Newton (Newton Haven)**	PPPPPPP					Sandy.
5	★★★★	**Beadnell Bay**	PPPPPPP	1	2,000 summer (1,200 winter)	Maceration	At LWM	Sandy. Dangerous undercurrents at times. Good windsurfing for all levels of ability.
	★★★★	**Seahouses (North)**	PPPPPPP	1	6,000	Screens/ maceration/ tidal tank	100 below	Sandy.
6	★★★★	**Bamburgh**	PPPPPPP	2	1,000 summer (700 winter)	Maceration/ tidal tank	At LWM	Sandy.
					100	Raw	At LWM	
		Holy Island		1	500 summer (200 winter)	Maceration/ tidal tank	At LWM	Pebbles. Water quality not monitored by NRA in 1992.
		Cocklawburn Beach		1	300	Raw	20 above LWM	Sand and rocks. Emergency outfall only. Water quality not monitored by NRA in 1992.
	f	**Spittal**	FFFPFFF					Improvement scheme to install fine screens planned.
	f	Spittal Quay	~~~~~FF					Improvement scheme.
		Berwick-upon-Tweed:		1		Raw	At LWM	Sandy.
	f	Upstream of sewage treatment works	~~~~~FF					

1 Druridge Bay, Cresswell, Northumberland   OS Ref: NZ2993

A 5 mile (8km) curving sweep of golden sand is fringed by dunes with rocky outcrops at Cresswell and Hadston Carrs at either end. Cresswell is the easiest point of access and may be busy on a sunny afternoon, but a short walk along the shore will bring you to miles of quiet sand. There are views north along the bay to Coquet Island and its lighthouse.

Water quality Water quality monitored by the NRA and found to meet the EC Guideline coliform standards for bathing water in 1992. ★★★★ in this year's listing section. One outfall serving 5,500 people discharges untreated sewage at low water mark.

Bathing safety Swim with extreme caution as the tides and currents are strong and unpredictable.

Access The A1068 leads to Cresswell and the Druridge Bay Country Park. The beach is a short walk from the car parks across the dunes.

Parking Near Cresswell there is a car park with 100 spaces; at Cresswell Ponds there is space for 10 cars, and on Druridge Links a National Trust car park has 150 spaces. Druridge Bay Country Park has parking for 200 cars and also coaches.

Toilets In Cresswell village and at Druridge Bay Country Park at the northern end of the bay.

Food A café and tea room in the village and also mobile ice-cream vans.

Seaside activities Swimming, sailing and fishing.

Wildlife and walks At the northern end of the beach is the Druridge Bay Country Park. There are also nature reserves at Druridge and Hauxley. Cresswell Ponds have been designated as a Site of Special Scientific Interest. It is a superb area for bird-watching; the Northumberland Wildlife Trust has recently opened its Druridge Pools Reserve to the public and hide facilities are available. The Trust also runs the Blakemoor Visitor Centre where details of bird numbers and species can be found. South of the bay, beyond the smaller Broadsands beach and the rocky outcrops of Snab Point, there is the sharply contrasting Lynemouth beach, blackened by coal dust washed from waste tips that line the beach.

2 Warkworth, Northumberland   OS Ref: NU2606

Between Warkworth Harbour at the mouth of the Coquet Estuary and the Aln Estuary lie 3 miles (5km) of fabulous sandy beach. Edged by sand dunes, the beach extends northwards for 2 miles (3km) to merge with Aln-mouth Links. The town of Amble lies on the southern banks of the estuary and here fishing cobles may be seen in the harbour and yachts moored in the river or at the Braid Marina. Coquet Island lies 1 mile (1.6km) off shore, sheltering the harbour entrance; boat trips are available from the harbour. The views back across the estuary with the backdrop of Warkworth Castle are most impressive. The near-perfect mediaeval village of Warkworth, an idyllic spot with a dramatic castle, hermitage and unique fortified bridge, is set 1 mile (1.6km) inland, almost enclosed by a meander of the river Coquet. The picnic site by the beach has panoramic views of the Coquet Estuary. There is access to Alnmouth Links south of Bilton on the A1068 but there is only very limited parking behind the dunes.

Water quality Water quality monitored by the NRA and found to meet the EC Guideline coliform standards for bathing water in 1992. ★★★★ in this year's listing section. One outfall serving 8,000 people discharges screened and macerated sewage at Amble.

Litter Some marine litter and fishing debris is washed on to the beach.

Bathing safety Bathing is dangerous at high tide. There is an inshore and offshore rescue boat and coastguard station at Amble.

Access North of Warkworth a turning off the A1068 is signposted to the beach.

Parking Car park at the picnic site with space for 50 cars.

Toilets The toilets are situated in the car park.

Food None at the beach. There are tea rooms in the village 1 mile (1.6km) away.

Seaside activities Swimming, golf course (Warkworth), river and sea fishing from Amble.

Wildlife and walks The picnic site and surrounding area at Warkworth beach is managed by the Northumberland National Park while the National Trust owns the land to the north. A coastal path stretches the 3 miles (5km) from Warkworth to Alnmouth and is described in a leaflet available locally. A walk to the south takes you through dunes to the long breakwater serving Warkworth harbour and some interesting salt marshes which were designated as a Site of Special Scientific Interest in 1988. Coquet Island is frequented by colonies of breeding seabirds – puffins, terns, eider. These may be viewed from boat trips around the island organised by the RSPB; information can be obtained at Amble Tourist Information Office.

3 Alnmouth, Northumberland   OS Ref: NU2410

This is a 1 mile (1.6km) expanse of sand that stretches from the picturesque village of Alnmouth north to the Marsden Rocks. At low tide over 440 yards (400m) of excellent sand is exposed. The beach is bordered by a large car park and golf course, behind which lies the village. Alnmouth was a port of some importance during the 18th century, but due to a change in the course of the river little can be seen of the old harbour; however, the old granaries have been carefully converted into pubs, shops, eating places and accommodation, retaining its unspoilt character.

Water quality Water quality monitored by the NRA and found to meet the EC Guideline coliform standards for bathing water in 1992. ★★★★ in this year's listing section. No sewage is discharged in the vicinity of the beach.

Bathing safety There are dangerous currents at some states of the tide. Bathing can be very dangerous – take care.

Access Alnmouth is signposted off the A1068 south of Alnwick. A road through the golf course north of the village leads to the beach car park.

Parking Parking for 150 cars adjacent to the beach.

Toilets In the village.

Food There are numerous cafés and restaurants in the village.

Seaside activities Swimming, surfing, windsurfing, fishing and sailing in the estuary. Two links golf courses north of the village.

Wildlife and walks There is an excellent coastal walk north from Alnmouth along the rocky shore with its series of small sandy bays to explore. Fulmars glide effortlessly along these cliffs where a wide range of seabirds can be seen. At Howick Haven you can either continue north along the low cliffs to the fishing village of Craster or turn inland and follow the wooded valley for 1 mile (1.6km) to the grounds of Howick Hall, where the gardens are open in summer.

4 Low Newton (Newton Haven), Northumberland   OS Ref: NU2525

Newton Haven's crescent of sand lies at the northern end of Embleton Bay. Low tide exposes a wide beach which is fringed by dunes. Sheltered by a grass headland to the north and an offshore reef, the beach is popular for watersports. It is overlooked by the village of Low Newton, an attractive square of fishermen's cottages and pub now owned by the National Trust. Behind the dunes lies Newton Pool, a freshwater lagoon which is a nature reserve.

Water quality Water quality monitored by the NRA and found to meet the EC Guideline coliform standards for bathing water in 1992. **** in this year's listing section. There is no sewage discharged in the vicinity of this beach.

Litter Some oil drums and fishing debris are washed up, particularly in winter.

Bathing safety Bathing is safe on the incoming tide; there are undercurrents on the ebbing tide.

Access From the car park on the approach road to Low Newton, signposted off the B1339 from High Newton. It is a short walk down to the village with direct access to the beach. A path leads along Low Newton beach to Embleton Bay.

Parking There is a car park 330 yards (300m) from Low Newton and on the roadsides with space for about 100 cars. Parking in the village is for residents and disabled badge holders only.

Toilets Adjacent to the beach.

Food There is a pub that serves snacks, and a tea room in High Newton ⅔ mile (1km) away.

Seaside activities Swimming, windsurfing, sailing, diving, canoeing and fishing.

Wildlife and walks There are bird hides at Newton Pool (one with access for disabled visitors) and a wide variety of species can be seen, particularly in winter. The Heritage Coast Path stretches south round Embleton Bay to Dunstanburgh Castle and north around Newton Point to the wide sweep of Newton Links and Beadnell Bay.

5 Beadnell Bay, Beadnell, Northumberland   OS Ref: NU2229

The golden sands of this superb beach sweep south on a 2 mile (3km) long curve to the rocky outcrop of Snook Point. A stream meanders across the sands in the centre of the bay and to the south of it is a good area for collecting shells. At the northern end of the beach is the tiny harbour of Beadnell, still used by the traditional east coast fishing cobles. Standing on the quay are some huge 18th-century limestone kilns. These impressive structures have been restored and are owned by the National Trust. This is a very clean beach: two wardens are employed to oversee the maintenance.

Water quality Water quality monitored by the NRA and found to meet the EC Guideline coliform standards for bathing water in 1992. **** in this year's listing section. One outfall serving approximately 2,000 people discharges macerated and screened sewage at low water mark.

Bathing safety Bathing is safe on the incoming tide; there are dangerous undercurrents on the ebb.

Access A road from the B1340 in Beadnell village leads to the harbour. It is a short walk from the car park to the sand.

Parking A large car park at the north end of the bay, near the harbour, has 200 spaces; a small car park at Newton Links at the south end of the bay has space for 30 cars.

Toilets In Beadnell car park.

Food There is usually an ice-cream van at the car park.

Seaside activities Swimming, windsurfing, sailing, diving, water skiing and canoeing. Outdoor sports hire centre at the car park. Good for windsurfing for all levels.

Wildlife and walks This stretch of coastline provides some splendid walking. South, a path around the edge of the bay leads to Newton Haven, the lovely Embleton Bay and the romantic ruins of Dunstanburgh Castle. To the north, the rocky shore gives way to sand that stretches to Seahouses.

6 Bamburgh and Seahouses, Northumberland   OS Ref: NU1834

A 150 foot (45m) rock outcrop towers above beautiful long sandy beaches and provides the magnificent setting for Bamburgh Castle. From the castle rock there are spectacular views of the sandy beaches stretching north to Holy Island and south to Seahouses. Seaward lies the panorama of the Farne Islands, their rocky cliffs falling steeply to the water below. It was from the Longstone lighthouse on Outer Farne that Grace Darling set off to rescue the crew of the *Forfarshire*. The deed that made her a national heroine is remembered in the Grace Darling Museum in Bamburgh. Today the trip to the Islands is made from the little harbour at Seahouses. Inland, Bamburgh village nestles below the castle among undulating fields. Between Bamburgh and Seahouses there are 4 miles (6.5km) of superb beach with sand that squeaks when walked over. Backed by the St Aidan's and Shoreston Dunes, the sands give way to rocky shore at Seahouses where the rock pools are full of marine life.

Water quality Both Bamburgh and Seahouses were monitored by the NRA and found to meet the EC Guideline coliform standards for bathing water in 1992. There are two outfalls at Bamburgh: one, serving approximately 1,000 people, discharges macerated sewage through a tidal tank at low water mark; the other serves 100 people and discharges untreated sewage at low water mark. One outfall at Seahouses serving 6,000 people discharges screened and macerated sewage through a tidal tank 110 yards (100m) below low water mark. ******** in this year's listing section.

Litter A little wood, plastic and fishing debris is washed on to the beach. Litter left by visitors is cleared by the National Trust.

Bathing safety Bathing is safe only on the incoming tide, due to under-currents as the tide ebbs; beware of offshore winds. Life belts are available at Seahouses. There is an inshore rescue boat and lifeboat.

Access From both Bamburgh and Seahouses on the B1340, with easy access to the beach across dunes.

Bamburgh
Parking Large car park in Bamburgh has over 200 spaces. Three dune car parks with approximately 25 spaces in each, plus space for about 50 cars along the road above the dunes.

Toilets In the village.

Food A café and hotel in the village and ice-cream vans on or near the beach.

Seaside activities Swimming, surfing, windsurfing, diving, sailing and fishing.

Wet weather alternatives Castle, Grace Darling Museum and her grave in the village.

Seahouses
Parking Car park in the village has 500 spaces. Space for 30 cars on the verge of B1340 north of Seahouses.

Toilets In the village.

Food In the village.

Seaside activities Swimming, golf course, amusements.

Wet weather alternatives Marine Life Centre.

Wildlife and walks This fantastic section of coastline falls within the Northumberland Heritage Coast and is also designated as an Area of Out-standing Natural Beauty. Below the lofty position of Bamburgh Castle, a walk north along the shore leads to Budle Bay. The saltmarsh, mud and sand flats are part of the Lindisfarne Nature Reserve which covers the whole of the Fenham Flats, Holy Island Sands and most of the island itself. The area provides feeding for thousands of waders and wildfowl. It is dan-gerous to cross the sands; access to the island is by the causeway which is covered for at least 11 hours each day. With its castle and priory, the island is steeped in history and its distinctive conical shape leaves a lasting impres-sion on the memory. The beaches around the island are wide and sandy but unsafe for swimming because of strong currents. The Farne Islands to the south of Holy Island are of international importance for their large colonies of seabirds and grey seals. The 30 islands that make up the Farnes are a National Trust Nature Reserve and landing is permitted on Inner Farne and Staple Island. Boats make the hour-long trip from the harbour at Seahouses in good weather. Further information about the service is available from the National Trust shop in Seahouses. Access is restricted during the bird breeding season from mid-May until mid-July.

North-West England

For the region that pioneered the concept of the seaside resort, it is tragic that there are no 'good beaches' from the north-west in a guide such as this. The north-west does have some lovely stretches of coastline; Morecambe Bay with the Lake District as a backdrop, the Victorian elegance of Southport and the extensive dune system at Aintree.

However, the whole region is affected by pollution. The Irish Sea is heavily polluted; it is the most radioactive sea in the world and it is more chemically contaminated than the North Sea. The Mersey Estuary and Liverpool Bay have suffered particularly, not only from accidental oil spills but also from the deliberate and unacceptable discharges of mercury, cadmium and lead that are released into the bay each day, mostly from industrial sources and contaminated sewage outfalls to the Mersey and its tributaries. In addition at least 1.5 million tons of sewage sludge and 3.5 million tons of dredged spoil (sediments dredged from the estuary usually contaminated with heavy metals and other persistent toxic chemicals) are dumped into Liverpool Bay each year. Some of the most famous seaside resorts in the country, for example Blackpool, look out on to this toxic mess.

Despite the plans for considerable investment in sewage treatment over the next few years, a legacy of terrible under-investment means that in 1992 the water quality at north-west beaches was no better than in 1991. In 1992 only the designated beaches in the north-west were monitored, leaving us with no definite idea of the state of many beaches in the area. Recently, a decision was made to permit the use of sodium hypochlorite as chemical disinfection on the Manchester Square outfall in Blackpool. This is a terrible backward step which must not be allowed to be taken up at other areas. Chemical disinfection is only disguising the problem by removing the indicators of sewage pollution and may indeed be adding to the problem by introducing powerful chemicals to an already hellish mixture entering the sea.

It will be many years before bathing will be advisable at most beaches in the north-west. This is certainly the worst region in the UK for polluted beaches.

North-West England

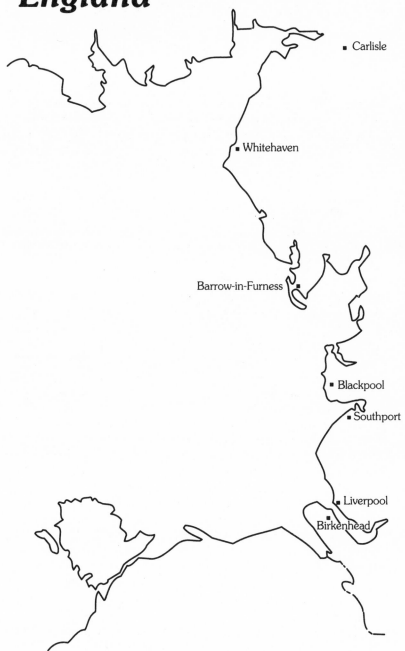

- Carlisle

- Whitehaven

Barrow-in-Furness ■

- Blackpool

- Southport

- Liverpool
■ Birkenhead

North-West England *See page 21 for further details*

Beach No on Map	Rating. The more stars the better. f=failed	Resort	Pass/Fail track record	Sewage outlets	Population discharging from outlet	Type of treatment	Discharge point relative to low water mark, unless otherwise stated. Distance given in metres	Remarks
f		**Skinburness (Silloth)**	~FF~FFF					
★		**Silloth (Lees Scar)**	FPFPFFP	1	3,000	Screened	60 below LWM	Sand and shingle. Sewage treatment works planned for 1995 providing secondary treatment and storm water management.
f		**Allonby South**	~FFFFFF	1	300	Screened/ tidal tank	50 below after high tide	Sand and rock slightly muddy. Popular beach. Secondary treatment works planned for 1995 Sewage and litter reported on beach.
f		**Allonby West Winds**	FFFPPFF					
		Maryport		1	11,500	Raw	Above LWM	Sand, shingle. Fishing port. Improvements planned – diversion of all flows to proposed primary treatment works with long sea outfall at Workington for 1995. Water quality not monitored by NRA in 1992.
		Flimby		3	100	Raw	150 above LWM	Sand and shingle. Improvements planned as above. Water quality not monitored by NRA in 1992.
					1,500	Raw	150 above LWM	
					50	Raw	150 above LWM	
		Siddick		2	3,500	Raw	Above LWM	Improvements planned. Water quality not monitored by NRA in 1992.
					50	Raw	200 below LWM	
		Workington		4	2,500	Raw	At LWM	Shingle/slag. Low amenity. Proposed primary treatment with long sea outfall planned for 1995. Water quality not monitored by NRA in 1992.
					6,000	Raw	10 above LWM	
					12,000	Raw	20 above LWM	
					5,500	Raw	Below HWM	

Beach No on Map	Rating. The more stars the better. f=failed	Resort	Pass/Fail track record	Sewage outlets	Population discharging from outlet	Type of treatment	Discharge point relative to low water mark, unless otherwise stated. Distance given in metres	Remarks
		Harrington		1	3,500 + industry	Raw	At LWM	Shingle/slag. Popular beach. Improvements planned as for Maryport. Water quality not monitored by NRA in 1992.
		Parton		1	200 + industry	Screened/ maceration	800 below LWM	Shingle/sand. Low amenity. Primary treatment planned for 1995. Water quality not monitored by NRA in 1992.
		Whitehaven		3	500 1,000 25,500	Raw Raw Raw	Above HWM Above LWM At LWM	Shingle and black sand. Cliffs. Little used. Industrial pollution from nearby works. Water quality not monitored by NRA in 1992. Diversion of foul flows to primary works at Parton for 1995.
f	**St Bees**		F~~PPPF	1	2,000	Primary/ tidal tank	Above LWM	Sand/shingle. Strong tank currents. Proposed long sea outfall and storm water management for 1995.
		Nethertown		1	500	Raw	At LWM	Sand/shingle. Water quality not monitored by NRA in 1992. Diversion of flows to primary treatment works for 1995.
		Braystones		1	9,000	Raw	50 below LWM	Sand/shingle. Proposed primary treatment works with long sea outfall for 1995. Water quality not monitored by NRA in 1992.
f	**Seascale**		FFFFFFF	1	2,200	Raw	Below LWM	Sand/shingle and rocks. Storm water management and a primary treatment works with long outfall proposed for 1995. Nearby radioactive discharges from Sellafield (Windscale).

Beach No on Map	Rating. The more stars the better. f=failed	Resort	Pass/Fail track record	Sewage outlets	Population discharging from outlet	Type of treatment	Discharge point relative to low water mark, unless otherwise stated. Distance given in metres	Remarks
		Ravenglass		1	250 + heavy tourist trade	Primary	To Esk at LWM	Shingle and mud. Water quality not monitored. by NRA in 1992.
	★★	**Silecroft**	FPPPPPP					Sand and shingle.
	f	**Haverigg**	FFFFFFF					Sand dunes. High amenity. Improvement scheme at Millom to ensure Haverigg compliance.
		Millom		1	7,500	Primary	At LWM	Sand and shingle. Proposed uprating to secondary treatment for 1995. Water quality not monitored by NRA in 1992.
	f	**Askam-in-Furness**	F~~FFFF	1	2,350	Secondary	To Duddon Channel	Sand. Pollution in Duddon Estuary. Ultra-violet disinfection of secondary treated effluent planned for 1995.
		Barrow-in-Furness		32	73,000	Raw/other		All discharge to Walney Channel. Secondary treatment planned for 1996. Water quality not monitored by NRA in 1992.
	f	**Roan Head**	FFFPFPF					
	★	**Walney Island: West Shore**	FFFPFPP					
	★★	**Walney Island: Biggar Bank**	PPPFPPP					
	★	**Walney Island: Sandy Gap**	PFPFPPP					Beaches to the west of the island have sand dunes and normal bathing facilities. Walney Channel is badly polluted and used by boats only.

Beach No on Map	Rating. The more stars the better. f=failed	Resort	Pass/Fail track record	Sewage outlets	Population discharging from outlet	Type of treatment	Discharge point relative to low water mark, unless otherwise stated. Distance given in metres	Remarks
	f	*Newbiggin*	~FF~FFF					Sandy. Ultra-violet disinfection of secondary effluent scheduled for late 1992.
	★	*Aldingham*	~FF~FFP					Sandy.
	f	*Bardsea*	FFFPPFF					Sandy. Country park. Improvement scheme to transfer flows to Ulverston treatment works planned.
		Grange-over-Sands & Kents Bank		3	11,500	Secondary		To Wyke Beck. Mud, shingle and sand. New sewage treatment works. Water quality not monitored by NRA in 1992.
		Arnside		1	2,000	Tidal tank		Mud, shingle and sand. New pumping station has reduced the number of occasions when overflow operates. Water quality not monitored by NRA in 1992.
		Hest Bank		2	2,850	Secondary	One above HWM and one below	Mud flats, sea retreats 4 miles (6.4km). No bathing. Water quality not monitored by NRA in 1992.
	f f	*Morecambe:* *Morecambe North* *Morecambe South*	F~FFFFF F~FFFFF	1	31,000	Raw	At LWM	North beach mud and shingle. South beach sandy. £20 m improvement scheme incorporating storm water management and secondary treatment works planned for 1996.
	f	*Heysham*	FFFPFFF					Sand. Popular beach. Foul flows are now transferred to primary works at Lancaster which discharges to the Lune Estuary via tidal tanks.

Beach No on Map	Rating. The more stars the better. f=failed	Resort	Pass/Fail track record	Sewage outlets	Population discharging from outlet	Type of treatment	Discharge point relative to low water mark, unless otherwise stated. Distance given in metres	Remarks
		Pilling Sands		1	1,000	Tidal tank	To Broadfleet	Mud flats/saltmarsh. Outfall has been moved. Water quality not monitored by NRA in 1992.
		Knott End-on-Sea						Sand/mud flats Water quality not monitored by NRA in 1992. Flows transferred to secondary works serving Pressail then discharging to the Wyre estuary.
f		**Fleetwood (Pier)**	FFFFFFF	1	31,000	Tidal tank	At LWM	Sand. Storm water overflow at high water mark which often overflows on to the beach. Linked to Fylde Coast scheme. Long sea outfall planned from new Fleetwood secondary sewage treatment works by 1996.
		Rossall	~~~~~F~					Water quality not monitored by NRA in 1992.
f		**Cleveleys**	FFFFFFF	1	81,000			To be linked to Fylde Coast scheme for 1996. Gross littering by sewage and related debris reported 1992.
f		**Bispham**	~FF~FFF					

Beach No on Map	Rating. The more stars the better. **f**=failed	Resort	Pass/Fail track record	Sewage outlets	Population discharging from outlet	Type of treatment	Discharge point relative to low water mark, unless otherwise stated. Distance given in metres	Remarks
		Blackpool:		2	105,000	Screened	Below LWM	Sand. Discharges of storm water directly on to the beach occur once or twice a year. Improvement scheme planned (the Fylde Coast scheme) Cleveleys, Bispham and all entries under Blackpool are planned to have storm water management and secondary treatment with a long sea outfall for 1995; whether this will happen seems rather unlikely at present. There are also plans to add sodium hypochlorite to the Manchester Square outfall on a trial basis in 1993. If the NRA is satisfied with this chemical treatment then all three outfalls will be disinfected in 1994 and 1995. This area is very badly polluted and remains highly unsuitable for bathing.
f		**Blackpool North**	FFFFFFF					
f		**Blackpool Lost Children's Post**	FFFFFFF					
f		**Blackpool South**	FFFFFFF					
		Blackpool Squire's Gate	~~~~~F~					Water quality not monitored by NRA in 1992.
		Blackpool Manchester Square	~~~~~F~					Water quality not monitored by NRA in 1992.
		Blackpool Coral Island	~~~~~F~					Water quality not monitored by NRA in 1992.
		Blackpool Anchorsholme	~~~~~F~					Water quality not monitored by NRA in 1992.

Beach No on Map	Rating. The more stars the better. f=failed	Resort	Pass/Fail track record	Sewage outlets	Population discharging from outlet	Type of treatment	Discharge point relative to low water mark, unless otherwise stated. Distance given in metres	Remarks
f		**St Anne's North**	FFFFFFF					
		St Anne's						
		Granny's Bay	~~~~~F~					
		Lytham Jetty	~~~~~F~					
f		**Lytham St Anne's**	FFFFFFF	1	42,000	Screened	At LWM	Water quality not monitored by NRA in 1992. Sand. Outfall discharges into channel of the Ribble Estuary. Diversion to Preston sewage treatment works to be upgraded to secondary treatment works 1995.
f		**Southport**	FFFFFFF	4	91,500	Primary	To Crossens Pool	Sandy beaches. Three storm water overflows, which are to be abandoned when the Southport sewage treatment works is extended, planned for 1995.
		Birkdale	~~~~~FF~					Water quality not monitored by the NRA in 1992.
	★	**Ainsdale**	FFFPPFP	0	12,000	Secondary		To inland waterway.
	★★	**Formby**	PPFPPFP	0	18,000	Secondary		To River Alt. National Trust property in the area – leaflet available from the National Trust.
		Hightown						Sand and some muddy areas around Alt estuary. Emergency overflow into Alt Estuary. Sewage is treated at Formby sewage treatment works. Water quality not monitored in 1992.
		Blundell Sands		2	48,100			An £8 m scheme commmenced in 1992 to shut these two outfalls. Water quality not monitored by NRA in 1992.
		Brighton-le-Sands						Water quality not monitored by NRA in 1992.

Beach No on Map	Rating. The more stars the better. **f**=failed	Resort	Pass/Fail track record	Sewage outlets	Population discharging from outlet	Type of treatment	Discharge point relative to low water mark, unless otherwise stated. Distance given in metres	Remarks
		Crosby	~~~~~F~					Water quality not monitored by NRA in 1992.
		Waterloo						Water quality not monitored by NRA in 1992.
		New Brighton, Victoria Road	~~~~~F~					All flows diverted to Wallasey screening plant. Water quality not monitored by NRA in 1992.
		New Brighton, Dalmorton Road	~~~~~F~					All flows diverted to Wallasey screening plant. Water quality not monitored by NRA in 1992.
	f	**New Brighton, Harrison Drive**	FPPFPPF					All flows now diverted to Wallasey screening plant.
		Wallasey (Leasowe Bay)	~~~~~P~					Water quality not monitored by NRA in 1992. Some litter and sewage debris reported 1992.
	★★★★	**Moreton**	PPPPPPP	1	65,000	Maceration	3000 below LWM	A long sea outfall discharges the macerated effluent through diffusers.
		Hoylake Red Rocks	~~~~~P~					Water quality not monitored by NRA in 1992.
		Hoylake Baths	~~~~~P~					Water quality not monitored by NRA in 1992.
	f	West Kirby	~~~~~~F					Reports of excessive sewage pollution in 1992.
	★	Meols	FFPFFFFP					

THERE ARE NO BEACHES IN THE NORTH-WEST REGION
CURRENTLY CONSIDERED TO WARRANT FURTHER DETAILED
INFORMATION AS ONE OF BRITAIN'S BEST BEACHES.

Scotland

If you are looking for a clean beach in the UK you are most likely to find one in Scotland. That is not to say that Scotland does not have problems around the coast: there are Scottish beaches that have failed to meet the minimum EC bathing water quality standard. Sea-borne rubbish is washed up on to the shore; sewage sludge and dredged spoil are dumped off the Clyde, Forth and Tay estuaries; industrial waste is discharged into coastal waters, particularly around the Clyde and the Forth. Nuclear installations at Chapelcross, Hunterston, Torness and Dounreay contribute to pollution of the sea by discharging warm water and contaminants from antifouling treatments of the intake pipes.

Development of the coastline has destroyed once scenic areas. The sea lochs of the west coat are studded with the floating cages of the troubled fish farming industry. The North Sea oil and gas industries have resulted in the growth of massive onshore terminals and the view along the Cromarty Firth is dominated by a string of massive platforms.

In contrast to this there is some of the most spectacular coastal scenery in the country, including the long sand dunes of the east coast and the rocky shore of Fife with its series of picturesque fishing villages. There are also the cliffs and stacks of Caithness, and of course the west coast, Highlands and Islands, sea lochs, towering mountains. There are hundreds (if not thousands) of tiny sandy bays, mostly remote, deserted and beautiful. Many can only be reached by the keen walker but without a doubt the effort is well worth while.

The beaches listed in this guide are those that are relatively easy to reach for a day at the sea or as a starting point to explore the delights of this coastline further. The Western Isles have not been included in the section; if you take the boat to the outer islands, beaches abound and every one is a good beach. If you are looking for peace and solitude combined with traditional hospitality, try Scotland.

4 Sandside Bay

6 Balnakeil Bay

3 Duncansby Head

5 Coldbackie

Wick

7 Scourie

9 Clachtoll · **8** Clashnessie Bay

10 Achmelvich

11 Achnahaird

12 Achiltibuie

Ullapool

13 Gruinard Bay

5 The Coral Beaches

14 Applecross

Inverness

Aberdeen

Scotland

16 Morar

17 Camusdarrach

18 Traigh, Arisaig

19 Sanna Bay

20 Calgary Bay

Oban

21 Erraid

2 Thorntonloch

1 Pease Sands

Edinburgh

Glasgow

Stranraer

Coastal walk
Forth Road Bridge to Newburgh 94 miles (152km).

Scotland   *See page 21 for further details*

Beach No on Map	Rating. The more stars the better. f=failed	Resort	Pass/Fail track record	Sewage outlets	Population discharging from outlet	Type of treatment	Discharge point relative to low water mark, unless otherwise stated. Distance given in metres	Remarks
BORDERS								
	f	Eyemouth	PPPFPFF	2	4,500	Other	Above LWM	Rocks and sand.
					1,000	Raw	Above LWM	Bathing can be unsafe due to currents..
	★★	Coldingham Bay	PPPFPPP	1	200	Raw	Above LWM	Sandy.
1	★★★	**Pease Sands**	PPPPPPP	1	1,000	Secondary	Above LWM	Red cliffs and sand.
LOTHIAN								
	★★★	Dunglass	~~~~~PP					Coarse sand and rocks.
2	★★★	Thorntonloch	PPPPPPP					Mostly sandy.
	★★★	Whitesands Bay	PPPPPPP					Sandy.
	f	Dunbar East	~~~~~FF					Sand and rocks.
	★	**Belhaven Beach**	PPPPPPP	1	4,200	Screens/ maceration	At LWM	Sandy. Beware undertow when swimming. New long sea outfall in 1992.
	★★★	Peffersands	PPPPPPP					Sandy. Dunes.
	★★★	Seacliff	~~~~~PP					Sandy sheltered bay. Car park and toilets on private land – a fee is charged.
	★	**Milsey Bay**	PPFPPPP	2	2,100	Raw	At LWM	Sandy and rock outcrops.
	★★	North Berwick Bay	PPFFFFP	2	2,800	Raw	At LWM	Sandy and rock outcrops.
	f	**Yellowcraig (Broad Sands Bay)**	PPPPPPF	1	300	Raw	At LWM	Sandy, some rocks.
	★★	**Gullane Bay**	PPPPPPP					Sand and dunes. Muirfield Golf Club nearby. Affected by sewage discharge onto beach due to broken outfall pipe in 1992.
	★★	Gosford Sands	PPPFFPP	1		Raw	At LWM	Sand with rocky upper shore.
	f	Longniddry	~~~~~PF	1	Secondary		At LWM	Sand and rocks. Popular with windsurfers.
	f	Seton Sands	FFP~FPF	1	3,700	Primary	At LWM	Sand and rocks.
	f	Fisherrow	~~~~~FF					Sandy.

Beach No on Map	Rating. The more stars the better. **f**=failed	Resort	Pass/Fail track record	Sewage outlets	Population discharging from outlet	Type of treatment	Discharge point relative to low water mark, unless otherwise stated. Distance given in metres	Remarks
	f	Portobello	FFFFPFF	1	4,500	Screened	At LWM	Mostly sand. Outfall due for removal. Reports of sewage-related solids and bathing-related illnesses in 1992. There are old wooded stands which used to hold an outfall pipe from the swimming pool – these can only be seen at low tide and are dangerous to users of the beach.
	★★	Silverknowes	~~~~~FP					Sand and mud.
	f	Cramond	~~~~~PF					Sand, very low tide.
FIFE								
		Dalgety	~~~~~P~	1	Secondary		At LWM	Sand and rocks. Water quality not monitored by RPB in 1992.
	★★	Aberdour Harbour	~~~~~PP					Sand and rocks.
	f	**Aberdour Silversands**	PPPPFFF	1	2,500	Primary and disinfection	At LWM	Sandy.
	f	Burntisland	PPP~~PF	2	2,200	Screens	At LWM	Sandy.
	f	**Pettycur**	FFP~PFF	1	1,120	Primary	At LWM	Sandy.
	f	Kinghorn	FFFFFFF	1	2,400	Primary	50 below LWM	Sandy. Localised problems in 1991. New long sea outfall in 1992.
	f	**Kirkcaldy Linktown**	FF~~FFF	2 1	50,000	Screens Screens	At LWM Long sea outfall	Sandy.
	★★	**Pathhead Sands (Kirkcaldy Harbour)**	~~~~~PP					Sand/coal spoil.
	f	Leven West	~~~~~FF	1	110,000	Screens	Long sea outfall	Sandy/rocks.
	f	Leven East	PPP~FFF	1	< 100	Septic tank	At LWM	Wide sands.
	f	Lundin Links	PPPPFPF	1	1,090	Primary	200 below LWM	Sandy to west. Rocks.
	f	Lower Largo	FFFFFFF	1	1,400	Screens	At LWM	Sandy.
	f	Upper Largo	~~~~~FF					Sandy.
	★★	Shell Bay	PPFFPPP	1	100	Primary	At LWM	Sheltered sandy bay.

Beach No on Map	Rating. The more stars the better. f=failed	Resort	Pass/Fail track record	Sewage outlets	Population discharging from outlet	Type of treatment	Discharge point relative to low water mark, unless otherwise stated. Distance given in metres	Remarks
	★★★	Elie/Earlsferry	PPPFFPP	1	1,200	Primary	Long sea outfall	Sandy. Reports of sewage-related debris in 1992.
	f	Pittenweem	PPP~FFF	1	500	Screens	At LWM	Rocky. Fishing port.
	★	Anstruther	PPPPPPP	7	3,115	Screens	At LWM	Sand and rocks.
	f	Roome Bay, Crail	PPPPPPF	4	1,200	Screens	At LWM	Sand and rocks.
	★	St Andrews East	PPFFFPP					
	★★★	**St Andrews West**	PPPPPPP	1	16,000	Primary	At LWM	Sandy.
	★★★	Tentsmuir Point	~~~~PPP					Sand and dunes. Excessive littering reported in 1992.
	f	Tayport	~~~~~FF			Primary		
	f	Broughty Ferry	FFF~~FF					
	f	Monifieth	FFF~~FF					
	★	**Carnoustie**	PPPFFFP	1	10,000	Raw	Above LWM	Sandy.
	★★	**Arbroath**	PPFFFFP	2	9,000 21,000	Raw Screened	At LWM 900 below LWM	Red sands. Diversion of flow to Inchcape late 1992.
	f	Arbroath Victoria Park	~~~~~FF					
	★★★	Lunan Bay	~~~~FPP					Sandy. Safe bathing except at river mouth.
	★★	**Montrose**	PPPPPPP	2	8,000 6,000	Maceration Raw	Below LWM Below LWM	Sandy. Do not bathe at mouth of river.
	f	Westhaven	~~~~~PF					
GRAMPIAN								
	f	St Cyrus	~~~PFFF	1	820	Maceration	At LWM	Sand/saltmarsh.
	★★	Stonehaven	PPPPPPP	2	9,000	Maceration/ primary	At LWM	
		Muchalls						Pebbles/rock. Bathing unsafe. Water quality not monitored by RPB in 1992.

Beach No on Map	Rating. The more stars the better. f=failed	Resort	Pass/Fail track record	Sewage outlets	Population discharging from outlet	Type of treatment	Discharge point relative to low water mark, unless otherwise stated. Distance given in metres	Remarks
	★★	**Aberdeen/ Ballroom**	PPPPPP	2	205,060	Screens/ maceration	2,500 below LWM	Sand. New long sea outfall soon.
	★★	Aberdeen/ Footdee	~~~~~PP					
	★★	Balmedie	~~PPPPP					16km of sand and dunes. Sewage-related debris and dog-fouling on the beach reported.
	★★	Collieston	~~~~PPP	1	200	Maceration	At LWM	Old fishing port.
	★★	Cruden Bay	~~PPFPP	1	2,200	Maceration	At LWM	Sand and dunes.
	★★	Lido Peterhead	~~PPPPP	1	20,450	Screened	Long sea outfall	Sand. Storm water receives primary treatment. Sand.
		Strathbeg Bay						Sand and dunes. Water quality not monitored by RPB in 1992.
	★★	St Combs	~~~~FPP					Small fishing port.
	★★	**Fraserburgh**	PPFPPPP	12	15,690	Raw	Variable	Sand and dunes. Improvement scheme under way. Sewage-related debris reported on the beach.
	★★	Rosehearty	~~~~PPP	1	1,250	Raw		Old fishing port. Golf course.
	★★	Banff Links	~~FFFFP	2	4,420	Raw	Variable	Sand. Improvement scheme under way.
	★★	Inverboyndie	~~~~~PP					Panoramic bay. Coastal rangers.
	★★	Sandend Bay	~~~~PPP	1	280	Settlement		Sandy. Parking for disabled visitors. Good facilities.
	★★	**Cullen**	PPPPPP	2	1,500	Raw	At LWM	Sandy. Golf club nearby.
		Findochty		2	1,050	1 raw, 1 macerated	1 at and 1 below LWM	Sand. Two raw outfalls closed. Water quality not monitored by RPB in 1992.
		Strathlene, Buckie	~~~~~P	12	15,000	Raw	Variable	Sand. Water quality not monitored by RPB in 1992.
	★★	Lossiemouth East	FFFPPFP	1	42,700	Screens	Long sea outfall	Sandy.

Beach No on Map	Rating. The more stars the better. **f**=failed	Resort	Pass/Fail track record	Sewage outlets	Population discharging from outlet	Type of treatment	Discharge point relative to low water mark, unless otherwise stated. Distance given in metres	Remarks
	★★	Lossiemouth West	PPPPPFP	2		Raw/ maceration	Short sea outfalls	
		Hopeman		1	1,663	Raw	At LWM	Water sports. Water quality not monitored by RPB in 1992. Rocks just under the water on either side of the bay are dangerous to swimmers and canoeists etc. Marine litter, especially fishing gear, reported 1992.
		Burghead		1		Raw	Via long sea outfall east of harbour	Sandy. District Council caravan site nearby. Bathing not recommended. Litter and oil reported 1992. Water quality not monitored by RPB in 1992.

HIGHLAND

Beach No on Map	Rating	Resort	Pass/Fail track record	Sewage outlets	Population discharging from outlet	Type of treatment	Discharge point	Remarks
		Nairn East/ Central	PPFP~P~	3		2 raw, 1 primary		Sandy. Improvement scheme. Water quality not monitored by RPB in 1992.
		Rosemarkie						Sand/gravel and shingle. Very popular in summer. Water quality not monitored by RPB in 1992.
		Cromarty				Raw		Untreated sewage discharges to beach. Water quality not monitored by RPB in 1992.
		Nigg Bay						Popular beach in summer. Water quality not monitored by RPB in 1992.
		Portmahomack						Sand/dunes. Fishing, sailing and windsurfing popular. Water quality not monitored by RPB in 1992.

Beach No on Map	Rating. The more stars the better. f=failed	Resort	Pass/Fail track record	Sewage outlets	Population discharging from outlet	Type of treatment	Discharge point relative to low water mark, unless otherwise stated. Distance given in metres	Remarks
		Dornoch						Sandy, famous Royal Dornoch golf course nearby. Reports of excessive littering in 1992. Water quality not monitored by RPB in 1992.
		Sinclair's Bay Wick		3	700	2 raw 1 primary	1 tank 2 above LWM	Sandy. Water quality not monitored by RPB in 1992.
3		Duncansby Head						Small, sandy. Water quality not monitored by RPB in 1992.
		Dunnet Bay/ Murkle Bay		2	200 1000	Maceration Primary	Above LWM Below LWM	Sand and dunes. Water quality not monitored. by RPB in 1992.
		Thurso		1	9,000	Maceration	450 below	Sandy. Water quality not monitored by RPB in 1992.
4		Sandside Bay						Dunes, rocky outcrops. Water quality not monitored by RPB in 1992.
5		Coldbackie						Sand/dunes. Water quality not monitored by RPB in 1992.
6		Sango Bay/ Balnakeil Bay		1	200	Primary	At LWM	Sand/dunes. Water quality not monitored by RPB in 1992.
		Sandwood Bay						Sand/dunes. Water quality not monitored by RPB in 1992.
7		Scourie		2	300	Primary	At LWM	Sandy. Water quality not monitored by RPB in 1992.
8		Clashnessie Bay						Sandy. Water quality not monitored by RPB in 1992.
9		Clachtoll						Sandy. Water quality not monitored by RPB in 1992.
10		Achmelvich						Sandy. Water quality not monitored by RPB in 1992.

Beach No on Map	Rating. The more stars the better. **f**=failed	Resort	Pass/Fail track record	Sewage outlets	Population discharging from outlet	Type of treatment	Discharge point relative to low water mark, unless otherwise stated. Distance given in metres	Remarks
11		Achnahaird						Sandy. Water quality not monitored by RPB in 1992. Dunes becoming badly eroded due to visitor pressure.
12		Achiltibuie						Shingle. Water quality not monitored by RPB in 1992.
13		Gruinard Bay						Sandy. Water quality not monitored by RPB in 1992.
		Gairloch		3		Primary		Sandy. Safe bathing. Water quality not monitored by RPB in 1992.
14		Applecross						Sand. Water quality not monitored by RPB in 1992. New village sewerage scheme including sewage treatment works for 1994.
15		Coral Beaches						Sand/shells. Water quality not monitored by RPB in 1992.
16		Morar						Sand. Water quality not monitored by RPB in 1992. New village sewerage scheme including sewage treatment works for 1994.
17		Camusdarrach						Sand/dunes. Water quality not monitored by RPB in 1992.
18		Traigh, Arisaig						Sand/dunes. Water quality not monitored by RPB in 1992.
19		Sanna Bay						Sandy. Water quality not monitored by RPB in 1992.
20		Calgary Bay						Sand/dunes. Water quality not monitored by RPB in 1992.

Beach No on Map	Rating. The more stars the better. **f**=failed	Resort	Pass/Fail track record	Sewage outlets	Population discharging from outlet	Type of treatment	Discharge point relative to low water mark, unless otherwise stated. Distance given in metres	Remarks
21		Erraid						Sand/dunes. Water quality not monitored by RPB in 1992.
STRATHCLYDE								
		Kilchattan Bay		1	170	Raw	At LWM	Water quality not monitored by RPB in 1992.
		Kames Bay		several	550	Raw		Sand and pebbles. Water quality not monitored by RPB in 1992.
		Dunoon (West Bay)		1	unknown	Raw	Below LWM	Sand and pebbles. Water quality not monitored by RPB 1992.
		Ganavan		1	100	Septic tank	Below LWM	Sand and rocky outcrops. Water quality not monitored by RPB in 1992.
		Machrihanish		1	200	Raw	At LWM	Sandy. Water quality not monitored by RPB in 1992.
		Carradale		2	480	Raw	At LWM	Water quality not monitored by RPB in 1992.
		Helensburgh		1	13,200	Maceration		Sand and pebbles. Water quality not monitored by RPB in 1992.
		Portkil/ Meikleross		1 1	<100 <100	Raw Raw	Below LWM Above LWM	Sand and rocks. Water quality not monitored by RPB in 1992.
		Gourock (West Bay)		4	2,600	Raw	Below LWM	Shingle and rocks. Water quality not monitored by RPB in 1992. Improvement scheme planned.
		Lunderston Bay		1	unknown	Septic tank	Above LWM	Shingle and sand. Water quality not monitored by RPB in 1992.
		Wemyss Bay		3	100 100 11,000	Other Other Maceration	Above LWM Above LWM Below LWM	Shingle and sand. Water quality not monitored by RPB in 1992.
		Largs		1	12,000	Other	Below LWM	Sand and rocks.

Beach No on Map	Rating. The more stars the better. f=failed	Resort	Pass/Fail track record	Sewage outlets	Population discharging from outlet	Type of treatment	Discharge point relative to low water mark, unless otherwise stated. Distance given in metres	Remarks
		Fairlie		2	1,000 500	Raw Raw	Below LWM At LWM	Sand and rocks. Water quality not monitored by RPB in 1992.
		Millport		11	2,700	Primary	At LWM	Sand and rocks. Reports of gross littering by sanitary towels. Water quality not monitored by RPB in 1992.
		Seamill		3	4,500	Raw	All at LWM	Sand and rocks. Improvements planned. Water quality not monitored by RPB in 1992.
		Ardrossan (Boydston)		1	4,000	Maceration	At LWM	Sand and rocks. Improvement scheme planned. Water quality not monitored by RPB in 1992.
	f	**Saltcoats**	PPFFFPF	2	13,500	Raw	Both below LWM	Sandy. Improvement scheme under construction.
		Stevenston		1	41,000	Screens	1km below LWM	Sandy. Water quality not monitored by RPB in 1992.
	f	**Irvine (Beach Park)**	FFFFFFF					Sandy. Improvement scheme completed in 1991.
		Gailes		1	100,000	Screens	1.5km beyond LWM	Sandy. Water quality not monitored by RPB in 1992.
		Brodick Bay		2	700	Both raw	1 below and 1 above LWM	Rocks and sand. Water quality not monitored by RPB in 1992.
		Lamlash Bay		6	950	Raw	All at LWM	Rocks and sand. Water quality not monitored by RPB in 1992.
		Whiting Bay		2	800	Raw	Below LWM	Sand and shingle. Water quality not monitored by RPB in 1992.
		Blackwaterfoot						4 discharges of septic tank effluent. Sand and shingle. Water quality not monitored by RPB in 1992.

Beach No on Map	Rating. The more stars the better. **f**=failed	Resort	Pass/Fail track record	Sewage outlets	Population discharging from outlet	Type of treatment	Discharge point relative to low water mark, unless otherwise stated. Distance given in metres	Remarks
		Troon (North)		1	6,300	Raw	At LWM	Sandy. Improvement scheme under construction. Reports of littering, sewage slicks and bathing-related illnesses in 1992.
	★★	**Troon (South)**	PPPPPPP					Sandy.
	f	**Prestwick**	PPPFFFF					Sandy.
	f	**Ayr**	FFFFFFF	1	16,200	Screens	140 below LWM	Sandy. Improvements planned.
		Doonfoot		1	8,000	Maceration	220 below LWM	Sand/rocks. Improvements planned. Water quality not monitored by RPB in 1992.
		Butlins (Heads of Ayr)		1	10,000	Secondary	Below LWM	Sandy. Water quality not monitored by RPB in 1992.
		Maidens		1	600	Primary	At LWM	Sandy and rocks. Improvement scheme planned. Water quality not monitored by RPB in 1992.
	f	**Turnberry**	PPF~FFF	1	Primary		Beyond LWM	Sand and rocks. Improvement scheme under consideration.
	f	**Girvan**	FFFPFPF	3	4,000	Screens/ maceration	10 below LWM	Sandy. Improvement scheme in preparation.
					500	Tidal tank	At LWM	
					2,500	Tidal tank	At LWM	
DUMFRIES AND GALLOWAY								
	f	Stranraer Marine Lake	~~~~~FF		10,000	Primary		Area affected by silt and effluent from local creamery.
	f	Stranraer Cockle Shore	~~~~~FF					Fine sand/silt. Creamery effluent discharged to beach
	★	Portpatrick Outer Harbour	~~~~~PP	1	600	Raw		Rocky.
		Portlogan Bay		1	75	Primary	200 below HWM	Sandy. Water quality not monitored by RPB in 1992.

Beach No on Map	Rating. The more stars the better. f=failed	Resort	Pass/Fail track record	Sewage outlets	Population discharging from outlet	Type of treatment	Discharge point relative to low water mark, unless otherwise stated. Distance given in metres	Remarks
	★★★	Drunmore	~~~~~PP	2	280 50		Primary	Sandy.
		Ardwell Bay		1	75	Primary	75 below HWM	Sand/shingle. Water quality not monitored by RPB in 1992.
	★★	Sandhead	~~~~~FP					Sandy. Some contamination by animal faeces.
	★★★	Monreith	~~~~~~PP					Sandy. Affected by sea-borne litter, especially after winter storms, although cleared for holiday season.
	★★	Mossyard	~~~~~PP					Sandy.
	★	Carrick Shore	~~~~~PP					Fine sand.
	★★	Brighouse Bay	~~~~~PP	1	400	Secondary	30 below LWM	Sandy. Strong tides and rocky shores outside bay.
	★★	Dhoon	~~~~~PP	2	6,000 200	Primary		Fine sand/silt.
	f	Rockcliffe	~~~~~FF	2	200 300	Secondary		Fine sand.
	★	**Sandyhills**	PPPPFPP	1	220	Secondary	To tidal watercourse	Fine sand. Sometimes affected by livestock faeces from inland.
		Southerness		1	3,500	Primary	500 above LWM	Sand/rock. Water quality not monitored by RPB in 1992.
	f	Powfoot	~~~~~PF	1	400	Primary		Silty.
	f	Annan Waterfoot	~~~~~FF	1	7,900	Primary		Unsuitable for bathing, due to deep channel and nearby Annan sewage outfall.

1 Pease Sands, Cockburns Path, Berwickshire   OS Ref: NT7971

The deep wooded valley of Pease Burn opens out on to the sandy cove of Pease Bay. Framed by red cliffs, a shrub- and grass-covered bank fringes the landward side of the sands beyond which is a large caravan and mobile home park. The ¾ mile (1.2km) of good sandy beach is very much dominated by the caravan site that rings the bay.

Water quality Water quality monitored by the River Purification Board (RPB) and found to meet the EC Guideline coliform standards for bathing water in 1992. ★★★ in this year's listed section. One outfall serving 1,000 people discharges secondary treated sewage.

Bathing safety Safe bathing.

Access A steep road from the A1107, just south of its junction with the A1.

Parking Car park with 100 spaces directly off the beach.

Toilets At the car park.

Food Small shop adjacent to the beach.

Seaside activities Swimming and fishing.

Wildlife and walks Good walks are available in Pease Dean. A cliff path can be followed north of the beach, passing the tiny village and harbour of Cove and leading to the Dunglass Gorge.

2 Thorntonloch, Lothian   OS Ref: NT752744

Shallow dunes back on to this beautiful sandy beach which is about 440 yards (400m) long. To the south there are beautiful views of the Berwickshire cliffs, while to the north is the Torness nuclear power station. There is a caravan site near the beach.

Water quality Water quality monitored by the RPB and found to meet the EC Guideline coliform standards for bathing water in 1992. ★★★ in this year's listed section.

Bathing safety There is a fairly strong undertow and swimmers should use extreme caution.

Access The beach is a short walk from the car park.

Parking Car park for approximately 40 cars.

Toilets At the caravan site.

Food There is a small shop at the caravan site.

Seaside activities   Swimming, fishing, windsurfing.

Wildlife and walks   This is a good bird-watching area.

3 Duncansby Head, John o'Groats, Highland   OS Ref: ND4173

Travellers taking the A9 north beyond Inverness are normally heading for John o'Groats as the most northerly point. Not to be missed is Duncansby Head, without a doubt one of the finest pieces of coastline in Britain. The road from John o'Groats takes you to the Duncansby lighthouse. From the small car park the view to the islands is hard to beat; on a clear day the panorama laid out before you can be breathtaking. Just off shore beyond the foaming tidal races are the Pentland Skerries and Stroma, on which you can see many abandoned dwellings. Beyond, Swona, South Ronaldsay, Hoy and the mainland of Orkney complete the picture. Tucked below the headland, just off the lighthouse approach road, is a tiny and delightful beach. A mere 110 yards (100m) in length, the narrow strip of sand is shadowed by the red sandstone of the headland. This may not be the beach to seek out for a day by the sea, but after enjoying a stroll on the headland, relax awhile and watch the seals that bob around offshore. This is one of many little beaches along the north coast between the Duncansby and Dunnet Headlands, although most are difficult to get to and are not as attractive, lacking the backdrop of sheer red cliffs.

Water quality   No sewage is discharged in the vicinity of this beach. The water quality was not monitored by the RPB in 1992.

Bathing safety   The beach shelves steeply and swimming is dangerous.

Access   Duncansby Head is signposted from the A9 south of John o'Groats. A short walk from the parking area down the hill across turf leads on to the sands.

Parking   Car park at Duncansby lighthouse with approximately 25 spaces.

Toilets   None.

Food   At John o'Groats and Dunnet.

Wildlife and walks   A short walk over the headland passes a narrow inlet or geo whose cliff walls rise nearly 200 feet (60m) above the waves. A short distance further and you are rewarded with a marvellous view of Duncansby Stacks, their steeple-like outlines pointing skywards. These are also known as Muckle Stack. Boat trips around this stretch of coast are available from John o'Groats.

4 Sandside Bay, Reay, Highland   OS Ref: NC9774

This area has some of the best exposed rocky coastline in Britain. Low cliffs, rocky outcrops and dunes bound the long, flat, sandy beach. At the western end of the bay is the tiny harbour of Fresgoe; a tranquil old-world air prevails around the little-used harbour, a sharp contrast to the view along the coast east to the Dounreay Fast Breeder Reactor. A remote and quiet beach.

Water quality No sewage is discharged in the vicinity of the beach. The water quality was not monitored by the RPB in 1992.

Bathing safety Safe bathing.

Access The road to Fresgoe runs alongside the bay, and it is a short walk from the road down a track between the dunes to the beach.

Parking In the area along the side road.

Toilets On the road close to the car parking area.

Food None. The closest shop is in Reay village 2 miles (3km) away.

Seaside activities Swimming.

Wet weather alternatives Dounreay Exhibition Centre (access for disabled visitors, tours limited to the over-12s).

Wildlife and walks There is a short cliff walk from the beach.

5 Coldbackie, Tongue, Highland   OS Ref: NC6160

The half-moon of Coldbackie Sands faces Tongue Bay at the mouth of the Kyle of Tongue, one of the three deep indents into the north coast. The undulating turf-covered moorland which dominates this corner of Scotland slopes down to the grass-covered dunes which border the sands. Below Meall Mor, low grass-covered cliffs flank the beach.

Water quality No sewage is discharged in the vicinity of this beach. The water quality was not monitored by the RPB in 1992.

Bathing safety Safe bathing.

Access From the A836 north of Tongue, banks of dunes descend to the beach. There is no proper footpath but it is an easy walk down to the sand.

Parking There is limited car parking in a layby off the main road above the beach.

Toilets None.

Food None.

Seaside activities Swimming.

Wildlife and walks The 1000 foot (300m) peaks of Cnoc an Fhreiceadan and Ben Tongue rise behind the beach. From the road a footpath inland skirts the sides of the hills, passing a tiny loch to reach Tongue and the shores of the Kyle.

6 Balnakeil Bay, Durness, Highland   OS Ref: NC3869

There are in fact three beaches at Durness, all worthy of note. All have clean white sands and are unspoilt and quiet, even at the height of the summer. To the east of Faraid Head Peninsula, below the steep limestone cliffs on which Durness stands, are the twin beaches of Sango Bay and Sangobeg. The best beach, however, is Balnakeil Bay, a long curve of white sand and dunes on the western side of the peninsula. There is easy access at the southern end of the beach close to the ruined Balnakeil Church. The extensive wind-sculptured dunes stretch north along the low, rugged headland. The bare and treeless landscape is dominated by wild, windswept moorland – a sharp contrast to the coastline, which is made up of warm red sandstone cliffs, folded and faulted limestone, collapsed caverns, geos, rocky shores and sandy bays.

Water quality One outfall discharges primary treated sewage from 200 people at low water mark. The water quality was not monitored by the RPB in 1992.

Bathing safety Safe bathing, although in this part of the country some might find it rather cold.

Access A road off the A838 from Durness village leads to a car park behind the beach, and from here an easy path leads to the sand.

Parking Car park with 30 spaces.

Toilets Portaloo at car park.

Food Sango Sands Oasis Restaurant in Sango.

Seaside activities Swimming.

Wet weather alternatives Half a mile (800m) inland is a craft village in the building of a disused early warning station; the workshops are open to the public during the summer months. Sixteenth-century church at Balnakeil.

Wildlife and walks There are walks on the cliffs surrounding the bay and much evidence of 1000 years of human activity, including the remains of an ancient fortress on the Faraid Headland. Steps lead down from Durness village to the beach at Sango Bay where the high arched entrance to the Smoo Cave can be found. The Allt (river) Smoo flows from the cave. The first of three chambers can be entered. The Highland Regional Ranger Service organises guided walks in the area, and further information can be obtained from the information centre in Durness. The remote north-western tip of Scotland, Cape Wrath, can be reached by a small ferry across the Kyle of Durness, followed by a minibus service to the Cape. The bus takes you across the wild moorland to the Cape Wrath Lighthouse and there is fantastic cliff scenery along this most isolated stretch of coastline. The most spectacular cliffs are along the northern coast, where, in places, the sheer cliffs fall 800 feet (250m) to the waters below.

7 Scourie, Highland   OS Ref: NC1544

Unlike most of the crofting villages along the west coast, Scourie has some facilities for the visitor; it boasts two hotels, a shop, a post office and a camp site, thus enabling the tourist to stop a while and enjoy this most picturesque district. Scourie is set at the head of a 1 mile (1.6km) rocky inlet, on the banks of a small river draining from a loch a short distance inland. There is a lovely sheltered beach on the southern flank of the bay. The wide, gently sloping sands are backed by a narrow storm beach, where small boulders and pebbles edge the sand. The irregular hummocks of this grey-green rocky landscape come down to the water's edge in the outer bay. This exposed rocky coast is coloured by bands of lichens and encrusted with barnacles and seaweed below high water mark, where there are many rockpools to explore. This is a deservedly popular spot.

Water quality Two outfalls, each serving 100-200 people, discharge primary treated sewage at low water mark. Water quality was not monitored by the RPB in 1992.

Bathing safety Safe bathing.

Access There are gentle grass-covered slopes down to the sand.

Parking Parking space available adjacent to the beach.

Toilets In the village.

Food Hotel and shop in the village.

Seaside activities Swimming.

Wildlife and walks A stroll around the loch, the village and its quay-side can be a most pleasant way to spend an afternoon. Alternatively, follow the path north of the bay to Tarbet. Handa Island, lying just across the Sound of Handa, is an RSPB reserve. The numerous ledges on its vertical cliffs provide nesting sites for thousands of seabirds, including guillemots, kittiwakes and fulmars. The island can be visited by boat from Tarbet daily, except Sunday, from April to August.

8 Clashnessie Bay, Lochinver, Highland   OS Ref: NC0631

Steep rocky cliffs, wide bays dotted with tiny islands, clean clear waters, beautiful sunsets, seabirds and seals: the perfect ingredients to make a good beach. Clashnessie is an attractive and safe beach. The 660 yards

(600m) of gently sloping pink sands are framed by red sandstone cliffs. There are superb views north towards Oldany Island and east along the rugged cliffs of the Stoer Peninsula.

Water quality No sewage is discharged in the vicinity of the beach. The water quality was not monitored by the RPB in 1992.

Bathing safety Safe bathing.

Access A side road from the B869 at Clashnessie leads down to the shore, and then there is a short walk down to the beach.

Parking Car park at the beach with 10–15 spaces.

Toilets None.

Food None.

Seaside activities Swimming.

Wildlife and walks To the east there is a cliff-top walk to Stoer Point with views of the fine cliff scenery, including the Old Man of Stoer, an isolated sea stack rising 200 feet (60m) above the waves. Further along the coast stands the Stoer lighthouse. A good variety of birds can be seen on the beach and cliffs. There are also a number of walks on the wide, flat moors inland.

9 Clachtoll, Lochinver, Highland   OS Ref: NC0427

This is one of a series of sandy coves along this stretch of coastline north of Loch Inver which is scenically stunning. Clachtoll is a small cove, 275 yards (250m) of beautiful white shell sand backed by machair banks and grey and red cliffs. The quiet beach is washed by clear waters and seals can often be seen close to the shore. There is a camp site situated behind the beach.

Water quality No sewage is discharged in the vicinity of this beach. The water quality was not monitored by the RPB in 1992.

Bathing safety Safe bathing within the bay.

Access There is car parking off the B869 which runs along this stretch of coast. It is a short walk across the dunes to the beach.

Parking Car park with 20 spaces.

Toilets Toilets and showers at the car park.

Food Takeaway meals and snacks at the camp site.

Seaside activities Swimming, windsurfing, diving, sailing, canoeing and fishing. Boats can be hired for fishing; details are available from the local ranger.

Wet weather alternatives Teas and games at Stoer village hall.

Wildlife and walks There is a diverse range of plant and animal life around the bay, and an interesting variety of birds and mammals, including seals and whales, can be seen. Many rare plants can also be found. There is a wealth of material for those interested in conservation and the history of the area. Full details are available from the interpretative centre at the beach, and coastal walks can be arranged by the local ranger.

10 Achmelvich, Lochinver, Highland   OS Ref: NC0625

This is a small sandy cove at the southern end of Achmelvich Bay which can be reached fairly easily. The white sands of the bay are backed by an area of machair grassland; this vegetation is very fragile and easily eroded, so great care must be taken not to cause damage. Rocky grey cliffs rise steeply on either side of the sands, creating a marvellous setting for the bay. Dogs are permitted on the beach under strict control but they are not allowed on the surrounding land. The beach is cleaned by local volunteers.

Water quality No sewage is discharged in the vicinity of this beach. The water quality was not monitored by the RPB in 1992.

Bathing safety Safe bathing.

Access A side road off the B869 north of Lochinver leads to Achmelvich. The car park gives direct access to the turf sloping to the sand.

Parking Car park with 60 spaces.

Toilets In the car park.

Food None.

Seaside activities Swimming, surfing, windsurfing, diving, sailing and fishing.

Wildlife and walks There is a 1 mile (1.6km) nature trail along the coast to the small sandy bay of Alltan na Bradhan. The walk leads from the machair grassland over the sandhills and then passes through heath and bog vegetation. A leaflet describing the whole trail is available from the Countryside Ranger Centre at the rear of the car park at Achmelvich. This area also has interesting geology; there is a combination of red sandstone and grey Lewisian gneiss (pronounced 'nice') with igneous dyke intrusions – dark rock squeezed in bands up through the surrounding rock.

11 Achnahaird, Enard Bay, Highland   OS Ref: NC0214

Flat windswept moorland with outcrops of grey gneiss leads down to the shore of Enard Bay, a magnificent island-dotted prospect. On the western side of the Rubha Mor headland is the narrow inlet of Achnahaird Bay. The bay, in the southern corner of Enard Bay, stretches nearly 1 mile (1.6km) inland and low tide reveals an expanse of flat white sand. On the western side of the inlet there are extensive dunes which give way to saltmarsh at the head of the bay. Irregularly layered sandstone cliffs flank the eastern side of the inlet and a stream meanders across the centre of the sands.

Water quality No sewage is discharged in the vicinity of this beach. The water quality was not monitored by the RPB in 1992.

Bathing safety Bathe with caution as there may be some currents that could cause problems for the swimmer.

Access A side road from Achnahaird village leads to parking behind the beach. There is access to the sands on a path down the rocks (can be diffi-cult) or through the camp site behind the dunes. Visitor pressure is causing damage to the dunes.

Parking Limited parking behind the dunes.

Toilets None.

Food None.

Seaside activities Swimming.

Wildlife and walks The shores of Enard Bay are part of the Inverpolly National Nature Reserve, a vast area of moorland which includes the huge bulk of Suilven. There is a visitors' centre at Knockan some way inland, where there is an interpretative centre, a nature trail and a geology trail. This helps to introduce the visitor to an area that abounds in wildlife, includ-ing red deer and otters. A hundred bird species and 300 types of plant have been recorded within the reserve. Achnahaird Bay combines a wide variety of vegetation types: dunes, saltmarsh and rocky and sandy shore. The salt-marsh attracts waders and wildfowl; the rocky shore is banded with lichen and there are pools among the barnacle-encrusted rocks.

12 Achiltibuie, Badentarbat Bay, Highland   OS Ref: NC0309

Smooth heather-clad slopes descend to the crofting village of Achiltibuie which straggles 3 miles (5km) along the shore of Badentarbat Bay. The beach, which curves round the bay, lacks the sand so common on the west coast but to compensate there is a marvellous view across to the Summer Isles. A patchwork of islands and rocky skerries lies just offshore and pro-vides the most wonderful seascape. From the pier the shingle and cobble beach stretches south to the rocky headland of Rubha Dunan.

Water quality No sewage is discharged in the vicinity of this beach. The water quality was not monitored by the RPB in 1992.

Bathing safety Bathe with caution as there may be some currents that could cause problems for the swimmer.

Access The road through the village continues along the edge of the bay and the sand can be reached across the grass which slopes below the road.

Parking Cars park on the grass between the road and the beach.

Toilets None.

Food Shops in the village.

Seaside activities Swimming and fishing.

Wildlife and walks The Summer Isles fall within the Ben More Coigach Nature Reserve (Scottish Wildlife Trust Royal Society for Nature Conservation). The 15,011 acres (6,075 hectares) include the peak which gives the reserve its name, and whose purple and red slopes dominate the views inland from Achiltibuie. There is good walking along the Coigach Peninsula west of the bay. The Summer Isles can be viewed at closer range by taking a boat trip from the pier at Achiltibuie.

13 Gruinard Bay, Laide, Highland   OS Ref: NG9092

There are several excellent beaches dotted around Gruinard Bay, all of which overlook the lovely Gruinard Island, centrepiece of the bay. The island was used for anthrax experiments during the last war and was out of bounds until 1992, when it was declared safe and returned to its owners. It is now possible to visit the island provided you have permission; enquiries should be made to the information office in Ullapool. The A832 skirts the southern and eastern shores of the bay, giving easy access to the three lovely cove beaches on the eastern shore. Their pink sands are set among sandstone rock outcrops. In contrast, the south-eastern shore at Little Gruinard has the bulging hummocks of Lewisian gneiss as a most attractive backdrop. Gruinard Hill provides the best views of the bay, the island, and the Summer Isles on the horizon. Wooded slopes above the beach provide a sharp contrast to the rocky grey outcrops. At Laide, the road runs parallel with the beach behind the machair turf, which slopes to the sand of this 1 mile (1.6km) beach. This most picturesque of bays, like most of the west coast beaches, is relatively quiet and unspoilt; facilities for the tourist are limited and there is restricted parking. In many parts of the bay parking along the back-shore causes severe erosional problems for the machair grass. It is important that the grass cover is maintained and parking should be limited accordingly.

Water quality No sewage is discharged in the vicinity of this beach. The water quality was not monitored by the RPB in 1992.

Bathing safety Safe bathing.

Access The A832 follows the shore round most of the bay with easy access to the beach.

Parking There are two car parks in the south-eastern corner of the bay near Little Gruinard and another at Laide.

Toilets In Laide.

Food Hotel and shop in Laide.

Seaside activities Swimming and fishing.

Wildlife and walks There are trips around the bay during the summer months which allow the visitor to take a closer look at Gruinard Island and enjoy the spectacular panoramas across the bay towards the mountains inland.

14 Applecross, Highland   OS Ref: NG7144

The dramatic and tortuous 'Pass of the Cattle' climbs over 2,000 feet (620m) as it twists its way from the A896 at the head of Loch Kishorn across the wild mountains and moorlands to Applecross. There is a wooded approach to the cluster of white cottages which make up this remote village on the southern shore of a wide bay. The sweeping sandy beach lies below limestone cliffs from which there are superb views across the Inner Sound to Raasay and Scalpay, with the Cuillins of Skye on the distant horizon. Having crossed desolate moorland, negotiated precipitous roads and revelled in vast panoramic views, one could be at the edge of the world. This lovely beach with its magnificent setting provides an ideal spot to rest and unwind.

Water quality No sewage is discharged in the vicinity of this beach. The water quality was not monitored by the RPB in 1992.

Bathing safety Safe bathing.

Access The Pass from Loch Kishorn should not be attempted by the caravanner or the faint-hearted; the alternative route which approaches the village along the coast from Loch Torridon is an easier drive. The village stands on the shore with easy access to the sands.

Parking Limited parking at Applecross.

Toilets None.

Food Shop in the village.

Seaside activities Swimming and fishing. Picnic site behind the beach.

Wildlife and walks There are good walks along this beautiful stretch of coast with eider duck, mergansers and other seabirds to be seen in the bays.

15 The Coral Beaches, Dunvegan, Skye   OS Ref: NG2354

A pleasant, easy, ½ mile (800m) walk across grassland takes you to two small beaches which are beautiful and totally unspoilt. Known locally as the Coral Beaches, they are in fact white sand made up of broken shells. Grass banks slope gently down to the sand. The bays, each about 220 yards (200m) in length, are separated by a low grassy promontory, around which there are rocky outcrops. There are lovely views across Loch Dunvegan, whose clean, clear waters wash the beach.

Water quality There is no sewage discharged in the vicinity of this beach. The water quality was not monitored by the RPB in 1992.

Bathing safety Safe bathing.

Access The road north from Dunvegan becomes a narrow lane beyond Claigan. From the lane-end there is a well-defined path across the grassland to the sand.

Parking Limited parking along the lane.

Toilets None.

Food None.

Seaside activities Swimming and snorkelling.

Wildlife and walks There is excellent walking to the Coral Beaches and along the beautiful peninsula beyond. Numerous seals can be seen in the waters of the loch. They are often visible close inshore, and a short boat trip from Dunvegan takes you to the rocky islands where they can be seen basking on the shore.

16 Morar, Highland   OS Ref: NM6793

This stretch of coastline between Mallaig and Arisaig has to be one of the most memorable in Scotland. When you try to imagine the silver sands of the west coast you probably create a picture closely resembling this stretch of shore. The green crofting land, dotted with white cottages, slopes down to the white sands of the bays. South of Mallaig, with its busy harbour that links to the Islands, is the wide, sheltered Morar Bay. Two-thirds of a mile (1km) of white sands fringes the wide, Y-shaped bay which is set below undulating hills. The bay was originally the mouth of a sea loch similar to many others that penetrate this coastline until the long finger of Loch Morar was cut off from the sea by an uplift of the land and glacial deposits. A fast-flowing river drains the freshwater lake over a weir, which is all that remains of once-impressive falls which were sacrificed to a hydro-electric power scheme. The river meanders across the southern edge of the bay to the narrow sea opening.

Water quality There have been reports that some sewage from Morar village and the other villages along this coast ends up on the sands. The water quality was not monitored by the RPB in 1992.

Bathing safety Bathing is only safe close inshore due to strong undercurrents 110 yards (100m) from the shore.

Access The main road runs parallel with the beach and it is a short walk across the turf banks that lead down to the sand. The railway runs alongside the road and some trains stop at Morar station.

Parking Along the road above the beach. Car park at toilets.

Toilets Male and female, including facilities for disabled visitors, now available.

Food None.

Seaside activities Swimming and sailing.

Wildlife and walks At the southern end of the bay a turning off the main coast road leads along the shore of Loch Morar. Beyond the tiny hamlet of Bracora the road gives way to a path which can be followed through some spectacular scenery to Tarbet on Loch Nevis. From the shoreline around Morar there are stunning views east to the Inner Hebrides.

17 Camusdarrach Beach, Glenancross, Highland   OS Ref: NM6592

This beach was made famous in Bill Forsyth's film *Local Hero* (although the actual village scenes were shot over on the east coast). The mile (1.6km) of gleaming white sands backed by dunes and undulating grassland is popular, but remains beautiful and unspoilt. There is easy access to the beach by paths from the road above the beach. A series of delightful secluded bays can be reached by walking over the hills edging the shore, forming rocky outcrops. The area is popular with tourists and in summer many caravans appear. The approach to the beach is vulnerable to erosion and visitors should use the paths to avoid damaging the dunes. Those staying at this beach until the late evening will enjoy seeing the most breathtaking sunsets, as the sun sinks behind the rugged mountains of Skye.

Water quality No sewage is discharged in the vicinity of this beach. The water quality was not monitored by the RPB in 1992.

Bathing safety Safe bathing but beware of some offshore currents.

Access Camusdarrach is situated just south of Morar Bay. The road runs parallel with the shore between Morar and Arisaig. There are paths giving access at various points across the low turf-banks that descend to the beach.

Parking Cars can park on the turf behind the beach.

Toilets None.

Food None.

Seaside activities Swimming and windsurfing. Golf course.

Wildlife and walks All along the western coast there is much of interest for the naturalist. Underwater there is a rich and varied marine life which can only be glimpsed from the shore. The bobbing heads of seals are common, the outline of the basking shark a rarer occurrence. On the rocks that edge these beautiful beaches cormorants, shags, gannets and terns may be seen.

18 Traigh, Arisaig, Highland   OS Ref: NM6492

This U-shaped beach, some 2 miles (3km) west of Arisaig village, is sheltered by the small dunes and elevated land behind it. The main road follows its perimeter and it is easily accessible. Immediately across the road is a small 9-hole course which is maintained by local voluntary effort – the greens may not be up to the standard of a professionally maintained course, but it provides good practice and fun. The area is popular with tourists. Sunsets over the Western Isles viewed from Arisaig are often superb.

Water quality No sewage is discharged in the vicinity of the beach. The water quality was not monitored by the RPB in 1992.

Bathing safety Bathing is safe within the bay.

Access The trunk road A830 follows the perimeter of the site.

Parking Limited parking in a lay-by and on adjoining land.

Toilets There are toilets behind the beach with facilities for disabled visitors.

Food None.

Seaside activities Swimming and sailing.

19 Sanna Bay, Sanna, Highland   OS Ref: NM4368

On the northern side of Ardnamurchan Point, the most westerly point of mainland Britain, are the lovely white sands of Sanna Bay. This is a beautiful and unspoilt beach backed by impressive marram-covered dunes and ringed by craggy hills. There are a series of island skerries off Sanna Point at the northern end of the bay, as well as rocky outcrops along the beach, dividing the bay into three sections. The sands are washed by clean, clear seas. The south side of the bay is covered by extensive rocks encrusted with barnacles and many types of seaweeds. To the south is a second sandy cove which is shadowed by cliffs and the nearby Ardnamurchan lighthouse.

Water quality No sewage is discharged in the vicinity of the beach. The water quality was not monitored by the RPB in 1992.

Bathing safety Offshore currents necessitate bathing with caution.

Access The B8007 from Kilchoran leads to the southern end of the bay, Portuairk, and from here it is a short walk across the dunes to the beach.

Parking Limited parking behind the dunes.

Toilets None.

Food   None.

Seaside activities   Swimming, sailing and fishing.

Wildlife and walks   There is a string of small sandy bays along the north coast of Ardnamurchan, only accessible on foot. These deserted beaches offer much to interest the naturalist. Ardnamurchan Point itself is notorious in sailing circles for its unpredictable weather so do not be surprised if you see boats motoring past as quickly as possible!

20 Calgary Bay, Mull   OS Ref: NM3652

Calgary Bay has been described as Mull's most beautiful bay. It might best be considered as a small sea loch with a sandy beach at its head. The gently sloping white sands are backed by small dunes and flat machair grassland. Rocky shores extend at right angles from both sides of the beach. There are areas of both flat rock and boulders, amongst which there are numerous rock pools rich in animal and plant life. Steep cliffs and grassy slopes rising behind the rocky shore enclose the bay. This lovely beach is understandably popular with visitors in the summer. Emigrants from this area may well have founded the Canadian city which bears the same name.

Water quality   No sewage is discharged in the vicinity of this beach. The water quality was not monitored by the RPB in 1992.

Bathing safety   Safe bathing.

Access   The B8073 from Tobermory leads south to Calgary. The road skirts the grassland behind the beach and continues along the southern shore.

Parking   There is a car park at the northern end of the beach and a small parking area at the southern end.

Toilets   At the southern end of the beach, on the road behind the dunes.

Food   None.

Seaside activities   Swimming and fishing.

Wildlife and walks   From the car park at the northern end of the beach a track leads to an old pier. This continues for a short distance as a footpath above the rocky shore where a series of lava dykes can be seen as grey bands where the molten lava has been pushed up between the surrounding rocks.

21 Erraid, Fionnphort, Mull   OS Ref: NM3120

Mull has 300 miles (500km) of breathtaking coastline including sheer cliffs, stacks and arches. There are also tiny bays nestling below the cliffs with a backdrop of brooding mountains. The Ross of Mull, a long, low peninsula to the south of the island, has some of the best coastal features. There are cliffs of basalt columns, the Carsaig Arches at Malcolm's Point, numerous caves and secluded sandy bays which can only be approached on foot. The extensive sands at the western tip of the Ross are much more accessible. A road from Fionnphort, point of departure for the ferries to Iona, proceeds south along the Sound of Iona to extensive sandy beaches sheltered by Erraid Island. Between the island and the mainland, the Sound of Erraid is a sandy beach at low tide backed by sand dunes and machair grassland. At either end of the Sound there are rocky outcrops, and a host of islets and skerries lie just offshore. The grassland behind the beach is used for camping and as a result the beach can be quite crowded in summer. Those wanting to get away from the busier beaches should seek out the bays along the southern coast. There is easy access to Ardchiavaig, with limited parking.

Water quality No sewage is discharged in the vicinity of this beach. The water quality was not monitored by the RPB in 1992.

Bathing safety Bathing can be dangerous due to the skerries and currents.

Access A side road from the A849 at Fionnphort leads south to Fidden skirting the dunes south to Knockvolgan.

Parking Parking space is available behind the dunes.

Toilets None.

Food None.

Seaside activities Swimming.

Wildlife and walks The lovely island of Iona is well worth a visit; boat trips leave from Fionnphort. There are sites of great historical interest including the St Oran Chapel and the Iona Cathedral. Scenically, the island has much to offer with its beautiful shoreline, clear blue seas and white sands.

Wales

Sand dunes of Anglesey, pounding surf on the Lleyn, miles of sand, the cliffs and secluded coves of West Wales and the beautiful Gower – this is the coast of Wales. There are many lovely beaches which are comparable with the best anywhere in the country and they have the added advantage of not being too crowded. Unfortunately there are individual beaches throughout the region that have failed to meet the minimum EC standards for bathing water due to the discharge of sewage from their shores. Major schemes are planned, but two of the largest are not due for completion until 1997.

The north and south coasts suffer from the close proximity of large industrial centres. Swansea, Cardiff, Port Talbot and Newport all contribute to the pollution of the south coast with discharges of domestic and industrial waste. The north coast is affected by pollution from Merseyside and the Wirral. Milford Haven has suffered from oil pollution problems from the terminals and refineries that line its shore and has also been affected by the antifoulants used on the oiltankers. Further west, away from centres of population, some beaches remain clean and unspoilt; definitely worth exploring.

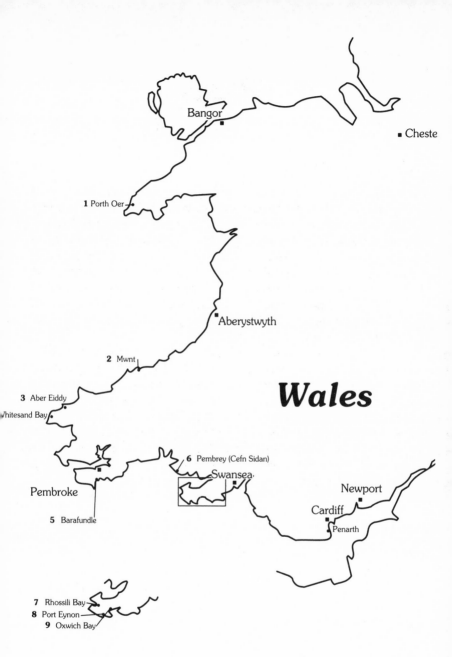

1 Porth Oer

2 Mwnt

3 Aber Eiddy

Whitesand Bay

Bangor

Cheste

Aberystwyth

Wales

6 Pembrey (Cefn Sidan)

Swansea

Pembroke

5 Barafundle

Newport

Cardiff

Penarth

7 Rhossili Bay
8 Port Eynon
9 Oxwich Bay

Coastal walk
Pembrokeshire Coast Path
Cardigan to Tenby 180 miles (290km) mostly in the
Pembrokeshire National Park.

Wales   *See page 21 for further details*

Beach No on Map	Rating. The more stars the better. f=failed	Resort	Pass/Fail track record	Sewage outlets	Population discharging from outlet	Type of treatment	Discharge point relative to low water mark. unless otherwise stated. Distance given in metres	Remarks
CLWYD								
	f	Point of Ayr Lighthouse	~~~~~PF					
	★★ ★★	**Prestatyn** Prestatyn: Barkby Beach	FPPPFFP ~~~~~FP	1	16,246	Screens/ maceration	1000 below LWM	Sandy. Safety patrols. Linked to Rhyl scheme. Marine litter and sewage debris reported 1992.
		Ffrith						Sandy. Water quality not monitored by NRA in 1992.
	f f	**Rhyl** Rhyl (Splash Point)	~~~~~FF FFFFFFF	1	22,600	Maceration/ tidal tank		Sandy. Safety patrols. Bathing unsafe near river mouth. Primary treatment to be added by 1994.
	f	**Kinmel Bay (Sandy Cove)**	FFFFFFF					Sandy. Bathing unsafe near river mouth. Linked to Rhyl scheme for completion in 1994.
	★★	Abergele (Towyn)	~~~~FPP	1	4,237	Screens/ maceration/ tidal tank	100 above LWM	Sand/shingle. Linked to Rhyl scheme.
	★★	Abergele (Pensam)	~~~~~~P	1	7,487	Screens/ maceration/ tidal tank	100 above LWM	Sand at low tide. Linked to Rhyl scheme.
	f	Llandulas	~~~~PPF	1	1,550	Screens/ maceration/ tidal tank	75 below LWM	Sand/shingle. Storm overflow on beach. Linked to improvement scheme at Colwyn Bay.
	★ ★ ★★	**Colwyn Bay** Colwyn Bay (end of Cayley Prom) Colwyn Bay (opposite Rhos Abbey Hotel)	PPPPPPP ~~~~~FP ~~~~~PP	1	25,800	Screens/ maceration/ tidal tank	1000 below	Primary treatment by 2000
GWYNEDD								
	f	Penrhyn Bay	~~~~FFF		3,500	Screens/ maceration/ tidal tank	100 above LWM	Sand/shingle.

Beach No on Map	Rating. The more stars the better. **f**=failed	Resort	Pass/Fail track record	Sewage outlets	Population discharging from outlet	Type of treatment	Discharge point relative to low water mark, unless otherwise stated. Distance given in metres	Remarks
★		Llandudno (North Jetty)	~~~~~FP					
	f	**Llandudno (North)**	PPPPFPF					Sandy.
	f	**Llandudno (West Shore)**	FFFFFFF	1	34,000	Screens/ maceration/ tidal tank	Long sea outfall	Sand/shingle. Some complaints due to unsatisfactory discharges in Conwy Estuary.
		Deganwy (North)						To be linked to Llandudno for primary treatment by 2000. Water quality not monitored by NRA in 1992.
		Penmaenmawr	~~~~FP~	1	3,700	Maceration	200 above LWM	Sand/shingle
		(Conwy Bay)		2	160	Raw	200 above LWM	Improvements planned. Water quality not monitored by NRA in 1992.
		Llanfairfechan						Beware tidal currents. Water quality not monitored by NRA in 1992.

ANGLESEY

Beach No on Map	Rating	Resort	Pass/Fail track record	Sewage outlets	Population discharging from outlet	Type of treatment	Discharge point	Remarks
		Beaumaris: West of Pier Opposite swimming baths	~~~~~P~ ~~~~~F~					Shingle/sand. Bathing dangerous on ebbing tide. Water quality not monitored by NRA in 1992.
		Llanddona	~~~~~P~					Water quality not monitored by NRA in 1992.
		Red Wharf Bay	~~~~~F~					Bathing unsafe at ebb tide. Algal blooms reported. Sewage debris and litter left by users a problem. Water quality not monitored by NRA in 1992.
★		**Benllech** Craig Dwllan (Benllech)	PFPPFFP	1	2,284	Raw	200 below LWM	Sandy. Long sea outfall planned.

Beach No on Map	Rating. The more stars the better. f=failed	Resort	Pass/Fail track record	Sewage outlets	Population discharging from outlet	Type of treatment	Discharge point relative to low water mark, unless otherwise stated. Distance given in metres	Remarks
		Moelfre (Treath Lligwy)		1	894	Raw	100 below LWM	Shingle. Water quality not monitored by the NRA in 1992.
		Amlwch (Bull Bay)		1	4,200	Raw	50 below LWM	Outfall 800m east of bay (to be extended). Storm overflow below LWM. Water quality not monitored by NRA in 1992.
		Cemaes Bay	~~~~FP~	1	1,000	Maceration/ tidal tank	70 below LWM	Sandy. Water quality not monitored by NRA in 1992.
		Penrhos Beach (Centre)	~~~~~P~					Water quality not monitored by NRA in 1992.
		Newry Beach, Holyhead	~~~~~P~	5	11,000	Raw	All above LWM	Docks area. Water quality not monitored by NRA in 1992.
★★		**Trearddur Bay**	FFPPPPP			Screening and disinfection		Sand and rocks.
		Traeth Llydan (Broad Beach)						Dunes. Water quality not monitored by NRA in 1992.
★★★★		**Rhosneigr**	~~~PPPP	1	1,532	Raw	150 below LWM	Outfall discharges from rocks. Many watersports. Sewage solids and related debris reported and excessive dog-fouling 1992.
★★		Aberffraw Bay	~~~~~~P	1	534	Screens/ maceration	At HWM	Sandy. Avoid the estuary area as tide ebbs. Extensive dune system.
		Llanddwyn						Sandy. Water quality not monitored by NRA in 1992.
★★		St George's Pier, Menai Bridge	~~~~~FP					
f		Porth Dinorwic Sailing Club (Menai Straits)	~~~~~FF					
★★		Plas Menai (Menai Straits)	~~~~~PP					

Beach No on Map	Rating. The more stars the better. f=failed	Resort	Pass/Fail track record	Sewage outlets	Population discharging from outlet	Type of treatment	Discharge point relative to low water mark, unless otherwise stated. Distance given in metres	Remarks
		Dinas Dinlle	~~PPPP~					Sandy. Water quality not monitored by NRA in 1992.
		Pontllyfni	~~~~~P~					Sandy. Water quality not monitored by NRA in 1992.
	★	Trefor	~~~~~~P	1	582	Secondary	At LWM	Sand/shingle.
	★★	Porth Nefyn	~~~~~~P	1	2,800	Maceration	At HWM	Sand. Surfing, boating.
	★★	Morfa Nefyn	~~~PPP	1	2,100	Maceration	At LWM	Sand/rocks.
	★	Porth Dinllaen	~~~FPP					Sand/rocks.
		Rhos-y-Llan		1	420	Primary	Off rocks.	Sandy. Water quality not monitored by NRA in 1992.
		Traeth Penllech						Sand and rocks. Water quality not monitored by NRA in 1992.
	★★	Porth Colman	~~~~~PP					Rock pools.
	★★★★	Porth Iago	~~~~PPP					Sandy. Surfing.
1	★★★★	Porth Oer	~~~~PPP					Sandy.
	★	Aberdaron	~~~~PPP					Sandy. Surfing. Litter collection in the summer.
	★★★★	Porth Neigwl Beach	~~~~~PP					Surfing beach. Strong Atlantic rollers. Also called 'Hell's Mouth'.
		Porth Ceriad Beach	~~~~~P~					Water quality not monitored by NRA in 1992.
		Machroes Beach, Abersoch	~~~~~P~					Water quality not monitored by NRA in 1992.
	★	**Abersoch**	PPFPPPP	1	1,356	Secondary	100 below LWM	Sandy. Sewage-related debris reported in 1992.
	★★	Afon Soch at Slipway	~~~~~PP					
	★	Llanbedrog	~~~FFFP	1	672	Maceration/ tidal tank	50 below LWM	Sandy.
	★★	**Pwllheli**	PPPPPPP	1	4,107	Maceration/ tidal tank	At harbour mouth.	Sandy. Long sea outfall planned by 2005. Fast currents.

Beach No on Map	Rating. The more stars the better. f=failed	Resort	Pass/Fail track record	Sewage outlets	Population discharging from outlet	Type of treatment	Discharge point relative to low water mark, unless otherwise stated. Distance given in metres	Remarks
		Morfa Aberech						Sandy. Water quality not monitored by NRA in 1992.
		Afon Wen		1	46	Maceration/ tidal tank	At LWM	Sand/shingle. Water quality not monitored by NRA in 1992.
	f f	**Criccieth** West Beach	PFPFFPF ~~~~~FF	1	800	Tidal tank	50 below LWM	Sand/shingle. Treatment and disinfection to be installed at most cost-effective option. Gross littering by sewage-related debris.
	f	**Black Rock Sands (Morfa Bychan)**	~~~~~PF					Windsurfing and surfing.
	★★	Morfa Bychan	FFPPPPP	1	800	Maceration	Long sea outfall	Sandy beach. Contaminated by local streams. Do not bathe at SE end. Litter frequent but is collected daily. Problem with weever fish reported 1992.
	★	**Harlech**	PPPPPPP	1	1,291	Primary	At LWM	Sandy beach. Bathing unsafe. Outfall to be extended and provided with screening.
	★★	**Llandanwg**	PPPPPPP	1	258	Primary	At LWM	Sand/rock. Bathing safe at high tide. Visible sewage slicks.
	★	Tal-y-Bont	~~~~~PP					Sand, dunes.
	★★	Llanaber	~~~~~PP					Smuggling village.
	★	**Barmouth**	PPPPPPP	1	2,200	Screened	Long sea outfall	Sandy. Estuary unsafe for swimming. Bathing-related illnesses reported 1992. Good area for walking.
	★★	**Fairbourne**	PPPPPPP	1	474	Tidal tank	400 below LWM	Sandy. Starting point of the smallest narrow gauge railway. Improvements under review.
	f	Llwyngwril	~~~~~FF	1	370	Raw	At LWM	Sand/shingle.

Beach No on Map	Rating. The more stars the better. f=failed	Resort	Pass/Fail track record	Sewage outlets	Population discharging from outlet	Type of treatment	Discharge point relative to low water mark, unless otherwise stated. Distance given in metres	Remarks
	**	**Tywyn**	FPPPPPP	1	2,811	Maceration/ tidal tank	Above LWM	Sandy. Surfing. Scheme under investigation, possibly including secondary treatment and disinfection.
	f	**Aberdyfi**	~~~FFPF	1	6,000	Primary/ tidal tank	At LWM	Sewage outfall in estuary. To be combined with Tywyn scheme.
	f	Aberdyfi Beach	~~~~~~F					
	f	Aberdyfi Beach East	~~~FFPF					
DYFED								
	****	Ynyslas (North)	~~~~~PP					
	*	East Tywyni, Ynyslas	~~~~~PP					
	****	Borth	PPPPPPP					Bathing dangerous near mouth of the estuary. Good elsewhere. Windsurfing good for more experienced sailors; prevailing winds cross/on shore giving a bad shore break. Sewage solids reported in 1992 by surfers.
		Clarach Bay:						
	f	South of River	~~~FFFF					
	f	North of River	~~~~~~F					
	f	Footbridge						
	*	**Aberystwyth North**	PPPPPPP	1	9,100	Screened		New secondary treatment works, UV disinfection and outfall planned for 1994.
	f	Aberystwyth Harbour	~~~~~FF					
	f	**Aberystwyth South**	FFPFFPF					
	f	Aberystwyth South	~~~~~FF					
	**	Tanybwlch Beach, Aberystwyth	~~~~~PP					
	*	Morfa Bychan Beach (slipway)	~~~~~PP					Rocky beach in break in cliffs. Difficult access via steep ramp.
	****	Llanrhystud	~~~~~PP	1	500	Primary		Shingle. Sand at low tide.
	**	Llansantffraid	~~~~~PP	1	1,160	Primary	At LWM	Sand and shingle.

Beach No on Map	Rating. The more stars the better. f=failed	Resort	Pass/Fail track record	Sewage outlets	Population discharging from outlet	Type of treatment	Discharge point relative to low water mark, unless otherwise stated. Distance given in metres	Remarks
	★	Llanon Slipway	~~~~PP					Access to beach by foot only.
	★★	Aberarth	~~~~PP	1	470	Primary	At LWM	Shingle beach.
	★★	Aberaeron: North of outfall	~~~~FP	1	5,000	Raw	At LWM	Sand and shingle. Improvement scheme under investigation.
	f	Fourth Groyne North Harbour	~~~~PF					
	f	South	~~~~PF					
	f	Lovers Bridge						
	★★	Little Quay Bay (Central Groyne)	~~~~PP					Sand.
	f	New Quay: New Quay (Centre)	~~~~PF	1	6,000	Maceration	1,300 below LWM	Long sea outfall off Llanina Point.
	★★	New Quay (South)	~~~~PP					
	★★	**New Quay (Traeth Gwyn)**	PPPPPPP					
	f	Cwmtudu						Secluded shingle and sand. Remains of lime kiln on beach.
	★	Llangranog	~~~~FFP	1	400	Primary	75 below LWM	Sand/shingle.
	★★	Penbryn	~~~~FP					Sand.
	★★	Tresaith	~~~~FPP	1	180	Maceration	75 below LWM	Sand and shingle. Lifeguards.
	★	Aberporth Beach East	~~~~FFP	1	1,842	Maceration	75 below LWM	Sandy. Lifeguards patrol from 11 July to 5 September. Sewage-related debris a problem. Improvement plans.
	f	Aberporth at Slip	~~~~FF					
2	★★★★	Mwnt Beach	~~~~PP					Sandy.
	f	Gwbert-on-Sea	~~~~FF					Affected by discharges from caravan park.
		Poppit Sands	~~~~P~			Secondary		Sand and shingle. Estuary polluted by outfalls at Cardigan. Bathing safe only at slack water and where there are lifeguard indicators. Water quality not monitored by NRA in 1992.

Beach No on Map	Rating. The more stars the better. **f**=failed	Resort	Pass/Fail track record	Sewage outlets	Population discharging from outlet	Type of treatment	Discharge point relative to low water mark. unless otherwise stated. Distance given in metres	Remarks
	**	**Newport**	PPPPPPP	1	1,400	Maceration	500 below LWM	Sand/shingle. Bathing safe in centre of beach except on ebb tide or when rough.
		Newport Sands South						Water quality not monitored by NRA in 1992.
		Pwllgwaelod		1	880	Secondary	At LWM	Grey sand. Water quality not monitored by NRA in 1992.
		Fishguard						Linked to Goodwick. Water quality not monitored by NRA in 1992.
		Goodwick Harbour (South) ~~~~~P~ Goodwick Sands ~~~~~PP~		1	2,710	Raw	At LWM	Ferry terminal. Sewage reported in the water. Extended outfall planned. Improved treatment under review. Water quality not monitored by NRA in 1992.
3	****	Aber Eiddy Bay (at slipway)	~~~~PPP					
4	****	**Whitesand Bay**	PPPPPPP					Surf bathing. Strong currents. Litter sometimes considerable. Lifeguards patrol. Good for intermediate to experienced windsurfers.
	****	Caerfai Bay	~~~~~PP					Sandy beach under cliffs.
	****	**Newgale Beach**	FPPPPPP					Shingle and sand. Surfing. Rip tides at low water. Windsurfing best in south-west and northerly winds.
	****	**Broadhaven**	FPPPPPP	1	2,200	Secondary	At HWM	Sandy. Surfing. Good area with easy access for wind-surfing, particularly wave sailing. Winds exposed.
		St Brides Haven ~~~~~P~						Many rock pools. Water quality not monitored by NRA in 1992.
		Musselwick Sands						Cliff-backed cove. Water quality not monitored by NRA in 1992.

Beach No on Map	Rating. The more stars the better. **f**=failed	Resort	Pass/Fail track record	Sewage outlets	Population discharging from outlet	Type of treatment	Discharge point relative to low water mark, unless otherwise stated. Distance given in metres	Remarks
		Marloes	~~~~~P~					Sand and rock. Water quality not monitored by NRA in 1992.
		Dale	~~~~PP~	1	600	Maceration/ tidal tank	Above LWM	Shingle and sand. Water quality not monitored by NRA in 1992. Protected site for windsurfing suitable for beginners and intermediate sailors. Shop and RYA tuition available. Some reports sewage when wind is onshore.
		Sandy Haven	~~~~~P~	1	1,360	Secondary	At LWM	Red sand.
		Milford Beach	~~~~~P~					Near major refinery town
		Neyland Slip	~~~~~F~					Shingle bank.
		Angle Bay		1	500	Secondary	At LWM	Shingle and muddy sand. Water quality not monitored by NRA in 1992.
		Broad Haven (South Beach)	~~~~~P~					Sand, dunes. Water quality not monitored by NRA in 1992.
5	★★★★	Barafundle Bay						Sand, good bathing.
		Freshwater East	~~~~PP~	1	600	Raw	At LWM	Sandy. Water quality not monitored by NRA in 1992.
		Manorbier Beach Manorbier West	~~~~PP~	1	520	Secondary	At LWM	Sand and shingle. Water quality not monitored by NRA in 1992.
		Lydstep Beach	~~~~~P~					Privately owned beach. Lydstep Point owned by NT. Water quality not monitored by NRA in 1992.
	★ ★★	**Tenby North South**	PFPPPPP FFPPPPP	1	25,000	Screened/ maceration	2.7km below LWM	Sandy. Highly effective beach management team on North Beach. Primary treatment to be provided by 2000.

Beach No on Map	Rating. The more stars the better. f=failed	Resort	Pass/Fail track record	Sewage outlets	Population discharging from outlet	Type of treatment	Discharge point relative to low water mark, unless otherwise stated. Distance given in metres	Remarks
	f	**Saundersfoot: Beach**	PFPPPPF	1	11,000	Primary	50 below LWM	Sand and shingle. Sewage-related debris reported. Extension to outfall planned for 1995.
	★	Amroth	FFPPPPP					Sand and shingle. At very low tides the remains of a drowned forest can be found in the sand.
	★	**Pendine Sands**	PPPPPPP					Sand and dunes. Part of beach often closed for MOD firing range.
6	★★★★	**Pembrey Sands**	PPPPPPP	1	2,500	Secondary	Above HWM into channel towards Burry Port	Sand and dunes. Bathing safe except on spring high water.
	★★	Burry Port Beach East	~~~~~PP	1	6,000	Primary	Below LWM	Industrial and muddy. Bathing unsafe. Linked with Llanelli scheme for secondary treatment and disinfection to be provided.
	f	Llanelli Beach (fourth groyne)	~~~~~FF					See above for treatment.
WEST GLAMORGAN								
	★★★★	Broughton Bay	~~~~~PP					Sandy, bathing unsafe.
7	★★★★	**Rhossili Bay**	FPPPPPP		360	Primary		Sandy. May on rare occasions be affected by animal faeces and algal blooms. Popular surfing beach. Suffers from marine debris, especially fishing gear.
	★★★★	Fall Bay	~~~~~~P	1		Primary		South of the Worm's Head. Access difficult.
		Ramsgrove		1	270	Primary	Below LWM	Sandy. Water quality not monitored by NRA in 1992.
8	★★★★	**Port Eynon Bay**	PPPPPPP					Sand and dunes.
9	★★★★	**Oxwich Bay**	PPPPPPP	1	500		Below LWM	Sand and dunes. See Swansea Bay. Some litter reported 1992.

Beach No on Map	Rating. The more stars the better. f=failed	Resort	Pass/Fail track record	Sewage outlets	Population discharging from outlet	Type of treatment	Discharge point relative to low water mark, unless otherwise stated. Distance given in metres	Remarks
		Three Cliffs Bay						Sandy. Water quality not monitored by NRA in 1992.
		Southgate		1	500	Secondary	Below LWM	Rocky. Water quality not monitored by NRA in 1992.
		Brandy Cove	~~~~~P~	1	2,000	Secondary	Below LWM	Rocky. Former smugglers' stronghold. Water quality not monitored by NRA in 1992.
f		**Caswell Bay**	PFPPPPF					Sandy. Do not surf on ebb tide. Very effective beach management with a high priority given to safety. See Swansea Bay.
		Langland Bay:						Sandy. See Swansea Bay.
★		**West**	FPPFPPP					
★★		East	~~~~~PP					Popular surfing beach.
★★		**Limeslade Bay**	FFPFPPP					Sandy. See Swansea Bay.
★		**Bracelet Bay**	PPPPPPP					Sandy. See Swansea Bay.
		Swansea Bay:		1	170,000	Screened/ tidal tank	Below LWM	Subject of many complaints about marine litter and sewage debris. New projects totalling over £50 m for whole bay area covering Swansea, Bracelet, Limeslade, Langland, Caswell and Oxwich Bays, but not due until 1997.
f		**The Mumbles**	FFFFFPF					
★		Knap Rock	~~~~~FP					
★★		Opposite Black Pill Rock	~~~~~PP					
★★		Mumbles Head Pier	~~~~~FP					
★★		Jersey Marine, nr Swansea	~~~~~PP					
★		Jersey Marine East						
f		Jersey Marine West						
		Baglan (Neath)		1	60,000	Screened	3.1km below LWM	Improvements planned to give secondary treatment by 2000. Water quality not monitored by NRA in 1992.

Beach No on Map	Rating. The more stars the better. **f**=failed	Resort	Pass/Fail track record	Sewage outlets	Population discharging from outlet	Type of treatment	Discharge point relative to low water mark, unless otherwise stated. Distance given in metres	Remarks
		Afan (Port Talbot)		1	60,000	Screened	2.4km below LWM	Improvements planned to give secondary treatment by 2000. Water quality not monitored by NRA in 1992.
	★	Aberafan: West	~~~~~FP					
	★	**Aberafan at Slip**	FPPPFPP					
	★★	East	~~~~~PP					
	★★	Margam Sands (opposite steel works)	~~~~~PP					Access difficult. Five km stretch of sand. Good surfing.
MID GLAMORGAN								
	★★	**Rest Bay**	FPPPPPP					Sand and rocks. Treatment works in operation. Surfing. Lifeguards.
		Porthcawl						Sand and rocks. Sewage transferred to Penybont treatment works. Water quality not monitored by NRA in 1992.
	★	**Sandy Bay**	FFFPFPP					Sand and rocks. Lifeguards. Bathing prohibited near rocks.
	★★	**Trecco Bay**	FFPFPPP					Sand and rocks. Surfing. Lifeguards.
		Newton Bay (Newton Point)	~~~~~F~					Sand and rocks. Power-boating. Bathing prohibited at Newton Point. Water quality not monitored by NRA in 1992.
	★	Ogmore by Sea	~~~FFFP	1	140,000	Secondary/ other	Into River Ogmore approx 1.6km from sea	Sand and rocks. Lifeguards. Bathing prohibited near estuary.
	★★	**Southerndown**	FPFPPPP					Sand and rocks. Bathing prohibited off Trwyn y Witch headland, Lifeguards. Do not surf at high tide.
		Dunraven Bay						Glamorgan Heritage Coast project nearby. Water quality not monitored by NRA in 1992.

Beach No on Map	Rating. The more stars the better. **f**=failed	Resort	Pass/Fail track record	Sewage outlets	Population discharging from outlet	Type of treatment	Discharge point relative to low water mark. unless otherwise stated. Distance given in metres	Remarks
SOUTH GLAMORGAN								
		Nash Point						Rocky. Bathing unsafe. Water quality not monitored by NRA in 1992.
		Tresilian Bay		1	8,000	Maceration	At LWM	Rocky. Bathing unsafe. Water quality not monitored by NRA in 1992.
	★★	Llantwit Major Beach	~~~~~FP					Easy access to a stretch of sand and shingle. Good walks on headlands either side of the bay.
	★★	Limpert Bay	~~~~~~P	1	4,500	Maceration	At LWM	Rocks. shingle and sand overlooked by power station
	★★	Font-y-Gary Bay	~~~~PFP	2	3,045 936	Raw Raw	At LWM At LWM	Rocky, difficult currents. Lifeguards. Sewage to be transferred to Barry West, long sea outfall planned.
	★	Watch House Bay, Barry	~~~~~PP					
		Bendrick's Beach	~~~~~F~					Water quality not monitored by NRA in 1992
	★★	Little Island Bay, Barry	~~~~~PP					
	★	**Cold Knap Beach**	FFFPFPP	1	23,000	Screening	Long sea outfall 1.5km below LWM	Pebbles and sand. Lifeguards. New scheme to transfer sewage to Barry West proposed for completion in 1997, with Whitmore and Jacksons Bay
f		Whitmore Bay: **Whitmore East Beach**	~~~~~PF	2	21,000 23,000	Maceration Raw	At LWM At LWM	Sand, shingle and mud. Beach patrolled.
f		**Jacksons Bay**	FFFFFFF					Sandy , falling rocks at back of beach. Lifeguards. Sewage to be transferred to Barry West. Reports showed that 30% of first aid cases treated were related to the litter problems on the beach. Bathing-related illnesses reported 1992.
f		St Mary's Well	~~~~FFF					Shingle and rocks.
f		Penarth	~~~~~FF	4				Shingle and rocks. Bathing dangerous.

1 Porth Oer, Gwynedd   OS Ref: SH1630

This is the last and most accessible in a series of long, secluded bays along the north coast of the Lleyn Peninsula. The small cove is ringed by steep grass-covered cliffs, typical of this whole coastline. It is also called 'Whistling Sands' because the white sands seem to whistle or squeak as they are walked on. To really get away from it all, try Porth Iago and Porth Colman further north.

Water quality Water quality monitored by the NRA and found to meet the EC Guideline standards for bathing water in 1992. ★★★★ in this year's listing section.

Bathing safety Bathing is safe.

Access From the B4413 south of Pen-y-groeslon lanes lead down to a car park just before Carreg. There is a steep path down from the cliff top.

Parking There is a car park on the cliff top, 220 yards (200m) from the beach.

Toilets At the car park.

Food There is a café on the beach.

Seaside activities Swimming and fishing.

Wildlife and walks Low tide reveals rock pools at the western end of the beach.

2 Mwnt, Cardigan, Dyfed   OS Ref: SN1952

A natural suntrap surrounded by National Trust land, this beautiful undeveloped sandy beach is quite easily accessible and can be very popular in summer. The 330 yards (300m) of gently sloping sands are fringed by folded and faulted shale and mudstone cliffs. The beach is shadowed by the imposing form of Foel-y-Mwnt, a conical hill on the headland. The tiny whitewashed church of the Holy Cross nestles in a hollow at its foot. The only other obvious sign of man is the remnant of a lime kiln adjacent to the path down to the beach; limestone was landed in the bay and fired ready for use by the local farmers. Dogs are banned from May to September.

Water quality No sewage is discharged in the vicinity of this beach. Water quality monitored by the NRA and found to meet the EC Guideline coliform standards for bathing water in 1992. ★★★★ in this year's listing section.

Bathing safety Bathing is safe inshore. Care is required as surface currents, due to waves breaking on the headland, deflect across the bay. There is an emergency phone on cliff path.

Access Mwnt is signposted from the B4548 north of Cardigan. Lanes lead to the car park above the beach. Steps and a steep path lead down the cliff to the beach.

Parking There is a National Trust car park with 250 spaces.

Toilets There are toilets at the head of the steps to the beach, with facilities for disabled visitors.

Food Refreshments are available from Easter to October.

Seaside activities Swimming.

Wildlife and walks National Trust cliff-top walks. A pack detailing walks in the Cardigan area is available from local tourist information centres. Foely-Mwnt hill on the headland provides good views of the bay south to Cardigan Island and the narrow rocky inlet to the north. On the cliff tops above the beach there is a small remnant dune system where marram grass covers the wind-blown sand. Dogs on leads are welcome on the footpaths.

3 Aber Eiddy Bay, Abereiddy, Preseli, Dyfed   OS Ref: SM8031

One of many small bays that have known a very different and more active past. The slate that gives the small beach its dark grey sand was quarried and the remains of the workings can still be seen at the northern end of the beach. A small harbour on the north side of the headland where the rock has been cut away forms a deep blue pool.

Water quality No sewage is discharged in the vicinity of this beach. Water quality monitored by the NRA and found to meet the EC Guideline coliform standards for bathing water in 1992. ★★★★ in this year's listing section.

Bathing safety There are dangerous undercurrents and undertows off parts of the beach. Life-saving equipment and an emergency telephone are available. Power boats are restricted to 8 knots in the bathing area.

Access Lanes from the A487 north of St David's lead to the hamlet of Abereiddy. This beach is suitable for people with limited mobility.

Parking There is a large car park with space for 200 cars.

Toilets At the rear of the car park.

Food Ice-cream van, and teas are available on the beach.

Seaside activities Swimming, diving, canoeing, surfing and fishing.

Wildlife and walks The Pembrokeshire Coast Path leads in both directions along this most impressive and unspoilt stretch of rocky coastline, several stretches of which are owned by the National Trust.

4 Whitesand Bay, St David's, Preseli, Pembs   OS Ref: SM7327

Gorgeous sunsets framed in the wide arc of Whitesand Bay, which reaches from the remote rocky headland of St David's to St John Point, are an added attraction of this lovely beach. There are splendid views away to Ramsey Island and the Bishops and Clerks; the South Bishop can be identified on the far horizon by its lighthouse. The wide white sands stretch for ⅔ mile (1km). Large pebbles are thrown to the top of the beach by the waves that frequently crash on to this beach, much to the delight of many surfers. Open fields slope down to the shore from the imposing craggy hill Carn Llidi, which provides good walking with excellent sea views. St David's Head is owned by the National Trust. There is a dog ban from May to September.

Water quality Water quality monitored by the NRA and found to meet the EC Guideline coliform standards for bathing water in 1992. ★★★★ in this year's listing section. No sewage is discharged in the vicinity of this beach.

Litter There are considerable quantities of litter on the beach.

Bathing safety There are dangerous and unpredictable currents off parts of the beach and at some states of the tide. Warning signs indicate where to bathe and flags indicate when it is safe; lifeguards patrol the beach during the summer. Power boats are restricted to 8 knots within the bathing area. Weever fish are present.

Access A road off the A487 north of St David's, signposted to Whitesand, leads directly to the car park adjoining the sand. This beach is accessible to wheelchair users and people with limited mobility.

Parking There is a car park behind beach, with approximately 400 spaces.

Toilets At the car park.

Food Café/shop at the car park.

Seaside activities Swimming, surfing, canoeing, diving, windsurfing and fishing.

Wildlife and walks The coast path north provides an interesting circular walk, taking in St David's Head with the remains of a fort and a burial chamber, and returning round Carn Llidi Hill. A guide describing the route is published by the Pembrokeshire Coast National Park and can be obtained at local information offices. Ramsey Island lies just south of the bay, and boat trips from Whitesand (12-person inflatables, May-September) take you round the island to view the seabird breeding colonies.

5 Barafundle Bay, Stackpole, Pembs   OS Ref: SR9995

The National Trust owns an 8 mile (13km) section of the coast around Stackpole, including the beautiful Barafundle Bay. The beach can only be reached by foot with a 1 mile (1.6km) walk along the cliff top from Stackpole Quay. One of many tiny harbours that once proliferated in West Wales, the stone quay in this tiny inlet has been restored by the National Trust. From the cliff-top path you get your first glimpse of the bay, an impressive view of soft golden sands backed by high dunes, with steep lime-stone cliffs rising on either side. The cliffs, with distinctive dark bands at their base due to the encrusting seaweeds, barnacles and lichens, extend to Stackpole Head which shelters the bay.

Water quality No sewage is discharged in the vicinity of this beach. Water quality monitored by the NRA and found to meet the EC Guideline coliform standards for bathing water in 1992. **** in this year's listing section.

Litter The beach is generally clean, although a small amount of litter is washed up. In summer it is cleaned daily by the National Trust.

Bathing safety Bathing is safe. There is life-saving equipment at the top of steps down the cliff.

Access A lane east of Stackpole, signposted to Stackpole Quay and Bara-fundle, leads to the car park at Stackpole Quay. A 10-minute walk along the coast path, signposted from the car park, leads to the bay; follow the steps down the cliff to reach the sands.

Parking There is a National Trust car park at Stackpole Quay with about 230 spaces.

Toilets At the car park.

Food None.

Seaside activities Swimming.

Wildlife and walks The coast path from Stackpole Quay crosses the beach and, climbing through the trees, tracks around Stackpole headland, passes Rame Blow Hole, and continues on to Broadhaven Bay. There are excellent views of the rocky coastline, and north-east the ranks of red sand-stone headlands extend to the horizon. Walking south-east there are views down on to tiny sandy coves which cannot be reached because of the steep limestone cliffs that tower above.

6 Pembrey Sands, Llanelli, Dyfed   OS Ref: SN3802

A marvellous beach with 7 miles (11km) of sand edged by a belt of sand dunes, known locally as Cefn Sidan. The beach falls within the Pembrey Country Park, which also covers the extensive grassland and forest behind the dunes. The middle of the beach near the visitors' centre can be very busy on a warm sunny afternoon, but the extremities remain relatively quiet although they are often used for marine sports. Land yachting by the local club is well worth watching. Whether you want to relax on the sand and enjoy the clear views to the Gower on the horizon or be more active, the country park has lots of facilities, both natural and man-made, to keep the whole family happy. Dogs are not permitted in the central ¾ mile (1.2km) section of the beach, although this may not always be observed by visitors.

Water quality Water quality monitored by the NRA and found to meet the EC Guideline coliform standards for bathing water in 1992. ★★★★ in this year's listing section.

Litter Flotsam and jetsam are washed up on this beach. This may be on the increase, but it is cleaned regularly.

Bathing safety Bathing is safe. Lifeguards patrol the beach near the main access point from June to September.

Access The country park is signposted from the A484. Board walks from the car parks lead through the dunes to the beach.

Parking Several car parks behind dunes offer about 1,000 spaces.

Toilets There is one toilet block with facilities for disabled visitors.

Food A permanent kiosk with outdoor seating provides snacks and drinks.

Seaside activities Swimming, windsurfing, sailing and fishing. Pitch and putt golf, miniature and narrow gauge railways, adventure play area and dry ski slope. Events such as sand sculpture competitions and treasure hunts are regularly staged on the beach.

Wet weather alternatives Kidwelly Castle and Industrial Museum, Pembrey Motor Sports centre. The Country Park Information Centre presents displays and exhibitions about the beach and country park (open all year).

Wildlife and walks There are four self-guided nature trails around the country park: woodland walk, floral trail, the yellow post walk (which includes the beach, dunes, forest and grassland), and the leisure route, suitable for wheelchairs and pushchairs. There is a permanent orienteering course, a programme of guided walks by the Ranger service and a nature quiz for children. Full information is available from the visitors' centre.

7 Rhossili Bay, Rhossili, West Glamorgan   OS Ref: SS4287

A spectacular 3 mile (5km) sweep of golden sands edges Rhossili Bay, stretching from Worms Head north to Burry Holms. The sands are shadowed by Rhossili Down; its grass slopes rise 650 feet (200m) above the beach and are popular with hang gliders. The southern end of the beach is ringed by steep cliffs which fall away northwards, where the Down is replaced by sand dunes. Worms Head, contrary to its name, is in fact an island, only linked to the mainland at low tide. The remains of a wreck can sometimes be seen at low tide. This lovely beach and the adjacent Down are owned by the National Trust.

Water quality Water quality monitored by the NRA and found to meet the EC Guideline coliform standards for bathing water in 1992. **** in this year's listing section. No sewage is discharged from this beach. Complaints of visible sewage have been received which may be linked to animal faeces washed from the north Gower marshes.

Litter Considerable quantities of marine litter, such as fishing gear, get washed up on the beach.

Bathing safety The beach is usually safe for bathing. However, sand banks sometimes build up, causing dangerous rip currents in rough conditions.

Access The B4247 leads to Rhossili village. There is a good path down the cliffs to the beach. This beach has a slipway which makes access to the beach easier for wheelchair users and people with limited mobility.

Parking There is a car park in village.

Toilets At the car park.

Food In the village.

Seaside activities Swimming, surfing (extremely popular) and fishing.

Wildlife and walks Worms Head island and the adjacent stretch of coast are a National Nature Reserve. The limestone cliffs are rich in flora, and nesting birds can be seen on the nature trail. The limestone rocky shore of the Gower is one of the best examples in Britain. There is a network of paths on the headland and the adjoining Down where superb views can be obtained.

8 Port Eynon, West Glamorgan   OS Ref: SS4685

The rocky headland, Port Eynon Point, to the south shelters this sandy cove. The road from the post office leads down to the shore, where a short section of newly built promenade gives access to the beach. On either side, high dunes back the wide, flat sands. High cliffs rise on either side of the bay with rocky outcrops at their base. On the eastern side of the bay stand the newly excavated remains of a salt house and workings. The wide, gently sloping sands are safe for bathing, and an ideal spot for building sandcastles or playing cricket. The beach is cleaned daily in summer and twice weekly in winter. A dog restriction by-law is being considered.

Water quality Water quality monitored by the NRA and found to meet the EC Guideline coliform standards for bathing water in 1992. **** in this year's listing section. One outfall serving 1,200 people discharges primary and secondary treated sewage at low water mark off Overton Mere, east of Port Eynon Point.

Bathing safety Warning notices indicate where it is safe to bathe. The beach is patrolled by lifeguards from 1 May until 31 August.

Access From the village a road leads to the main access point where there is direct level access to the sands. Board walks and marked paths run through the dunes. This beach has a slipway which makes access to the beach easier for wheelchair users and people with limited mobility.

Parking There is a car park behind the dunes with 500 spaces.

Toilets At the beach entrance.

Food Shop and café at the beach entrance.

Seaside activities Swimming, surfing, windsurfing, diving, canoeing and fishing. A boat ramp leads from the car park to the tidal sand, providing easy access to the beach for boats.

Wildlife and walks The South Gower Coast Nature Reserve stretches from Port Eynon to Worms Head at Rhossili, comprising 6 miles (10km) of rocky shore with faulted and folded grey limestone cliffs. There is most interesting limestone flora, and nesting birds can be seen on some ledges. The limestone rocky shore of the Gower is one of the best examples in Britain. A footpath on to Port Eynon Point climbs the cliff from the eastern end of the beach. The path leads to the Culver Hole, a deep cleft in the cliff which has been sealed off with a wall. There is a nature trail from the Rhossili Bay car park at the opposite end of the Nature Reserve.

9 Oxwich Bay, Oxwich, West Glamorgan   OS Ref: SS4986

A superb beach; from the steep tree-clad slopes of Oxwich Point a sweep of very fine soft sand backed by high dunes curves 2 miles (3km) round the bay to Great Tor – a stretch of towering, rocky, limestone cliffs. At low tide, wide, flat sands are revealed. There is only one indentation into the crescent of sand, where the dunes are interrupted by the river Nicholaston Pill which meanders through marshland before crossing the beach. The main access is from Oxwich village, where there are full facilities. The North Devon Coast can be seen on the horizon and in the evening it appears as a string of lights. At low tide Oxwich Bay links with Three Cliffs Bay to the east, giving 3 miles (5km) of continuous south-facing sands.

Water quality Water quality monitored by the NRA and found to meet the EC Guideline coliform standards for bathing water in 1992. ★★★★ in this year's listing section. No sewage is discharged in the immediate vicinity of this beach.

Bathing safety Bathing is safe.

Access Narrow lanes lead to Oxwich village at the western end of the bay, and a car park next to the dunes faces directly on to the beach. There is a ramp for launching boats that could be used for easier access to the hard tidal sand. There is also access to the other end of the beach: a 15-minute walk from Penmaen along the footpath marked Tor Bay leads to a steep path down the cliff.

Parking There is a large car park at Oxwich village, plus limited parking at Penmaen. In summer there is a National Trust car park (a farmer's field) at Penmaen.

Toilets Two toilet blocks at the Oxwich car park.

Food The Oxwich Bay Hotel which stands at the eastern end of the beach provides meals and bar snacks. There is a kiosk for refreshments at the car park, and cafés and a shop within the village.

Seaside activities Swimming, windsurfing, sailing, diving, canoeing and fishing. A slipway across the sand enables boats to be launched and makes the bay popular with waterskiers. There is a windsurfing school on the beach.

Wildlife and walks The Oxwich National Nature Reserve covers most of the beach, back-shore and the Oxwich Point headland. The reserve includes a wide variety of habitats: sandy beach, dunes, salt- and freshwater marshes, cliffs, woods and grassland. There are marked footpaths throughout the reserve, and board walks give access to the dunes. A path west of the hotel leads through the trees past St Illtyd's Church to steps which climb to the headland and along the coast to Horton. There is an interpretative centre at the car park at Oxwich. At the western end there are barnacle- and mussel-encrusted rocks below the cliffs, and low tide reveals pools full of life.

Northern Ireland

The coast of Northern Ireland remains largely undiscovered to those outside the province although its most famous feature, the Giant's Causeway, is one of the natural wonders of the world. The Causeway consists of huge basalt columns that disappear into the waves like a stairway to the depths.

The whole coast has a rich and varied geology with a succession of bays and rugged headlands. The strands of County Londonderry have popular holiday resorts, and the nine glens of County Antrim, each with a little beach nestling at its mouth, provide a quieter alternative. There are also the magnificent sea loughs of County Down: Belfast, Strangford and Carlingford, rich in wildlife and scenery. It is unfortunate that undiscovered does not mean unthreatened – Strangford Lough has suffered from the effects of scallop dredging in recent years. Dredging for scallops may not necessarily affect the quality of the beaches but the rape of such a beautiful and unique habitat should concern anyone who cares for our coasts and coastal life. The implementation of an effective management plan is essential to maintain the balance in Strangford Lough. Fortunately, the issues concerning the Lough are being widely discussed and debated and progress is being made.

The year of 1992 was not kind to beaches in Northern Ireland. In 1991 there was 100 per cent compliance with the EC Bathing Waters Directive, in 1992 this dropped to 89 per cent. Let's hope that 1993 sees a return to 100 per cent compliance.

Northern Ireland

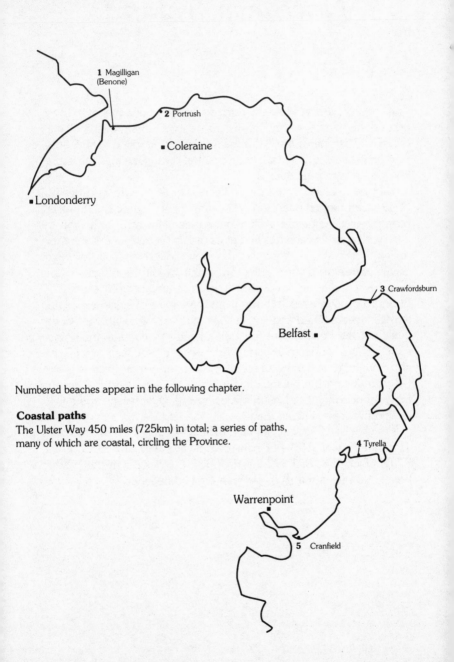

1 Magilligan
(Benone)

2 Portrush

■ Coleraine

■ Londonderry

3 Crawfordsburn

Belfast ■

Numbered beaches appear in the following chapter.

Coastal paths
The Ulster Way 450 miles (725km) in total; a series of paths,
many of which are coastal, circling the Province.

4 Tyrella

Warrenpoint
■

5 Cranfield

Northern Ireland   *See page 21 for further details*

Beach No on Map	Rating. The more stars the better. f=failed	Resort	Pass/Fail track record	Sewage outlets	Population discharging from outlet	Type of treatment	Discharge point relative to low water mark. unless otherwise stated. Distance given in metres	Remarks
1	★★★★	Magilligan (Benone)	~PPPPPP					Miles of sandy beach.
	★★	Castlerock	~FPPPPP	1	1,060	Maceration	At LWM	Sandy.
	★★	Portstewart	PPPPPPP	1	6,040	Maceration	Above LWM	Miles of sandy beach. This area is owned by the National Trust and a leaflet with further information is available from them.
2	★★★★ ★★★★	Portrush: Curran Strand Mill Strand	PPPPPPP PPPPPPP	1	5,560	Maceration	Above LWM	Sandy.
	★	Ballycastle	~FFPPPP	1	3,920	Maceration	At LWM	Sandy.
		White Park Bay						Sandy, dunes. Water quality not monitored by DoE-NI in 1992.
	★	Brown's Bay	~PPPPP					Sandy. Safe swimming.
	★★	Helen's Bay	~PPPPPP	1	1,600	Tidal tank	At LWM	Sandy. Safe swimming.
3	★★★★	Crawfordsburn	~PPPPPP	1	1,200	Secondary	Discharges to stream	Sandy.
	f	Ballyholme	FFPPPPF					Sandy.
	★	Groomsport	PFPPPPP	1	40,000	Screened	At LWM	Sandy.
	★★	Millisle	~PPPPPP	1	1,000	Primary	At LWM	Sandy.
4	★★★★	Tyrella	~PPPPPP					Sandy and very safe beach. National Nature Reserve.
		Murlough						Sandy. Water quality not monitored by DoE-NI in 1992.
	★	Newcastle	FFFPFPP	1	20,000	Secondary	285 below LWM	Sandy. New treatment works should ensure continued compliance in future.
5	★★★★ ★★	Cranfield: Nicholson's Strand Cranfield Bay	~~~~~~P ~PPPPP	1	2,200	Fine screens	410 below LWM	Long sandy south-facing beach.

1 Magilligan, Benone, Limavady, Co. Londonderry   OS Ref: C7037

Probably one of the best beaches in the United Kingdom. From Magilligan Point at the entrance to Lough Foyle, 7 miles (11km) of firm, flat, golden sand stretch east to the cliffs at Down Hill. Half of the beach is owned by the Ministry of Defence and is used as a firing range and so is out of bounds to the public. Dunes fringe the wide, curving beach, with sand hills covering the peninsula. The eastern end of the beach is backed by 750 foot (225m) cliffs, which are themselves shadowed by a heather-clad plateau and the Binevenagh Mountains. The new leisure complex provides excellent facilities close to the beach. If you prefer to get away from the sandcastles and games, the miles of sand offer solitude with only the sea and sky for company. The 110 yards (100m) of sand virtually disappear at high tide. Dogs must be on a lead. The beach is cleaned regularly.

Water quality Water quality monitored by the Department of the Environment for Northern Ireland (DoE–NI) and found to meet the EC Guideline coliform standards for bathing water in 1992. ★★★★ in this year's listing section. No sewage is discharged in the vicinity of the beach.

Bathing safety Bathing from some areas of the beach is unsafe due to currents; notices indicate where not to bathe. The beach is patrolled by lifeguards from June to September.

Access It is a short walk from the car park to the beach.

Parking There is a car park behind the dunes with 300 spaces. Car parking is also permitted on the sands but should be avoided on any beach.

Toilets Public toilets at the beach and also facilities at the leisure complex.

Food Refreshments are available at the leisure complex.

Seaside activities Swimming, surfing, windsurfing, sailing and fishing from the beach. Golf course, tennis and children's activity area are available at the leisure complex. A concrete ramp to the beach allows access to launch boats.

Wet weather alternatives Benone Tourist Complex.

Wildlife and walks It is claimed that up to 120 different species of shell have been found on Benone beach in one day, and an outdoor field studies recreation centre at Magilligan reflects the fact that the whole area is excellent for those interested in flora and fauna. One hundred and forty acres (56.6 hectares) of the sand dune system around the Martello Tower on Magilligan Point form a Nature Reserve and there is restricted access to protect this fragile environment. The coastline is the limit of the North Derry Area of Outstanding Natural Beauty. Inland, the Binevenagh mountains are good for hill walking and afford good views of the coast.

An interpretation centre has been highly commended for its imaginative approach to the local marine environment.

2 West Bay Strand, Portrush, Co. Antrim   OS Ref: C8740

Portrush is the largest and most popular seaside holiday centre in Northern Ireland. This Victorian and Edwardian resort is located on rocky Ramore Head and has all the facilities and amusements that might be expected of a traditional holiday town. From its elevated position there are excellent views along the coast to Donegal in the west and Rathlin Island in the east. A low sea wall bounds the soft sands of the west bay which curves gently south from the small harbour. The promenade which runs along the sea wall is on two levels separated by grassy banks. The larger East or Curran Strand is also backed by a sea wall but this gives way to dunes and a links golf course.

Water quality Water quality monitored by the DoE-NI and found to meet the EC Guideline coliform standards for bathing water in 1992. ★★★★ in this year's listing section. One outfall serving 5,000 people discharges macerated sewage at low water mark.

Bathing safety Beware of currents that may affect bathing safety.

Access Steps and a ramp from the promenade.

Parking 150-200 spaces at West Strand, 250-300 at East Strand.

Toilets At each end of West Strand and on East Strand.

Food Promenade café.

Seaside activities Swimming, surfing, windsurfing, sailing, diving and fishing. Boat trips from the harbour.

Wet weather alternatives 'Water World' alongside the old harbour has a swimming pool complete with flumes and jacuzzis, an aquarium and light entertainments. Amusements.

Wildlife and walks A section of the rocky shore on the eastern side of Ramore Head between the Portandoo Harbour and Bath road is a Nature Reserve noted for its fossil ammonites. Adjacent to the reserve is the Portrush Countryside Centre, an interpretative centre which can provide further information about the reserve and surrounding area. East of Portrush there is superb cliff scenery, including towering limestone cliffs eroded by the waves to form arches and caves. The white cliffs are replaced by the brown basalt which forms the famous Giant's Causeway further east; leaflets about the area are available from the National Trust. The coastal path follows the cliff top to the picturesque ruin of Dunluce Castle which offers superb views along the coastline (the castle is closed on Sunday mornings and on Mondays during the winter).

3 Crawfordsburn, Bangor, Co Down   OS Ref: J4783

Crawfordsburn and Helen's Bay are both within very easy reach of Belfast by road along the A2 and also by train. As a result they can be very popular in summer. The 550 yard (500m) sandy beach at Crawfordsburn is divided in two by the stream that flows from the glen behind the sands. The beach and the glen fall within the Crawfordsburn Country Park. On the right bank of the stream stands the house of the Scottish family who settled here in the 17th century and gave the bay their name. For those wishing to escape from the busy part of the beach, Swineley Bay to the east is more secluded.

Water quality Water quality monitored by the DoE-NI and found to meet the EC Guideline coliform standards for bathing water in 1992. **** in this year's listing section. A sewage treatment works serves the visitors' centre and toilets, discharging fully treated effluent into a nearby watercourse which flows across the beach.

Bathing safety Safe bathing.

Access Crawfordsburn Halt is ¾ mile (1.2km) from the beach along the road through the country park. The country park car park is 440 yards (400m) from the beach.

Parking A large car park is available in the country park.

Toilets There are toilets in the car park with facilities for disabled visitors.

Food Café.

Seaside activities Swimming, golf course. Orienteering courses held in the country park. Visitors' and interpretation centre.

Wildlife and walks The stream from Crawfordsburn village flows through a steep-sided valley, wooded with some exotic species. Below the village, it descends to a waterfall and flows under one of the railway viaduct's 80 foot (24m) high arches. Marked footpaths provide circular walks of varying lengths. Information about the park, including its walks and wildlife, is available from the interpretative centre. The beach is part of the North Down Coastal Path and also forms part of the Ulster Way. The path follows the coast from Hollywood, passes through the glen to the Clandeboye Estate and on to Newtownards.

4 Tyrella Beach, Clough, Co Down   OS Ref: J4535

Situated in Dundrum Bay, Tyrella is a 3 mile (5km) stretch of unspoilt sandy beach facing south and backed by dunes. The clean, shallow water and safe bathing make this a very popular beach on sunny Sundays in the holiday season: at other times it is blissfully quiet. There are six golf courses within a 12 mile (20km) radius of the beach, including the excellent Royal County Down. There is a tourist information and interpretation centre next to the toilets.

Water quality Water quality monitored by the DoE-NI and found to meet the EC Guideline coliform standards for bathing water in 1992. ★★★★ in this year's listing section. No sewage is discharged in the vicinity of the beach.

Bathing safety Safe bathing.

Access The A2 between Clough and Killough passes directly behind the beach.

Parking At present, some cars do park on the beach; this practice, of which the Marine Conservation Society strongly disapproves, will be restricted in 1993. Alternative parking should be found.

Toilets A new toilet block should be completed for 1993.

Food Snack vans visit the site.

Seaside activities Swimming.

Wet weather alternatives Leisure centres at Newcastle and Downpatrick, each about 6½ miles (10km) away.

Wildlife and walks The Murlough Nature Reserve, a dune system with plenty of wildlife and vegetation, is close by. There are signs of man's early habitation of the area: castles, dolmens (ancient cairns) and some of the earliest Christian remains (a result of St Patrick landing in the area). The Ulster Way goes past the beach.

5 Cranfield, Kilkeel, Co Down   OS Ref: J2611

An Area of Outstanding Natural Beauty and adjoining an area of Special Scientific Interest, Cranfield Bay is situated at the entrance to Carlingford Lough. The south-facing sand and shingle beach is backed by dunes and has the magnificent Mourne mountains as a backdrop. The beach stretches from the rocky outcrops at Greencastle Point to the boulders at Cranfield Point. There are good views across the Lough to Ballagan Point and away down the coast beyond Dundalk Bay.

Water quality Water quality monitored by the DoE-NI and found to meet the EC Guideline coliform standards for bathing water in 1992. ★★★★ in this year's listing section. No sewage is discharged in the vicinity of the beach.

Bathing safety Safe bathing.

Access A road leads from Cranfield to the car park, from which there is a short walk across the grass to the beach.

Parking Car park with 150 spaces.

Toilets There are public conveniences available.

Food Hotel, two cafés and three shops.

Seaside activities Swimming, windsurfing, diving, waterskiing and fishing. Beach entertainment and band concerts. Golf course.

Wet weather alternatives Analong cornmill and marine park.

Wildlife and walks The Mourne mountains are excellent for walking, with the Silent Valley Reserve just north of Kilkeel. A 3,000 million gallon (14,000 million litre) reservoir is set among the peaks and there is some fine parkland on the approaches to the dam.

Isle of Man

Lying in the middle of the Irish Sea yet separate from the British Isles is the Isle of Man, offering an incredible variety of scenery with a fiercely rugged coastline contrasting with the delicate beauty of the famous Manx Glens. Easily reached by air or boat, the island has been a favourite holiday destination since the development of resort-type holidays in Victorian times. The Island is renowned for its hospitality, the Tourist Trophy (TT) motorcycle races and the famous Manx kipper.

Most of the sewage produced in the Isle of Man is discharged to the sea via short sea outfalls with absolutely no treatment. The EC Bathing Water Directive is not applicable to the Isle of Man but in March 1990 Tynwald, the Manx government, decided that the EC Bathing Water Directive standards should be accepted as a target for the island.

There are some beautiful beaches on the Isle of Man. However, in 1992 only 1 of the 11 bathing beaches tested passed the minimum legal requirements of the bathing water directive. This situation should change drastically. The IRIS project – an ambitious scheme that aims to achieve Integrated Recycling of the Islands Sewage – will make the Isle of Man's beaches some of the best in the UK. The programme, which has the full support of the Marine Conservation Society, is designed to give improvements to some beaches in three years with the whole Island complying in eight years. The IRIS scheme represents what can be done with a little imagination and it is a model that many mainland water companies should learn from.

Details of public transport around the island are available from Isle of Man Transport on 0624-663366.

Beach No on Map	Rating. The more stars the better. f=failed	Resort	Pass/Fail track record	Sewage outlets	Population discharging from outlet	Type of treatment	Discharge point relative to low water mark, unless otherwise stated. Distance given in metres	Remarks
	f	Douglas Summerhill	PFPF					
	f	Douglas Palace	PFPF					
	f	Douglas Broadway	FFFF	3		Raw Raw Screened	All at LWM	The island's capital There is a 3km curving beach of sand, shingle and mud.
	f	Laxey	PPPF					Site of the famous Laxey Wheel – The Lady Isobella.
	f	Ramsey	FPFF			Raw	Below LWM	Two sandy beaches near the river mouth, sheltered from the prevailing south-westerlies. Interesting harbour town.
	f	Peel	FPFF			Poorly screened	100m from shore	Sandy beach, harbour and Peel castle. Sewage-related debris on Fenella Beach reported 1992.
	f	Port Erin	PPFF			Raw	Tidal tank below LWM - rarely uncovered	Sandy beach in sheltered bay on south of Island. Good cliff walks nearby.
	f	Port St Mary	PFFF			Raw	At LWM	Two beaches of firm, dry sand at Chapel Bay and Mary Bay.
	f	Castletown	~~PF			Raw	At LWM	Sheltered area, rocks and seaweed. Used extensively for watersports such as windsurfing. Domestic and industrial sewage discharge from leather/shoe factory.
	★	Derbyhaven	~~PP			Screens	At LWM near the pier	Sheltered shingle area. Used extensively for mooring boats.
		Gansey Bay (Bay Ny Carrickey)						Sand and shingle beach. New water sports centre. Water quality not monitored in 1992.

Beach No on Map	Rating. The more stars the better. **f**=failed	Resort	Pass/Fail track record	Sewage outlets	Population discharging from outlet	Type of treatment	Discharge point relative to low water mark, unless otherwise stated. Distance given in metres	Remarks
f		Kirk Michael	~~~F					Narrow shingle and sand beach. Exposed. Not extensively used for bathing.
		Jurby		1		Raw		Narrow shingle/sand beach backed by cliffs. Exposed.
		Fleshwick						North-facing shingle beach amid clusters of rocks. Good walking. Water quality not monitored in 1992.
		Port Cornaa						Shingle beach. Water quality not monitored in 1992.
		Port Soderick						Shingle beach. Water quality not monitored in 1992.
		Port Grenaugh						Shingle beach. Water quality not monitored in 1992.
		Niarbyl						Shingle beach. Water quality not monitored in 1992.

THERE ARE NO BEACHES ON THE ISLE OF MAN WITH GOOD ENOUGH WATER QUALITY TO WARRANT FURTHER DETAILED INFORMATION AS ONE OF BRITAIN'S BEST BEACHES.

Guernsey

Guernsey is a picturesque island off the north-west coast of France with a coastline of spectacular cliffs and sandy beaches. The capital of Guernsey is St Peter Port, known as one of the finest harbour towns in Europe. The island has its own government, issues its own coins and stamps but is subject to the Crown. The islanders are English-speaking, although French patois can be heard. Guernsey has had a turbulent history which is reflected in the archaeology that ranges from Neolithic remains and Royalist castles to concrete defences constructed by the Germans during the occupation of the island in the Second World War.

There are three main outfalls on the island and several minor discharges. Of the population of 60,000, approximately 37,000 are directly connected to the sewage network, while the majority of the remainder use cesspits which are regularly emptied and then discharged into the sewers at designated emptying points. There is very little contamination from industrial sources in the island's sewage.

The outfall at Bellegrave discharges sewage that has undergone preliminary treatment, maceration and screening. The sewage is then discharged via a long sea outfall. This outfall serves a population of 51,000. The outfall at Creux Mahie caters for 8,000 people and discharges raw and septic sewage, although this is to be updated for the 1993 season. Sewage from the Fort George outfall is macerated and then discharged to sea. There is a dog ban in effect between 1 May and 30 September at all the beaches listed below.

All Guernsey beaches reached a very high standard of water quality, with all but one of the monitored beaches being of three-star standard. None of the beaches qualified for the four-star rating since no monitoring was carried out for faecal streptococci. There is no track record available for the beaches in Guernsey since this is the first year that comprehensive monitoring has been carried out.

Details of public transport for the island are available from Guernsey Bus on 0481 724677.

Beach No on Map	Rating. The more stars the better. f=failed	Resort	Pass/Fail track record	Sewage outlets	Population discharging from outlet	Type of treatment	Discharge point relative to low water mark. unless otherwise stated. Distance given in metres	Remarks
	★★★	Grand Havre						No sewage is discharged in the vicinity of this large sandy beach edged by granite outcrops.
1	★★★	Pembroke Beach						No sewage is discharged in the vicinity of this large sandy beach with a narrow band of pebbles near the sea wall.
		Havelet Bay						Water quality not monitored in 1992. Fort George sewage outlet to the south of the beach. Sandy. Aquarium nearby and picnic area. Only beach on the island designated for water skiing. Good rock-pooling.
	★★	Fermain		1	1,000	Maceration	800m from the beach	Popular beach; pebbles give way to sand at low tide.
		Moulin Huet Bay						Sandy. Fascinating rock formations and pools. Café. Steep path to beach.
2	★★★	Petit Bot Bay		1	8,000	Maceration and screening	3km from the beach	Pebbles with large expanse of sand at low tide.
3	★★★	L'Eree						No sewage discharges in the vicinity of this beach. Large sandy beach with good bathing. Prone to seaweed deposits.
		Perelle Bay						Sandy. Surrounded by rocks. Not very good for swimming.
4	★★★	Vazon Bay						No sewage discharges in the vicinity of this beach. Sandy beach with safe bathing.
5	★★★	Cobo						No sewage discharges in the vicinity of this beach.

Beach No on Map	Rating. The more stars the better. f=failed	Resort	Pass/Fail track record	Sewage outlets	Population discharging from outlet	Type of treatment	Discharge point relative to low water mark, unless otherwise stated. Distance given in metres	Remarks
		Saline Bay (Grandes Rocques)						Water quality not monitored in 1992. No sewage discharges in the vicinity of this beach. Sandy/shingle. Large rocks. Rock pools
6	★★★	Porf Soif						No sewage discharges in the vicinity of this beach. An almost circular, very sheltered bay with fine dry sand.

1 Pembroke Beach, North Coast, Guernsey

Pembroke Beach is a large, almost unbroken expanse of sandy beach with a narrow band of pebbles near the sea wall. This beach boasts the best sunshine record in Guernsey and is sheltered from most winds. It is ideal for serious sunbathers and for beach games. The beach is cleaned on a daily basis throughout the summer season.

Water quality There is no sewage discharged in the vicinity of this beach. Water quality monitored and found to meet the EC Guideline coliform standards for bathing water in 1992. ★★★ in this year's listing section.

Bathing safety This beach is particularly suited to bathing.

Access There are slipways at either end of the beach, together with a number of flights of steps.

Parking There is plenty of parking available immediately above the beach.

Toilets At either end of the beach.

Food Two beach kiosks and the Pembroke Bay Hotel nearby.

Seaside activities Swimming and windsurfing. There is zoning of activities on this beach.

Wildlife and walks Immediately behind the beach is the L'Ancresse common, where a number of Neolithic burial chambers can be found.

2 Petit Bot Bay, South Coast, Guernsey

This popular bay lies at the foot of two wooded valleys. The beach is pebbly at high tide but at low tide a large expanse of sand is exposed. The beach is cleaned on a daily basis throughout the summer season.

Water quality There is a sewage outlet serving 8,000 people 2 miles (3km) from the beach which discharges macerated and screened sewage. Water quality monitored and found to meet the EC Guideline coliform standards for bathing water in 1992. ★★★ in this year's listing section.

Bathing safety Safe for bathing.

Access Access to the beach is via a slipway and is accessible to wheelchair users.

Parking Available along the road that leads to the beach.

Toilets Immediately above the beach.

Food A small kiosk on the beach serves food.

Seaside activities Swimming.

Wildlife and walks Petit Bot Bay is surrounded by the steep, wooded cliffs characteristic of the south coast of the island. It should be noted that although perfectly safe the cliff paths are steep and include long flights of steps and are not suitable for people with limited mobility.

3 L'Eree Beach, West Coast, Guernsey

The beach offers a large area of sand with good bathing. It is sheltered from the north-west wind but is prone to deposits of seaweed. The beach is cleaned daily between June and September and is cleaned every other day for the rest of the year

Water quality No sewage is discharged in the vicinity of this beach. Water quality monitored and found to meet the EC Guideline coliform standards for bathing water in 1992. ★★★ in this year's listing section.

Bathing safety Safe bathing.

Access A slipway at the northern end provides access for disabled visitors. There is also a flight of steps.

Parking Ample parking along the top of the beach.

Toilets Immediately above the beach.

Food There are a number of cafés and hotels on the other side of the road which runs above the beach.

Seaside activities Swimming.

Wildlife and walks The Catioroc Nature Trail and Shingle Bank are located near this beach. A leaflet which describes the wildlife which can be seen around this area is available from the tourist office.

4 Vazon Beach, West Coast, Guernsey

Vazon Beach is a crescent of lovely clean sand which gets the sun from early morning until sunset. However, it is exposed to wind from most directions. The beach is cleaned on a daily basis throughout the summer season.

Water quality There is no sewage discharged in the vicinity of this beach. Water quality monitored and found to meet the EC Guideline coliform standards for bathing water in 1992. ★★★ in this year's listing section.

Bathing safety Safe bathing.

Access There are slipways at either end of the beach providing access for disabled visitors and flights of steps at several other places.

Parking Several car parks immediately above the beach.

Toilets There are toilets with facilities for disabled visitors at several places along the beach.

Food Two beach kiosks and a number of restaurants and hotels in the area.

Seaside activities Swimming, surfing and windsurfing. All activities are carefully zoned.

Wildlife and walks The Fort Hommet Nature Conservation Area is found at the northern end of the beach and is of considerable interest historically and for its wildlife.

5 Cobo Beach, West Coast, Guernsey

A large stretch of sandy beach edged by spectacular rocky granite outcrops which provide excellent opportunities for rock-pooling. The beach is cleaned daily between June and September and every other day for the rest of the year.

Water quality No sewage is discharged in the vicinity of this beach. Water quality monitored and found to meet the EC Guideline coliform standards for bathing water in 1992. ★★★ in this year's listing section.

Bathing safety Safe bathing except in clearly marked areas to the northern end of the beach.

Access There are slipways at both the northern and southern ends of the beach providing access for disabled visitors, together with several sets of steps along the length of the beach.

Parking Plenty of free parking immediately above the beach.

Toilets At the southern end of the beach between the slipway and the car park.

Food A beach kiosk and a number of pubs, hotels and shops along the road that runs above the beach.

Seaside activities All activities at the beach are zoned. A windsurfing school operates from this beach. The main activities are swimming, rock-pooling, canoeing and windsurfing.

Wildlife and walks The Saumarez Nature Trail starts at Cobo Beach and winds 2 miles (3km) inland to Saumarez Park. An information leaflet describing what can be seen along the length of this walk is available from the tourist office.

6 Port Soif Bay, West Coast, Guernsey

Port Soif is an almost entirely circular bay which offers shelter from virtually any wind. It has a foreshore area of wonderful fine, dry sand. The beach is cleaned on a daily basis throughout the summer season.

Water quality There are no sewage outfalls in the vicinity of this beach. Water quality monitored and found to meet the EC Guideline coliform standards for bathing water in 1992. ★★★ in this year's listing section.

Bathing safety Safe bathing.

Access Access to the beach is via a flight of steps. There is also a gap in the dune system which forms the back of the beach where there is a gentle slope suitable for accompanied wheelchair users.

Parking There are car parks at either end of the bay.

Toilets In both car parks.

Food A beach kiosk.

Seaside activities Swimming.

Wildlife and walks The Port Soif Nature Trail lies just behind the beach. A leaflet available from the tourist office describes a walk along this section of coast.

Jersey

Jersey was established as an independent state over 700 years ago. It originally belonged to Normandy, then, when England was invaded by the Normans, it became English. When King John lost the island to France in 1204 the islanders chose to remain loyal and, although they are not governed by Parliament, they are subject to the Crown.

Jersey is famous for its wild, unspoilt coastline. Its record for water quality is excellent and it has one of the most comprehensive sewage treatment works in Britain. There is full sewage treatment for the island which includes screening, primary settlement, activated sludge oxidation, secondary settlement and ultra-violet disinfection. With 50 miles (80km) of coastline ranging from high cliffs to sweeping bays and bathing waters within EC standards, Jersey must surely be a prime destination for the discerning beach-lover.

No track record is available for Jersey since this is the first year that comprehensive monitoring has been carried out.

For details of public transport on the island, call JMT Express on 0534-21201.

Beach No on Map	Rating. The more stars the better. f=failed	Resort	Pass/Fail track record	Sewage outlets	Population discharging from outlet	Type of treatment	Discharge point relative to low water mark, unless otherwise stated. Distance given in metres	Remarks
	**	Grouville						Sandy. Occasionally affected by run-off from land. In general a pleasant beach.
1	****	Archirondel						Shingle beach with views of St Catherine's Breakwater.
2	****	St Brelade						Popular family beach.
	f	Beauport						The failure of Beauport was caused by run off and leaching from a trench at the head of the beach which contained several tons of potatoes dumped in June 1992. Action is being taken to remedy the situation and the beach should meet required standards in 1993.
3	****	Portelet						Sandy and sheltered.
4	****	St Ouen's Bay						8km long west coast, good for surfing. Recommended for strong swimmers only. Surfing school and hire facilities.
5	****	Plemont						Sheltered bay with many interesting caves.
6	****	Greve de Lacq						Sandy with rocky outcrops.

1 Archirondel, Jersey   OS Ref: 7151

Archirondel is a quiet shingle beach situated on the east coast of the island. The beach is unspoilt and offers spectacular views of St Catherine's Breakwater. Litter bins are provided and are emptied daily between May and September.

Water quality Water quality monitored and found to meet the EC Guideline coliform standards for bathing waters in 1992. ★★★★ in this year's listing section.

Bathing safety Safe bathing.

Parking A small car park specifically for the beach is available.

Toilets No public toilets in the area but the local café has toilets on the premises.

Food A café with indoor and outdoor seating next to the beach serves a range of food.

Seaside activities Swimming and canoeing.

Wildlife and walks St Catherine's Breakwater is a popular walk. There are picnic and barbecue areas nearby.

2 St Brelade's Bay, Jersey   OS Ref: 5848

The most popular family beach in Jersey with a large expanse of white sand and many beach activities. At the west end of the bay lies the picturesque St Brelade's parish church. A promenade stretches along the full length of the beach and is floodlit at night. There is a popular garden area set back from the promenade with floral displays and plenty of benches.

Water quality Water quality monitored and found to meet the EC Guideline coliform standards for bathing waters in 1992. ★★★★ in this year's listing section.

Bathing safety A safe bathing flag system is in operation and the area is patrolled by beach guards from Easter to September.

Parking Three main car parks with nearly 400 spaces.

Toilets There are toilets at four different sites. These are clearly signposted and are accessible for disabled users.

Food Several cafés and kiosks along the beach.

Seaside activities Funboats, windsurfers, trampolines, deck chairs, loungers, changing tents, pedalos and canoes for hire. Also waterskiing available.

3 Portelet, Jersey   OS Ref: 6046

This is a quiet, sandy beach occupying a sheltered position. Litter bins are emptied daily May to September,

Water quality Water quality monitored and found to meet the EC Guideline coliform standards for bathing waters in 1992. ★★★★ in this year's listing section.

Bathing safety Safe bathing.

Access Access to the beach is via steep steps unsuitable for people with limited mobility.

Parking Parking available behind the beach.

Food Café.

Seaside activities There are facilities for hiring deckchairs and windbreaks.

4 St Ouen, Jersey   OS Ref: 5651

St Ouen is the longest stretch of beach in Jersey and is commonly referred to as 'the Five Mile Beach'. It is a vast, sandy beach backed by Les Mielles conservation area, designated to conserve and protect the dunes and their flora and fauna. Situated to the south of the bay is La Rocco Tower, which can be visited at low tide but is cut off at mid to high tide. Litter bins are emptied daily between May and September and dog waste bins are provided.

Water quality Water quality monitored and found to meet the EC Guideline coliform standards for bathing waters in 1992. ★★★★ in this year's listing section.

Bathing safety This is a popular surfing beach but bathing can be dangerous. Lifeguards patrol the beach between Easter and September. There are flagged bathing areas.

Parking Ample car parks, some of which have been landscaped to be inconspicuous.

Toilets At three places along the bay with facilities for disabled users.

Food Numerous cafés and beach kiosks.

Seaside activities Surfing and windsurfing.

5 Plemont, Jersey   OS Ref: 5655

This is a relatively quiet beach popular with the locals. It is in a compact, sheltered bay situated in the north-west of the island. This beach is ideal for the beach explorer as there are many fascinating caves. There are litter bins in the car park.

Water quality Water quality monitored and found to meet the EC Guideline coliform standards for bathing waters in 1992. ★★★★ in this year's listing section.

Bathing safety Lifeguards are in attendance from May to September.

Access There is a steep climb down to the beach from the car park.

Toilets There are public facilities near to the café.

Food There is a café on the final approach to the beach selling food and beach-type merchandise.

Parking Car park behind the beach.

Wildlife and walks There are cliff walks along either side of the path down to the beach.

6 Greve de Lacq, Jersey   OS Ref: 5558

This beach is particularly popular with local people and can get very busy in the summer. It is a sandy beach with outcrops of rocks visible at low tide. There is a jetty at the end of the bay which is used by the local fishermen.

Water quality Water quality monitored and found to meet the EC Guideline coliform standards for bathing waters in 1992. ★★★★ in this year's listing section.

Bathing safety This beach is not patrolled by lifeguards. There is a flag system: when the flag is red it is not safe to bathe.

Parking Car parking facilities are available.

Toilets Public toilets are available.

Food There is a kiosk on the beach and several cafés serving local seafood nearby.

Wildlife and walks There are cliff path signs from the main car park taking the walker all the way to the famous 'Devil's Hole' or to Plemont.

Europe

As an introduction to the European Chapter it is important to look at how the different member states assess their beaches and bathing waters. There has been considerable argument that some countries are more honest than others over complying with the EC Bathing Water Directive. And if we can't trust each of the member states, how can we compare their beaches?

Below is a table, giving the results of the 1991 season – sadly this is the most up-to-date information available from all the member states. They are listed according to the percentage of their beaches passing the Imperative standards of the EC Bathing Water Directive. However, it is also very important to note the number of designated beaches that each country monitors, the frequency with which the bathing waters are sampled and the number of designated bathing waters that are not sampled enough.

Performance of the Member States

Member State	% pass	No. of bathing waters	No. not sampled sufficiently	Av. no of samples per year
Greece	97	1094	83	12.2 (see below)
Denmark	96	1165	2	12.3
Ireland	94	65	1	9.0
Netherlands	92	591	41	8.2
Italy	91	3824	76	11.7
Spain	90	1316	26	14.7
France	87	1526	63	11.3
Portugal	86	155	5	8.9
Belgium	85	39	2	44.7
United Kingdom	76	453	0	21.0
Germany (excl. Bavaria)	65	563	11	9.7

As you would expect the Mediterranean countries of Greece, Italy, Spain and France account for a very large number of Europe's designated bathing beaches. The United Kingdom has designated about one third of all its recreational beaches. The big surprise is

Denmark – with nearly 1200 designated bathing beaches, Denmark clearly takes the EC Bathing Water Directive seriously.

The number of samples taken per year makes a significant difference to the percentage of bathing beaches passing the minimum standards of the EC Bathing Water Directive. In this category Belgium is the clear leader, sampling on average 44 times a year. The United Kingdom also had a good record here, sampling 20 times a year between May and September.

Many European countries reported that they failed to take sufficient samples at some of their designated beaches. The United Kingdom was the only country to successfully monitor all its designated beaches. Greece and Italy top the table in failing to monitor properly. Interestingly, the Greek report pointed out that samples taken after rainfall were ignored. This is a highly doubtful practice – any water engineer will tell you that rainfall floods sewers and may cause a major decline in coastal water quality. This is certainly the case at some famous seaside resorts in the United Kingdom, but at least we don't try to pretend it doesn't happen.

In short, it is impossible to compare the different waters of the different member states until they use the same methods to monitor their waters. Until this happens, then percentage pass league tables will hide the dishonest and appear to punish the honest. The United Kingdom is certainly one of the more honest in its monitoring programme. It appears that perhaps the Greeks are less so.

So what is the solution? We hear a great deal about the idea of a level playing field in Europe. The Marine Conservation Society wholeheartedly supports our own Department of the Environment in its efforts to bring all the monitoring programmes into line and to seek a Euro-watchdog to check that all member states follow the same regulations.

Until then, all we have been able to do for this Euro-chapter is to pinpoint those most popular destinations in France, Spain, Portugal, Italy and Greece and to give the reported results for water quality. We also indicate whether European Blue Flags were awarded to these resorts in 1992. However, bear in mind that the source of most of this information is the government of the country involved; and we can only offer a very broad brush guide to these beaches.

A beach listed in this section is just popular – not necessarily clean.

If you, like us, are not satisfied with not knowing whether to believe all you are told, write to the Marine Conservation Society and give us your support. Write to your tour operators also. Remember there is no point in freedom of information if you can't be sure of the information you are being fed!

Key To The European Chapter Entries.

Microbiological quality

P – the waters passed the Imperative standards of the EC Bathing Water Directive. The water may be clean – ask your tour operator for more details.

F – the waters failed the Imperative standards of the EC bathing Water Directive. The water is badly polluted by sewage.

I – insufficient samples were taken to give a P or F rating

? – the waters were not monitored for sewage pollution.

Remember that 'P' only means that the waters have passed the Imperative standards of the EC Bathing Water Directive. The Marine Conservation Society recommends that only waters passing the Guideline standards (which are 20 times stricter) are used for recreational purposes. Only those beaches with a Blue Flag will definitely have passed these Guideline standards; look for this in the table.

European Blue Flag 1992

The beach will only have been awarded a European Blue Flag in 1992 if the bathing waters achieved the Guideline standards for water quality in 1991, and the resort has good landward facilities, including toilets, freshwater supplies and sources of information about, for example, first aid and lifeguards.

PORTUGAL

Although Portugal is a newcomer to the EC Bathing Water Directive, it has 39 mainland Blue Flag beaches. It has been helped by grants from EC regional funds to improve sewage treatment at the coast. More information is available from:

Associacao Bandeira Azul da Europa
Pavilhao ANL
Doca de Belem
P-1300
Lisboa
PORTUGAL

	Blue Flag 1992	Microbiological Quality	
COSTA VERDE			
Caminha			Fine sweeps of golden sands.
Priara da Ancora	No	F	
Caminha	No	P	
Moledo	Yes	P	
Viana do Castelo			There are hidden beaches either
Afife	Yes	P	side of the resort only accessible
Carreco	Yes	P	by boat.
LISBON COAST			
Lisbon			Soft sandy beaches about 20km
Cascais	No	?	from the capital.
Estoril	No	?	
Sintra			Sandy beaches seeming to
Adraga	No	I	stretch away endlessly.
Grande	No	I	
Magito	No	I	
Sesimbra			Sandy and sheltered.
California	No	F	Snorkelling and scuba diving.
Moinho de Baixo	Yes	P	
ALGARVE			
Silves			The longest beach on the Algarve,
Armacao de Pera	No	P	with soft golden sand encircling the bay to the east and a series of smaller sandy bays to the west. Water sports available.
Portimao			Golden beaches provide
Pria de Roche	No	P	excellent bathing, windsurfing
Alvor Praia	No	P	and waterskiing. Strange and beautiful rock formations.
Albufeira			Crescent beaches of fine golden
Gale leste	No	P	sand at the foot of red rocky
Oura	No	P	slopes.
Rocha baixinha leste	No	F	
S. Rafael	No	P	
Loule			A long stretch of gently sloping
Vilamoura	No	F	golden sand. Water sports are available.
MADEIRA			
Machico	No	?	Small shingle beach with some watersports available.

SPAIN

Spain and her island territories have 206 Blue Flag beaches. There is a phone-line (900-17-15-17) to call for up-to-date information about Spanish beaches free of charge.

Further information can be obtained from:

ADEAC
Salustioano Olozaga 5
S-28001 Madrid
SPAIN

	Blue Flag 1992	Microbiological Quality	
COSTA DEL SOL			
Torremolinos			Extremely popular with the British. All you would expect from Costa del Sol beaches.
Playa Los Alamos	No	P	
Fuengirola			
Los Boliches	Yes	P	
COSTA ALMERIA			
Roquetas de Mar			Shingle beaches. Windsurfing and waterskiing.
Cerrillos	Yes	P	
Aguadulce	Yes	P	
COSTA BRAVA			
Lloret de Mar			Shingle beaches and tree-lined promenades. Waterskiing and windsurfing.
Playa Cala Canyelles	No	F	
Playa de Lloret	Yes	P	
Playa de Fanals	Yes	P	
IBIZA			
Eivissa			Longest beach on the island. Gently sloping sand. Waterskiing, windsurfing and paragliding.
Playa d'en Bossa	Yes	P	
Santa Eularia des Riu			Man-made gently shelving beach with good all-round watersports.
Playa de Santa Eularia	Yes	P	
MALLORCA			
Alcudia			Almost 10km of soft white sand. Watersports and safe bathing.
Plata Alcudia	Yes	P	
Santanyi			Sheltered coves of gently sloping sand. Some windsurfing and diving.
Cala Santanyi	Yes	P	
Cala d'Or	No	P	
Sant Llorenc			Over 3km of golden sand. Safe bathing.
Cala Millor	Yes	P	
MINORCA			
Mercadal			Wide, curving sandy beach with all-round water sports.
Arenal d'en Castells	Yes	P	
Ferreries			Horseshoe bay of fine white sand. Diving and windsurfing.
Cala Galdana	Yes	P	
FUERTEVENTURA			
La Oliva			Sandy beach, but strong currents may make bathing unsuitable for children and poor swimmers. Diving available.
Corralejo	No	P	

GRAN CANARIA
Las Palmas de Gran Canaria

Las Canteras	Yes	P

San Bartolome de Tirajana

Maspalomas	Yes	P	
Playa del Ingles	Yes	P	Dunes of soft golden sand. Wide variety of watersports.

LANZAROTE
Teguise

Las Cucharas	Yes	P	One of five beaches at the Costa Teguise. Fine golden sand. Windsurfing.

Yaiza

Playa Blanca	Yes	P	Sheltered bay with small sandy beaches.

TENERIFE
Adeje

Playa de les Americas	No	P	Dark volcanic sandy beach. Windsurfing.

Arona

Playa Los Cristianos	No	P	Dark sandy beach in a sheltered bay. All-round watersports.

FRANCE
France has a total of 248 European Blue Flags. Some of her Mediterranean resorts have waters surprisingly unpolluted by sewage. For further information contact:

FEEEF
127 Rue de Flandre
F -75019 Paris
FRANCE

Alternatively, use the Minitel network (Code 3615 or 3616, IDEAL) or the Info-plage phonelines in France.

	Blue Flag 1992	Microbiological Quality	

NORMANDY

Etretat	No	P	Two natural arches in local cliffs that inspired Monet.
Deauville			Sandy beach and long
Plage des Six Fusilles	No	F	promenade.

BRITTANY
Perros-Guirec — Sheltered sandy beaches.

Trestignel	Yes	P	
Ploumanac'h – Saint Guirec	No	P	

Cotes d'Armor

St Michel en Greves	Yes	P	Sandy beach where the tide goes out for miles.

VENDEE
St Jean de Monts

Grande Plage, Palais Congres	Yes	P	Golden sandy beach. Deep sea fishing and sailing available.

CHARENTE MARITIME
Le Bois Plage en Re

Les Gollandieres	Yes	P

La Rochelle
Chef de Baie	No	F
Les Minimes	No	P

GIRONDE
Arcachon

Jetée Thiers	Yes	P	Superb beaches backed by some
Pereire	Yes	P	of the largest sand dune systems
Le Moulleau	Yes	P	in Europe.

LANGUEDOC – ROUSSILLON
Valras Plage

Bel Horizon	Yes	P	Golden sandy beaches with a
Poste de Secour Central	Yes	P	wide variety of water sports
Allee de Gaulle	Yes	P	available.

COTE D'AZUR
St Tropez

Les Canebiers	Yes	P
La Bouillabaisse	Yes	P

Cannes

Du Trou	Yes	P	Home of the famous film festival.
Roches de la Bocca	Yes	P	

Antibes

			Twenty-four beaches near
Hollywood	Yes	P	Antibes were awarded the
Siesta	Yes	P	European Blue Flag and have
			excellent water quality.

Nice

			Twenty two beaches in the
Miami	Yes	P	Nice region were awarded
Lido	Yes	P	European Blue Flags and have
			excellent water quality.

ITALY

Italy has 25 Blue Flag beaches. There have been problems on her Adriatic coast with algal blooms causing large quantities of bad-smelling foam to be washed on to the beaches. Further information can be obtained from:

Bandiere Bleu d'Europa
c/o CESVAM
Via del Tritone 46
I-00187 Roma
ITALY

	Blue Flag 1992	Microbiological Quality	
TUSCANY			
Camaiore			
Lido di Camaiore	Yes	P	
Viareggio			Superbly picturesque coastline.
Viareggio	Yes	P	
CAMPANIA			
Amalfi			
Spiaggia S. Croce	No	P	Gently sloping volcanic sand
Spiaggia Le Sirene	No	P	and shingle beach.
Maiori	No	P	Pale volcanic sand and pebbles. Long promenades.

Sorrento	No	P	A few beaches with small pebbles. Bathing platforms.

ADRIATIC COAST
Friuli Venezia Giulia

Lignano Sabbiadoro	Yes	P	
Emilia Romagna Forli			Over 15km of soft golden sand.
Rimini	No	P	Good water sports facilities.

SARDINIA

Golf Aranci	Yes	P	Only Blue Flag beach on Sardinia.

SICILY
Messina

Leotjanni	No	P	Both a public pebbly beach and an excellent private beach. Some water sports in high season.

Messina

Taormina – Lido Pizzichelli	No	P	Secluded beaches. Some charges apply. Cable car access.
Taormina – Lido Tropicana	No	P	

GREECE.
There are thousands of beaches in Greece. The European Blue Flag is run in Greece by the Hellenic Society for the Protection of Nature. They awarded 232 Blue Flags in 1992. Bear in mind that the monitoring process in Greece does ignore any results taken after rainfall when sewage contamination is likely to be at its worst.

More information can be obtained from:

Hellenic Society for the Protection of Nature
24, Nikis Street
GR-105 57 Athens
GREECE

	Blue Flag 1992	Microbiological Quality	
CORFU			
Sidari	No	?	Long, wide beach of golden sand with gently shelving shallow waters. All-round water sports.
Messonghi	No	?	Long sand beach backed by forest and olive groves. Windsurfing and waterskiing.
KEFALONIA			
Sami			
Antisamos Beach	Yes	P	
Argostoli			
Makri Gialos Beach	Yes	P	Sandy beach with superb water sports.
HALKIDIKI			
Neos Marmaras			Coarse sand and numerous
Europa Beach	Yes	P	secluded rocky coves. A wide
Neos Marmaras Beach	Yes	P	range of water sports is available.

Ouranoupolis Eagles Palace Beach	Yes	P	Sandy beach fringing the rugged rugged coastline. All-round water sports.

KOS
Kardemena	No	?	Long wide beach of fine sand stretching the length of the vil- lage. Excellent watersports.
Kos Town	No	?	Lambi beach is the main beach – sand and shingle. Tingaki beach is a short distance away. Wide and sandy.

RHODES
Ialyssos			
Rhodes Palace Beach	Yes	P	
Trianda Bleu Horizon Beach	Yes	P	
Trianda Golden Beach	Yes	P	
Lindos			All Ialyssos and Lindos beaches
Lindos Megalos Aigialos Beach	Yes	P	offer excellent water sports. Golden sandy bays.
Vlycha Beach	Yes	P	
Rhodos			Long shingle beaches near
Elli	Yes	P	Rhodes Town. Full tourist
Enidrio	Yes	P	facilities available.
Kanari	Yes	P	
Reni	Yes	P	

ZAKYNTHOS
Kalamaki			Long, sandy beach with gently
Kalamaki Beach	Yes	P	shelving shallow water. Famous as a nesting area for Caretta turtles; access is restricted as a result. Please observe all restric- tions to ensure the survival of these animals.
Planou			Long, white, sandy beach. All-
Tsilivi Beach	Yes	P	round water sports including paragliding.

CRETE
Aghios Nikolaos			Small public beach of sand
Almyros Beach	Yes	P	and shingle. Private beach of
Ammos Beach	Yes	P	shingle and pebbles.
Elounda			Sandy beach in the middle of a
Elounda Beach	Yes	P	small village.
Shisma Beach	Yes	P	
Rethymnon			Part of a 6km stretch of soft
Creta Palace Beach	Yes	P	golden sand and shingle beach. All-round water sports.

IF YOU GO ON HOLIDAY TO CONTINENTAL EUROPE, PLEASE WRITE TO
US. LET US KNOW IF THE BEACHES WERE CLEAN OR NOT AND TELL US
IF THE WATERS APPEARED TO BE POLLUTED.

The European Chapter,Marine Conservation Society,
9 Gloucester Road, Ross-on-Wye, Herefordshire HR9 5BU.

What Can You Do To Help Clean Up The Beaches Of The UK?

We compiled the 1993 *Heinz Good Beach Guide* using our own research, water quality data supplied by the National Rivers Authority and information given to us by the local authorities and other organisations concerned with the sea and the beach.

However, the most important source of information is YOU. We ask you to act as our ears and eyes around the beaches of the UK to help us know more about the problems around the coast. We cannot always act on individual cases, but we use your information in our national campaign to end sewage pollution of the seas off the UK. We can also supply you with expert knowledge of the issues to help you in your own campaign. Write to the Pollution Officer, Marine Conservation Society for details.

If you have a complaint about a beach you visit, or think that we may have got something wrong in the 1993 Guide – or if you have found a beach to be clean or waters especially clear – then please write and tell us about it, or use the special card enclosed in this Guide.

Please tell us all you can. The more we know, the more we can try to do about the problems around the UK coast. Better than that, send us photographs of the worst and best beaches in the UK.

How to make an official complaint and report pollution

If you go to a beach and find dirty water, badly littered beaches or dangerous items washed up, register your complaint and report what you have found. If the authorities don't know about the problem, or think that people don't care, nothing will ever improve. We cannot rely on government or industry to clean up the beaches and the water without prompting from us.

There are various local and national government bodies and water companies with which to register your complaint (after you have told us about it!). Here is a guide to whom to contact:

Local Authority Environmental Health Departments

Environmental Health Departments are responsible for keeping beaches clean of litter and safe from dangerous items washed up, such as chemical drums and canisters washed overboard or dumped at sea.

If you find items that you think may be dangerous call the Environmental Health Department straight away – do not touch whatever it is you find.

If the beach is badly littered with drink cans, plastic bottles, discarded fishing nets or whatever, register your complaint with the Environmental Health Department. The local authority has a legal duty under the Environmental Protection Act 1990 to keep beaches and other public places clean and free of litter. Tell them where the litter is and ask them to clear it up.

These departments are also responsible for displaying the results of bathing water monitoring at the beaches in line with government policy. There should be posters giving the results in a clear, easy-to-understand form at the beaches themselves. If there are no posters, contact the Chief Environmental Health Officer to ask why not. Ask him or her to put posters near the beach showing water quality monitoring results. The address and phone number of the local authority will be in the phone book.

Please send us copies of letters from the Environmental Health Department.

Local tourism departments

Although these departments have no responsibility for pollution on the beach or out at sea, they have a lot to lose if a resort gets a bad name. When they get complaints, they act quickly to get those other departments in the local authorities and the NRA (see below) to do something about the problem.

The National Rivers Authority, the River Purification Boards and the DoE – Northern Ireland

The NRA has responsibility for water quality and pollution incidents and also carries out the routine monitoring of bathing waters on which compliance with the EC Bathing Waters Directive is assessed. The River Purification Boards (RPBs) in Scotland and the Department of the Environment for Northern Ireland (DoE-NI) carry out broadly similar roles to those of the NRA in England.

If the waters appear to be badly polluted with sewage or there is any other pollution (such as oil) in the water, contact the local National Rivers Authority. They will be able to investigate the pollution and may even be able to track down and prosecute the polluter.

Also, if you suspect that the water may be affected by an algal bloom (heavy frothing of the water, excessive foam on the beach or possible red-brown discoloration of the water – 'red tides'), ask the NRA to investigate. Here are the addresses and telephone numbers of the regions of the NRA, RPBs and DOE-NI:

THE NATIONAL RIVERS AUTHORITY

Head Office NRA Head Office
Rivers House, 30–34 Albert Embankment, London SE1 7TL
Tel: 071-820 0101

South West NRA – South West Region
Manley House, Kestrel Way, Exeter, Devon EX2 7LQ
Tel: 0392-444000

Wessex Region
NRA – Wessex Region
Rivers House, East Quay, Bridgwater, Somerset TA6 4YS
Tel: 0278-457333

Southern Region NRA – Southern Region
Guildbourne House, Chatsworth Road, Worthing, Surrey BN11 1LD
Tel: 0903-820692

Thames Region NRA – Thames Region
Kings Meadow House, Kings Meadow Road, Reading RG1 8DQ
Tel: 0734-535000

Anglian Region NRA – Anglian Region
Kingfisher House, Goldhay Way, Orton Goldhay, Peterborough
PE2 0ZR Tel: 0733-371811

Severn-Trent Region
Severn Estuary
NRA – Lower Severn Region
Riversmeet House, Newtown Industrial Estate, Northway Lane,
Tewkesbury, Gloucestershire GL20 7JG Tel: 0684-850951

Trent Estuary
NRA – Lower Trent Region
Trentside Offices, Scarrington Road, West Bridgeford,
Nottingham NG2 5SA Tel: 0602-455722

NRA – Severn Trent Region
Sapphire East, 550 Streetbrook Road, Solihull, West Midlands
B91 1QT Tel: 021-711-2324

Yorkshire Region NRA – Yorkshire Region
Rivers House, 21 Park Square South, Leeds LS1 2QG
Tel: 0532-440191

Northumbrian Region NRA – Northumbrian Region
Eldon House, Regent Centre, Gosforth, Newcastle-upon-Tyne
NE3 3UD Tel: 091-213-0266

North West Region NRA – North West Region
PO Box 12, Richard Fairclough House, Knutsford Road,
Warrington WA14 1HG Tel: 0925-53999

Welsh Region NRA – Welsh Region
Rivers House, St Mellons Business Park, St Mellons, Cardiff
CF3 0FT Tel: 0222-770088

SCOTTISH RIVER PURIFICATION BOARDS

Highlands RPB
Carr's Corner, Lochybridge, Fort William, Inverness-shire
PH33 6TQ Tel: 0397-704351

North East RPB
Greyhope House, Greyhope Road, Torry, Aberdeen AB1 3RD
Tel: 0224-248338

Forth RPB
Heriot Watt Research Park, Avenue North, Riccarton, Edinburgh
Tel: 031-449-7296 (out of hours Pollution Callout 031-449-7292)

Clyde RPB
Rivers House, Murray Road, East Kilbride, Glasgow G75 0LA
Tel: 03552-38181

Tweed RPB
Burnbrae, Mossilee Road, Galashiels TD1 1NF Tel: 0896-2425

Solway RPB
Rivers House, Irongray Road, Dumfries DG2 0JE Tel: 0387-720502

Tay RPB
1 South Street, Perth PH2 8NJ Tel: 0738-27989

DEPARTMENT OF THE ENVIRONMENT FOR NORTHERN IRELAND (DOE-NI)

DOE-NI Environmental Protection Division
Calvert House, 23 Castle Place, Belfast BT1 1FY Tel: 0232-230560

The Water Service Companies

The Water Service Companies (WSCs), the newly privatised 'water plcs', are responsible for the operation of the coastal sewage works and outfall pipes around the coastline of the UK. They are currently investing large sums of money in a range of projects, but the pressure must be maintained to ensure the job is done properly. Some water companies say they will do the minimum required of them by the NRA. We must make them see that this is neither in our interests nor in theirs.

If you see an outfall pipe discharging raw sewage near a beach, write to the water company and ask them:

• Whether they think it is still acceptable in 1992 to pump raw sewage into the sea and expect the public to swim in it?

• Whether they are aware of the damage that sewage pollution causes to marine life?

• How many outfall pipes there are in the area and how many people do they serve?

• What sort of treatment is given to the sewage before it is discharged to sea?

• Are all these outfalls clearly marked with signs giving details of how much sewage is discharged and what sort of treatment it has received? If not, why not?

• Are there are any improvement schemes planned? What sort of treatment is considered to be adequate and why? When will the improvements be completed?

The 10 water service companies of England and Wales are:

South West Water, Peninsula House, Rydon Lane, Exeter EX2 7HR Tel: 0392-219666

Wessex Water, Wessex House, Passage Street, Bristol BS2 0JQ Tel: 0272-290611

Southern Water, Southern House, Yeoman Road, Worthing BN13 3NX Tel: 0903-64444

Thames Water, Nugent House, Vastern Road, Reading RG1 8DB Tel: 0734-591159

Anglian Water, Ambury Road, Huntingdon PE18 6NZ Tel:0480-433433

Yorkshire Water, Broadacre House, Vicar Lane, Bradford BD1 5PZ Tel 0274-306063

Northumbrian Water, Abbey Road, Pity Me, Durham DH1 5FJ Tel: 091-384-4222

North West Water, Dawson House, Great Sankey, Warrington WA5 3LW Tel:0925-234000

Severn-Trent Water, 2297 Coventry Road, Sheldon, Birmingham B26 3PU Tel: 021-722-4000

Welsh Water, Plas-y-Ffynnon, Cambrian Way, Brecon, Powys LD3 7HP Tel: 0874-3181

Please send us copies of any replies you receive from the WSCs.

The Coastguard

The Coastguard is available to help anyone in danger at sea or on the beach. If you think that someone needs help at sea, don't hesitate – dial 999. Don't leave it to someone else!

The Coastguard must also be told immediately of any dangerous items washed up on the beach, such as chemical drums and old wartime explosives. If you're in doubt, call anyway. Simply dial 999 and ask for the Coastguard. The call is always free.

Index